AMERICAN
CRUSADE

AMERICAN CRUSADE

OUR FIGHT TO STAY FREE

PETE HEGSETH

CENTER
STREET®

NEW YORK   NASHVILLE

Center Street
Hachette Book Group
1290 Avenue of the Americas, New York, NY 10104
centerstreet.com
twitter.com/centerstreet

First published in hardcover and ebook by Center Street in May 2020.
First Trade Paperback Edition: May 2021

Center Street is a division of Hachette Book Group, Inc. The Center Street
name and logo are trademarks of Hachette Book Group, Inc.

The publisher is not responsible for websites (or their content)
that are not owned by the publisher.

The Hachette Speakers Bureau provides a wide range of
authors for speaking events. To find out more, go to
www.HachetteSpeakersBureau.com or call (866) 376-6591.

Print book interior design by Timothy Shaner, NightAndDayDesign.biz

Library of Congress Cataloging-in-Publication Data has been applied for.

ISBNs: 978-1-5460-9874-4 (hardcover), 978-1-5460-5927-1 (signed edition),
978-1-5460-5926-4 (B&N.com signed edition), 978-1-5460-9906-2 (ebook),
978-1-5460-9937-6 (trade paperback)

Printed in the United States of America

LSC-C

Printing 1, 2021

This book is for our children—Gunner, Jackson, Peter Boone, Kenzie, Luke, Rex, and Gwendolyn.

And for yours.

CONTENTS

AMERICAN CRUSADE

PART ONE

A CONSEQUENTIAL MOMENT

"There is not room in the country for any fifty-fifty American, nor can there be but one loyalty—to the Stars and Stripes."

—Theodore Roosevelt

ONE

OUR AMERICAN CRUSADE

Take a moment to consider your part in the miracle of the 2016 election; the history we made as sons and daughters of freedom. For the Left, that humiliating defeat strengthened their resolve to achieve their ultimate goal: erasing America's soul, culture, and institutions. We are the ones standing in their way—and have been targeted for annihilation.

We the People must understand this moment. You feel it. I feel it. We all feel it. The other side—the Left—is not our friend. We are not "esteemed colleagues," nor mere political opponents. We are foes. Either we win, or they win—we agree on nothing else.

The United States has the top economy and military in the world, but our cultural and educational institutions—America's soul—have succumbed to leftist rot. Military might and worldly wealth alone are not enough to preserve our founding principles, nor are once-in-a-generation electoral miracles such as the 2016 election. Our future existence as sons and daughters of freedom requires the satisfaction of a single paramount objective: the categorical defeat of the Left. America cannot, and will not, survive otherwise.

This time in our history calls for an AMERICAN CRUSADE. Yes, a holy war for the righteous cause of human freedom.

One thousand years ago, after years of ceding land to conquering Muslim hordes, the pope ordered military action to save Europe. "Deus vult" ("God wills it") was the rallying cry of Christian knights as they marched to Jerusalem. Two hundred and fifty years ago, as King George III exercised more power over the colonists in North America, they rebelled. "Give me liberty or give me death!" they exclaimed. America was born and then battle tested.

The most important rallying cry of our era—"Make America Great Again"—catalyzed a political miracle of similar proportion and consequence so shocking that it still confounds those who proclaimed it. Like crusaders and patriots past, Donald Trump's red hat rebellion demonstrates that unapologetically going on offense is the only tenable strategy for the defense of our republic. Surrounded by the Left, with the odds stacked against us, only a crusade will do.

Mobilized for victory, we will save the republic in 2020 and beyond. But the battle is not for the meek or the weak. Those who make excuses that distract from decisive political triumph—such as petty grievances over President Trump's tweets, feigned civility standards, or stale, status quo thinking—are not worthy to populate the crusading ranks. We need informed, inspired, unapologetic patriots, and we need them now.

Lest we forget, the United States of America is the grandest—and greatest—freedom experiment in human history. The most free, most fair, most tolerant, most equal, and most powerful. We should never, ever apologize for her. If you don't agree with that statement, at best you are utterly ignorant of human history; at worst, you are a willing enemy of freedom—and America.

The Left's 2016 calamity is our opportunity and therefore requires urgent, radical steps to win in 2020 and engrave that victory on the soul of America. As we embark on this noblest of causes, remember the plan the Left has for you—utter annihilation—and prepare yourself to lock shields with fellow Americans in the defense of our simple and sacred shared objective: freedom.

Let's begin. And let's get personal. Millions of patriots—including you and me—love the founding ideals of America. But there are hordes of people within our borders (remember those?!) who don't share our allegiance—and their ignorance and ideologies threaten America's very survival. As such, we are two Americas; a house divided.

TWO AMERICANS, TWO AMERICAS

To begin our journey, it is necessary to demarcate the bitter division between America and the Left. To illustrate this, consider the lives and views of two immigrants from distant, war-torn lands: "Samarra" Omar and "Somali" Omar.

Having previously fled the tyranny of Saddam, Samarra Omar—along with his brother Bakr and father, Mr. Assad—returned to Iraq in 2003 to rebuild their life and fight Al Qaeda. I had the honor to fight alongside them in the battered city of Samarra in 2006. A decade later, Bakr and Omar earned the opportunity to immigrate legally to the United States and are now assimilated in the suburbs of Houston, Texas. Hereafter, I'll call my friend Texas Omar.

Somali Omar is a member of the United States Congress. Ilhan Omar came to America as a young girl, fleeing the civil war in Somalia. Following four years in a refugee camp in Kenya, she was granted asylum in the United States, eventually settling in Minneapolis, Minnesota. She graduated from high school there, attended college in North Dakota, and secured a prestigious policy fellowship at the

University of Minnesota. A few years later, the people of Minnesota elected her to the state house—and then to Congress. Yet despite all that privilege, referring to her as "Somali" Omar still fits best.

Somali Omar has chosen to return our goodwill with grievances, not gratitude. She views her time in Somali as "blissful," while criticizing the United States as racist, oppressive, and "torturous." Unlike Texas Omar, Somali Omar did not choose America—America chose her, from the squalor of a refugee camp in Kenya. We opened our doors and welcomed her. The state of Minnesota housed her, educated her, empowered her, enriched her, elevated her, and then elected her.

Through the lens of gratitude, America looks much different. Texas Omar's victories on the battlefield, killing Al Qaeda terrorists—who the delusional, hateful Somali Omar asserts are merely the product of Jewish-financed American imperialism—earned his family a life in the land of liberty. Texas welcomed them as sons and daughters of freedom.

Theodore Roosevelt once stated, "There is not room in the country for any fifty-fifty American, nor can there be but one loyalty—to the Stars and Stripes." My friend Texas Omar and his beautiful family embrace 100 percent Americanism. Somali Omar sees the land of opportunity much differently.

But don't take my word for it; consider their words on multiple subjects.

On America:

Texas Omar: "There is an American way to live, and it's unlike any other place on earth. The flag of the United States means sanctuary to me."

Somali Omar: "We export American exceptionalism, the Great America, the land of liberty and justice. . . . but we don't live those values here."

On equality:

Texas Omar: "Honestly, the media, and social media, paints America as racist. These people haven't lived where there was a real culture of racism. Where we came from, people were labeled and oppressed based on a few characteristics—even our first names—and there was so much division. Go live in Iraq or most other countries for six months, and then you will think differently about America."

Somali Omar: "I grew up in an extremely unjust society, and the only thing that made my family excited about coming to the United States was that the United States was supposed to be the country that guaranteed justice to all. So, I feel it necessary for me to speak about that promise that's not kept."

On race:

Texas Omar: "In our first weeks here [in Texas], we were very surprised," he explained. "I just knew we would face racism—even maniacs. My wife wears a hijab [a traditional Muslim head covering], and I feared she would be mistreated. But our experience has been the opposite. People open doors for her, smile, and greet her at the mall."

Somali Omar: "I would say our country should be more fearful of white men across our country because they are actually causing most of the deaths within this country."

On opportunity:

Texas Omar: "I've traveled and lived in twenty-eight countries before we came here. The American flag is respected—even if people don't always express their admiration, they feel it. Anything you want, you can achieve it here. But we will lose this way of life if we don't protect it."

Somali Omar: "I arrived at the age of 12 and learned that I was the extreme other. I was black. I was Muslim. I also learned I was extremely poor and that the classless America that my father talked about didn't exist."

Both Omars are Americans—technically, anyway.

What does Somali Omar embrace? The death squads of her native land? Antisemitism? Her brother? I mean, husband. There is no excuse for her behavior: America does not have room for even one fraction of a percent of her bigotry and blatant anti-Americanism.

INSHALLAH, TEXAS STYLE

I first met Texas Omar on a 2006 combat tour in Samarra, Iraq. He was young but streetwise and spoke English fairly well. His family had been raised with the understanding that English was the language of enterprise and freedom.

"We loved America before we ever set foot here," Texas Omar's brothers told me years later. "When we met the soldiers and other Americans helping our country, our beliefs were confirmed. They treated people with respect and fought alongside us."

It was a chaotic and violent time—before the surge, when Al Qaeda was battling to fill the vacuum of power left by sectarian violence. Texas Omar's father, Mr. Assad, had fought against Saddam Hussein's tyranny for years and as a result had been forced to flee Iraq with his family. When the murderous regime had fallen, they returned to rebuild their beloved—and battered—hometown of Samarra. Mr. Assad was soon nominated to be the city council president—a courageous move that Islamists viewed as blasphemy.

"We met Pete at one of the hardest points of our life," Texas Omar confided. "Our community was constantly being threatened by Al Qaeda, and our people were being killed by their snipers and bombs. The US military joined us to fight for our communities and families. We also saw how Iran wanted to take advantage of the situation, and we needed to stand against their influence. We were willing to die to fight that evil. Die standing."

As our combat tour progressed, this family of warriors risked their necks to rebuild their fractured city. Al Qaeda took notice and published an "announcement" targeting several leaders in Samarra for death. Texas Omar's father, Mr. Assad, and his entire family were the focus of the fliers posted throughout the city. A translated excerpt of the Al Qaeda death threat is below. As you read, imagine your name on this poster in your hometown:

> In the name of the great God, Al Qaeda will clean the city from the agents such as Assad and whoever stands as a bodyguard for him after he convicted himself by his tongue when he called the Occupational Forces the "American Forces" instead of telling the truth about the occupation of the country. . . . He convicted himself by accepting in the city council all the orders that come from the Jews and Crusaders. . . . We issued a statement to all his cells and companies inside and outside the city to target the families of the killers and criminals who are working with the Jews and Crusaders. . . . Demolish their houses, burn them down, possess their assets, burn their cars, burn their shops and steal all their money. . . . Signed, the Advisory Council of the Al Mujahadeen, Al Qaeda Organization in Mesopotamia.

They were crusaders even then.

Texas Omar recalls that one night: "Our home was surrounded by Al Qaeda snipers and machine gunners. Their mission was clear. I called Pete and said, 'We're trapped! We have no time. Send help.

Now!' We went to the roof with our rifles, knowing we would die, but hoping we could at least kill some terrorists first. A few minutes later, I saw an angel. It was an army helicopter. Within seconds, the enemy scattered, and my family was saved. Our second life began that day."

To Texas Omar, the sight of a US helicopter looks like an angel. To Somali Omar, the same American helicopter looks like Satan.

She said so herself.

In response to a tweet pointing out that nineteen Americans had been killed and seventy-three wounded during the Battle of Mogadishu in 1993—portrayed in the film *Black Hawk Down*—Somali Omar tweeted, "In his [Joshua, a patriotic Twitter user] selective memory, he forgets to also mention the thousands of Somalis killed by the American forces that day! #NotTodaySatan."

Her accusation that "thousands" had been killed by US troops is a detestable lie that reveals her contempt for all who wear our flag on their uniforms. Her image of a satanic US helicopter stands in stark contrast with Texas Omar's experience: an angel of America routing death's advance.

"Someday, brothers, we will see you in America," I would often cheerfully remark to Texas Omar and his family. "Inshallah" (if God wills it) they would reply, and we would laugh together. Behind the smiles and gallows humor was faint optimism.

Many members of Texas Omar's family met the terrible fate threatened by Al Qaeda. A car bomb attack by Al Qaeda destroyed their home, killing many of their loved ones, but Texas Omar's father and brothers survived and continued to fight the Islamist terrorists.

Before I left Iraq, Texas Omar and his father, Mr. Assad, wrote a generous letter of recommendation for me—which I'm sure was part of the reason I was accepted into graduate school at Harvard University. I am still awed by the kindness and the irony. They gave me a letter of recommendation and never asked me to write one for them so they might leave the fight in Iraq.

Years later, I had the chance to return the favor and started the process of officially inviting Texas Omar and his family to the United States. Because of the nightmare of US State Department bureaucracy and a lack of paperwork (their house had been bombed!), it took three long years. Three years. Undeterred, they patiently waited in line for the slow gears of government to turn on the green light. They came legally ready to fulfill their roles as 100 percent Americans.

My friends eventually landed in Texas, where Middle Eastern Muslims are supposedly feared and hated by gun-toting, pickup-driving Bible thumpers. They were about to meet the real America.

"A few weeks after arriving in this country, it was the Fourth of July. I didn't know what to expect but knew the holiday was a big deal. After work, I took my family to the local park, where a celebration was held. There were hundreds of people picnicking and hundreds of US flags. People welcomed us and gave my family little flags, too. It was like an initiation." After an emotional pause, he continued, "We felt like we belonged. We stayed for the fireworks, and we knew this would be a family tradition."

"This is God's country!" Texas Omar's brother declared.

What he and millions of other Americans refer to as "God's country" is the giant canvas of amber waves and purple mountains on which one may author their destiny, inscribing hopes and dreams as vigorously as one's ability to muster. It is the recognition of our God-given rights with a formal acknowledgment of the source of those rights. For those who fought tyranny and proclaimed America to be a force of good, this is their just reward. Muslim, Christian, or Jew, Zoroastrian or Hindu—all are welcome in our righteous crusade for human freedom!

Texas Omar and his family actively perpetuate the preservation of these tenants of freedom. They have Americanized their kids' names because they want their kids to be Americans. They make sure their kids learn English. They still love Iraq, embrace their faith, and respect their traditions, but they want to be part of this nation. Only this nation.

We cannot be afraid to say it just as Texas Omar's brother did: "My children will grow up here. It's their home. And they will defend this country. We've never been treated better than here in the United States. Anyone who comes here has the right of free speech and equal opportunity. The law applies to everyone equally. You are not identified by race or color, like we've seen in other countries. You can build a life here."

AMERICA THEN, IS NOW

If the most lethal Islamist terrorist organization in the world hung posters throughout your hometown announcing its intent to assassinate you, would you say, "This only makes me stronger"? That's what Texas Omar would say to me with a defiant laugh. They fought real bullets, not weenie social justice warriors.

It's not unlike King George III, the commander of the greatest military force of the age, putting your name on a "most wanted" list at city hall on the eve of our revolution. Or, today, the federal government arbitrarily targeting your business, your family, or your rights because it doesn't like what you stand for. It happened then, and—without President Trump in office—it would continue today.

Would you be willing to lose your home and livelihood to fight for real freedom? Would you stand with the signers of the Declaration of Independence and "pledge to each other our Lives, our

Fortunes, and our sacred Honor"? Really, truly, ask yourself that question. The battle for freedom is not one we can wage from the margins; it requires a personal investment.

In 1775, a year before that declaration, the hope of freedom and personal honor sent volunteers to a town square in Lexington, and a bridge in Concord. So-called common citizens took a deep breath and decided that liberty was worth it—even if it cost them their lives and possessions. New taxes on items such as paint, paper, and tea led humble men to stand their ground; a bunch of preachers, tavern owners, blacksmiths, farmers, tradesmen, and philosophers thirsting for freedom in America decided to stand up to the most powerful empire in the world. They didn't invade England. The British Empire slowly and systematically invaded their liberty. The same has happened to us over the course of decades; could you muster such courage?

The fate of freedom is what is at stake in the 2020 election. The immediate years that follow will, once and for all, determine whether the American experiment in human freedom—the America of our founding—will die, get a national divorce based on irreconcilable cultural and political divisions, or return to its founding principles. It sounds dramatic, but not if you appreciate history, human nature, and what we're up against.

FIFTY-FIFTY AMERICAN?

Lacking grittiness and historical perspective, fifty-fifty Americans too often delight in the warm comfort of toothless proclamations. Never inconveniencing themselves with the minutiae of grassroots or cultural activism—except in short spurts for limited reasons—their half measures, excuses, and ineffectiveness have earned them a fitting nickname: squishes.

Squishes don a hard veneer but lack the supportive inner structure of American vertebrates. So when the pressure mounts, they scurry away like roaches. For too long, this was the cycle of politics. While the Left advanced its agenda, we slogged through an internal battle between 100 percent Americans and fifty-fifty Americans.

The fifty-fifty Americans promulgated a number of compelling justifications for their complacency:

Well, the pendulum always swings back . . . we'll be okay.

America once fought a civil war, you see, and came out stronger. Surely common sense will prevail in this great country.

I know there are radical ideas out there, but it's been like this since the 1960s. We'll work it out.

I care about my country, but don't want to be seen as "overly political." That just makes the problem worse.

I run a business and pay my taxes; that is how I contribute. The Left protests; we work.

I can't stand Congress, but I love my congressman—because he [or she] really cares.

Most public schools are failing kids, but my local school is great. You should see the new library!

I've been a squish at times, and so have you. At some point, we have probably all subscribed to at least one of these statements. I know I have. For me, awakening has been a progression over many years, informed by multiple iterations of learning—and mostly failure. First I had to get informed. Then I denied the magnitude of the leftist problem. Next, being idealistic, naive, and new to the political arena, I played within the confines of the status quo. Now, as I have some worldly success and a large family, protecting my nest is tempting. I understand what is required of a 100 percent American: the sacrifice, the struggle, the uncertainty. You will face similar personal roadblocks—all personal, all powerful.

I used to be the poster boy for the Republican status quo. Then, in 2016, tens of millions of patriotic Americans rejected the status quo of the Republican Party—the think-tank, Beltway, cowardly retreat from our core principles. We the People elected an America First Disrupter in Chief.

God willed it, and I finally learned that establishment Republican politicians—squish Republicans—have been complicit in the decline of America.

Like their counterparts across the aisle, the squishes often have the connections, the salaries, the pensions, and the power—but those they pretend to serve, the forgotten men and women, have awakened to their betrayal. As for the Left, we know who they are and the philosophy of hate to which they subscribe. This book will reveal the core of their sedition. They are zero percent Americans.

I've personally seen the newsrooms, cloakrooms, and ivory towers of our so-called elites—and they don't want debate, they want destruction. They deplore you and believe they know better than you do. You and I must face the fact that at this moment the usual activities and attitudes of "good citizens" will not cut it. Following the lead of President Trump and beyond, American Crusaders must lead the cultural fight from here. Imagine if Texas Omar had been only fifty-fifty in the fight against Al Qaeda.

Ask yourself: *What percent American am I?*

OUR MOMENT

Three realities are central to understanding our moment. *First, history is not over. Trump was not the end, he was the turning point.* The miracle of 2016 still rings hope, but four years later the gravity of our situation has not lessened. Though many squish Republicans have relegated themselves to irrelevancy, American Crusaders still have work to do within our ranks. There is room for only *100 percent Americanism*. Trump's appointment of judges, the booming economy, his fight for the wall, and the defeat of ISIS are all spectacular achievements. But remember that although they have been necessary for the preservation of freedom, they are not sufficient. Only the categorical defeat of the Left will secure the blessings of liberty to ourselves and our posterity. We must reelect Donald Trump in 2020 and continue the cultural counterattack until Leftists are no longer electorally viable.

Second, America is not inevitable. America is an *experiment*. A free people, governing itself and reining in government is the exception to the rule in human history. For thousands of years, the vast majority of people have been led by kings, butchers, and theocrats. The norm is the dysfunctional gash on Africa's horn that produced Somali Omar, not the United States of America. Our ability to perpetuate self-governance is very much an open question.

Finally, if the twenty-first century is not an American-dominated century, it will not be a free century. The forces of despotism, collectivism, Islamism, and globalism are on the march. China is expanding. Europe is demographically and culturally overrun. America is a flickering light of freedom on a surrounded hill.

The hour *is* late for America. Beyond political success, her fate relies on exorcising the leftist specter dominating education, religion, and culture—a 360-degree holy war for the righteous cause of human freedom. As Abraham Lincoln remarked, "The philosophy of the school room in one generation will be the philosophy of government in the next." These nonpolitical fronts are where we will fight to ensure that our political victories continue for an age.

In the chapters that follow, we'll face every enemy that threatens our nation and undergo a basic training in the fight for freedom: the American Crusade. Our first objective is the reelection of Donald Trump. Crusaders, welcome to the Warring Twenties!

"You're a sleaze."

—Candidate Donald Trump to reporter from ABC News, 2016

"You're a warrior, Pete. A fucking warrior!"

—President Donald Trump, November 2019

TWO

2020: DEATH, DIVORCE, OR DAWN?

H i, my name is Pete Hegseth and I was almost a Never Trumper. In 2015, few people saw Donald Trump as a serious contender. God bless those who did—but I didn't.

For far too long, the conservative movement and Republican Party had been stale and shortsighted, stuck in the conventional wisdom of Washington, DC, think tanks and corporate interests—not to mention invested in wishful-thinking foreign nation building. I was stuck squarely in that prism, and it showed. I had revered the "compassionate conservatism" of George W. Bush, especially after 9/11, enthusiastically supported the "Country First" candidacy of John McCain, and dutifully backed the vanilla campaign of Mitt Romney.

Leading up to the 2016 election, I wanted the most cogent, elegant, and consistent conservative voice to be atop the Republican ticket. I wanted the best possible conservative contrast to the disastrous Barack Obama years. I looked for the type of candidate who would quote the Declaration of Independence, Alexis de Tocqueville,

Ronald Reagan, and the Heritage Foundation. The so-called front-runner, Jeb Bush, wasn't that person—barely distinguishable from his blue-blooded doppelgänger, Hillary Clinton. So as the 2016 campaign began, I was squarely in Marco Rubio's camp, donating to him on day one so I could get my signed campaign poster.

At the beginning, I mocked Donald Trump's candidacy. *He's an armchair tough guy and was a New York City liberal; why should we trust him?*, I reasoned. His celebrity left me unfazed and his style, unnerved.

I was a loyal Republican and took much else for granted. Having spent so much time around Republican stalwarts who spoke wistfully of Ronald Reagan, I defaulted to applying his leadership of the 1980s to every issue of our moment. If "The Gipper" did it, we should, too. It was blind faith based on an outdated view, and it didn't work. We weren't winning anymore. Worse, when our candidates lost, we made shallow excuses for them. When politicians failed us, we justified their weakness. When our policies failed, we ignored reality. We were losers—and good at it.

The process was familiar, the issue set largely static, and the fight for our values righteous. Or so we thought. But our righteousness was couched in comfort. We were used to losing—and rationalized it by reading history instead of making it! All the while, I told myself: *America will be just fine.*

After Rubio bowed out, I jumped aboard the Ted Cruz ship—all the while slamming Donald Trump's candidacy. As a staunch conservative, I loved what Cruz said and appreciated how he stood up to the establishment. He quoted the Constitution by memory and ruffled DC feathers. His filibuster on the Senate floor was a thing of beauty.

Then Cruz sank. Trump had officially crashed the party and pooped in the Republican punch bowl.

In January 2016, *National Review* magazine published its infamous "Against Trump" issue, featuring a cover with those two words in gold letters and the names of several Republican establishment "thinkers." The magazine argued that true conservatives must reject Trump to preserve the integrity of their principles. I remember emailing the publisher, Rich Lowry, after the magazine came out, saying "I wish you had asked me to put my name on that cover." That's how invested I was. In retrospect, it makes me cringe—but it is the truth.

I still could not handle Trump's roughness, bravado, and off-color comments. Not only did he not speak like politicians, he made fun of them! He ignored the traditional conservative lexicon and gave biting nicknames to his opponents—nicknames that had helped sink my "Little Marco" and "Lyin' Ted." He was a bull in the china shop, unafraid to take on anyone and everyone no matter the topic—large, small, and seemingly petty.

It just didn't click for me. Did not compute. Who was this guy? Why did people love him so much? What was his compass? I'd spent two decades marinating in traditional conservatism and Republican Party talking points—and had become more loyal to those than to what was best for America. I didn't have a properly calibrated America compass; I had just been following the well-worn path of Republican losers.

MY TRUMP CONVERSION

Then, watching the Left lose its mind over Donald Trump's candidacy, the light bulbs turned on: the Left hates him because they hate us! If they take him out, they can take out anyone. We're almost finished. We are surrounded. We need a fighter who truly loves America and will take the gloves off. *Break glass in case of war!* I was mugged on my own road to Damascus; it was a conversion moment many years in the making—but hastened by the fury of the political climate.

My "Trump conversion moment" was actually two moments.

My first conversion moment was watching a televised Trump rally in April 2016 in southern California. The protests on the street were so fierce that Trump and his staff had to leave their cars, walk along a highway, and be escorted into a back entrance of the venue. Helicopters followed his every move, and leftists were delighted. What was he talking about that was so controversial? *America?* Make America great again? Build the wall? America first? Outside the arena, the left-wing protesters seethed with rage; many of them waved Mexican flags and confronted police.

Man, they hate this guy, I thought. *He's not talking about policy issues such as reforming Social Security or making some radical tax cut. He's defending basic American values. They never hated Romney or McCain like this. And why the hell are they waving Mexican flags? This is America.*

I finally started to internalize how far the Left had taken the country away from Americanism. We were not just debating the future of the country, we were debating *the country.*

My second Trump conversation moment was a press conference in May 2016, when Trump held court and expressed his raw frustration with dishonest reporting about his rallies and fund-raising for veterans. He pointed to ABC News reporter Tom Llamas and, without the usual political genuflecting of Republicans past, proclaimed, "Like this sleazy guy right over here from ABC. He's a sleaze in my book. You're a sleaze, because you know the facts and you know the facts well." He mocked multiple left-wing reporters that day—to their faces and without hesitation.

Then, when asked later by another reporter if he'd treat the press this way if he became president, his answer was characteristically blunt: "Yes." Rush Limbaugh immediately called it "the press conference Republicans had been waiting for for twenty years"—and he was right. No more playing the game on their terms. The media have been in the tank for Democrats for longer than anyone realized, but still Republicans played along. No more. America needed a blunt instrument.

The election of 2016 was not about what *party* I was for but instead what *country* I was for. Since that realization, I've been all in for Trump—fully converted. Just as with a convert to a new religious faith, first being on the outside (an unbeliever) gives you an even clearer sense of where you stand and why. I didn't support Trump because he's a reality TV star or a successful businessman but because he showed his fighting spirit for our nation at the very moment we needed it.

We needed a Crusader in Chief, and we got one.

Winston Churchill is often quoted as saying, "America always does the right thing, but only after trying everything else." In this case, the "right thing" rode in on a gold-plated escalator in Manhattan. At the exact moment our republic required it, Donald Trump challenged every premise, ignored every norm, threw every bomb, and pissed off everyone. He rejected conventional wisdom, ridiculed "the haters and the losers," and thrived on chaos. Most important, he knew how to win. He threw out the political playbook, which was stacked against Republicans, and did it his way. He mocked political correctness and eviscerated the left-wing media. While typical, poll-tested politicians put on freshly-ironed flannel shirts to barnstorm the Iowa State Fair, he showed up in his private helicopter wearing a pinstripe suite and bold tie. He was Donald Trump, he was a billionaire, he loved America. And he apologized for none of it.

He didn't just talk and tweet—he acted. And when he did talk, he said the things we were all thinking but were too afraid to say in polite company. It's why I eventually started calling him the "see-something, say-something president." He said what *real people* were thinking and feeling, without hesitation or filter. Policies were "dumb," politicians "stupid," and outcomes "a disaster." Before Trump, issues such as illegal immigration, trade imbalance insanity, and foreign policy mistakes were ignored by insular Republican think tanks even though regular voters cared about how those realities impacted their lives. Establishment Republicans had put themselves first; Trump put America first—and everything else flowed from there. In doing so, he called the establishment of both parties corrupt, boring, and uncaring. And I couldn't argue with him.

But this movement is more than Trump himself. He has emboldened the American people and by extension, this author. Ironically, if you read my first book, IN THE ARENA: GOOD CITIZENS, A GREAT REPUBLIC, AND HOW ONE SPEECH CAN REINVIGORATE AMERICA, it reads a lot like Trump, minus the mojo. It was America first, without the political guts. Now liberated from the confines of conventional thinking, when I see something, I say something. When the traditional types scream about "norms," I embrace the chaos. When the media punches, I punch back. When the Left attacks, I counter-attack. Or attack first! If a former establishment type like me can wake up to the reality of our moment, anyone can. But it's going to take brutal honesty—about both ourselves and our county.

We are on the offense—which drives the Left and its lapdog media insane. I've been to combat, but Trump taught me how to fight political combat and live the lyrics of my favorite rock band: I feel safe inside the violence. He taught me and millions of other Americans to grow a spine. I call it a "Trump spine." When we finally face the fact that the very idea of America is at stake, we know it's time to fight back unapologetically on all fronts. In doing so—and in the service of winning a free future—we need to mock, humiliate, intimidate, and crush our leftist opponents in the national conversation, in the culture, and at the polls—the opposite of Jeb and just like Trump.

But still doubt lingers. Not doubt in Trump but doubt about the resolve of average Americans—citizens like me who played by the traditional conservative rules and a generation of Americans indoctrinated by leftist public schools, universities, movies, music, churches, and even our military. Basic truth has been upended by the Left. Up is down, and left is right. Men are women, and women are men—and then they scream at you for not celebrating their ever-changing identity. Oh, yeah, and America is terrible, too.

THE REAL 2016 STAKES

Once I removed my elephant-colored glasses and recalibrated, I started to see that the 2016 election was not between the platform of conventional left and right political parties. Whereas in the past, Republicans and Democrats shared a common civic understanding, that was no longer the case. Eight years of President Obama, in conjunction with decades of leftist cultural and educational indoctrination, had completely shifted the political grounds. It was no longer a debate between patriotic parties—about more or less spending, the level of marginal tax rates, or finer points of foreign policy. The central question of 2016 was—and even more in 2020 is—"Do you love America or not?"

Do you believe in national borders or not?

Do you believe in citizenship and the rule of law or not?

Do you support the police or not?

Do you say the Pledge of Allegiance or not?

Do you stand for the national anthem or not?

Do you support free markets or socialism?

Do you want a large, strong military or not?

Do you want to give veterans the best health care or not?

Do you support the celebration of life and faith or not?

Trump's unbending courage to put America first changed nearly every aspect of political and cultural perspective. If Trump can stand up under attack, so can I. He's not perfect—neither am I—but he's willing to risk everything for America. He doesn't back down from the left-wing mob. He doesn't apologize. He ignores the lie of political correctness. He's a street fighter for the core American values we have, for too long, taken for granted.

Allow me to put our task into army infantry terms. For decades, the United States has been lured into a giant L-shaped near ambush—the most deadly kind, with almost no escape. In more ways than you can imagine, leftists have surrounded traditional American patriots on all sides, ready to close in for the kill: killing our founders, killing our flag, and killing capitalism. The only option for survival in a near ambush is to charge; to close with, and destroy, the enemy. Now, while President Trump gives us cover fire, is our moment to reload, fix bayonets, and charge toward the enemy. Attack! (Metaphorically, of course, for triggered bed wetters.) Only that way, by regaining the initiative and closing with an exposed enemy, will we be able to survive, let alone win.

Donald Trump has proven to be an unflinching warrior for America—and his counterattacks have caused the enemies of freedom to expose their positions. The Left is not used to Republicans fighting back, let alone regaining the initiative. When President Trump charges into its ambush, the Left is forced to expose its position. It has to pop out of the tall grass and is no longer hidden. We now know who its members are and what they really stand for. It was all a quiet shell game before; now it's all in the open—all in plain sight.

The ways in which the Left has entrenched itself in our country have been quite effective: in ivory towers, behind elite titles, in newsrooms, in Hollywood, in the political correctness of liberal churches.

And it has a stranglehold on businesses that are so "woke" that they bow to agitating grievance groups—in spite of their bottom lines. Until now, the Left had hidden itself in plain sight because no political figure dared to step into its territory.

Then Trump came out with all of his bombast, insults, and truth telling with the courage to stand up for the people of this country. For years we watched politicians cower to the legacy, left-wing media—but Trump refused to do so. Asked a tricky question in his first debate about whether he would not abide by the Republican endorsement, Trump confidently raised his hand. Nobody else did. In another 2015 debate classic, the moderator prefaced a question by saying "You've called women you don't like 'fat pigs, dogs, slobs, and disgusting animals.'"

"Only Rosie O'Donnell," Trump shot back.

Then, when hit with the *Access Hollywood* Billy Bush tape in the home stretch of the campaign, Trump responded by bringing all of the women who had accused Bill Clinton of sexually accosting them to the debate. He gave them the microphone. He invited them to sit in the front row. He punched back, not playing by the rules of a game that was stacked against him—and against all patriotic Americans.

Name another politician in America who has the guts to stare down everyone and not waver? Republican candidates, the media, the deep state, Hillary Clinton, all of them tried to take him down. But Trump won in 2016. In 2020 and beyond, we don't need perfect messengers; we need fighters.

(DON'T) VOTE FOR PETE

To understand our moment even better, indulge me in a quick personal story. Did you hear about the time I ran for the US Senate in 2012 from my home state of Minnesota? No? I'm not surprised. Few Minnesota voters did, either.

The year prior to running, I had been the senior counterinsurgency instructor at the Counterinsurgency Training Academy in Kabul, Afghanistan. My job during that tour was to train incoming military units on the nature of the battlefield, what the Taliban was up to in different regions, how it used shadow governance, and recent happenings at the tribal level. The units had already been training at home for months; now they were in Afghanistan, and our job was to give them the latest intelligence and strategy so they would be fully prepared for the fight they were about to encounter.

Without going into details, one of the first rules of counterinsurgency that we always emphasized was "Know your terrain." In war, understanding the physical terrain—the geography—of your area is obvious. Where can the enemy hide? How can I gain a tactical advantage? But in Afghanistan and any other counterinsurgencies, the *human* terrain is even more important. Who are the local players? What tribe is in control? Is there a shadow government that's actually running things? What do the people really think? You have to know the people and the history, their culture, and their motivations.

After a yearlong mission, I came home and naively threw my hat into the Republican ring to run for the US Senate, with the hope of eventually running against—and defeating—Democrat Amy Klobuchar. Yes, that now-fizzled, eat-salad-with-a-comb presidential candidate. But in order to take her on, I first had to win the Republican endorsement and then the nomination. *I'm a conservative guy, Ivy League schooling, combat veteran, from a nice family in Minnesota*, I thought. *Shouldn't be a big problem.*

The day I announced, the communist *Star Tribune*—the Minnesota "paper of record"—put me on the front page, describing my candidacy as "a picture-perfect outsider to pick up the GOP mantle in the race." It was all downhill from there. There was a problem with this self-appointed political poster boy. I violated the first rule we taught in

Afghanistan: know the human terrain. Though I wanted to defeat Amy Klobuchar and Barack Obama as much as anyone, I still didn't understand the grassroots swell forming in America. I didn't understand, or appreciate, the depth of the grassroots Ron Paul Liberty movement, which was making waves in Minnesota and across the country. I assumed I'd be embraced by freedom-loving, patriotic Republican activists. But a growing number of Minnesotans—like millions of other Americans during Barack Obama's reelection year—were skeptical of elitists, globalists, and establishment types. I was none of those things in reality, but my résumé sure read otherwise.

Having attended Princeton and Harvard was one thing, but I was also a term member of the Council on Foreign Relations, which I viewed as a prestigious foreign affairs think tank, headquartered in New York City. Years earlier I had applied for membership and Democrat senator Joe Lieberman had written one of my letters of recommendation, based on a mutual respect formed while supporting war fighters in Iraq. The columnist Max Boot, who later devolved into a rabid Never Trumper, also helped me gain membership. In New York and Washington, DC, my membership was viewed as a prestigious résumé builder. In Minnesota—regular America—my affiliation meant I was a globalist who put international institutions first and wanted to nation build the globe. I wasn't a globalist—never have been. But I also did not understand the threat of globalism. I was coloring inside the lines. I didn't yet understand the full nature of the threat. I was America always but not yet America first.

Then, in May 2012, I was crushed in delegate voting at the Minnesota Republican Party convention—the de facto primary, since I had pledged to abide by the endorsement, yet again coloring inside the lines. The vote wasn't even close. And although we had clearly been out-organized by more liberty-minded delegates focused on America's first principles, I still had almost no clue why. I wanted to serve my country. I was passionate about politics. I was running for all the right reasons, but I was out of touch with the commonsense, liberty-loving grass roots—the "shadow" government of forgotten men and women who were fed up with the bullshit of establishment Republicans. Thank God for these patriots—I'm grateful they *didn't* vote for me.

To add insult to minor injury, the Republican who beat me in that race ended up losing to Amy Klobuchar in the single largest defeat in Minnesota statewide history. I didn't just lose, I lost to the biggest loser of *all time*!

For decades, establishment Republicans had campaigned as conservatives, governed as "moderates," and done the bidding of liberals—rejecting the will of the freedom-minded people who had sent them to Washington. I might have been yet another establishment senator. Instead, my real political education began in 2012, even if I didn't realize it at the time. Republican activists had rejected me, calling *me* a leftist, a globalist, and a squish instead. They were both wrong and right. In hindsight, freedom-minded people were whispering about issues that Donald Trump would soon shout about. The winds were changing.

In ways I only now realize, I was an enemy of Trump before Trump was even a candidate because I was beholden to stale thinking. I didn't understand the roots of our political moment and the nature of the leftist opponents we were up against. I was beholden to scripted talking points, establishment endorsements, party politics, and small-ball thinking. Thank God I didn't win my Senate race in 2012.

BREAKING RANKS

At first, I concealed my Trump conversion—for fear of being kicked out of the unwritten, but very real, conservative cool-kids club.

In the summer of 2016, I distinctly remember a guest segment on *FOX & Friends* where I came out of the closet in my support for then candidate Trump: "You may not love everything he says. You may not love how he says it. You may not love every single tweet he sends out, but he's our man in the arena. He's fighting for America, putting America first. And that's what matters the most to me." Better late than never. Considering my background, I'm glad I figured it out at all.

I didn't know if he could win the election, but I didn't care. I believed he could, believed in him, and desperately wanted to stop the Clinton machine. I backed our fighter. As time went on, I became bolder in my support, but his chances remained ambiguous at best— and that's when the whispers started.

"Pete, what are you doing throwing in with Trump?" asked one Ivy League friend.

"When he loses, you're going to look like a fool," said another colleague.

"This is not a good look for you, Pete," said a prominent conservative in private.

All that was happening as an accidental career in television was taking some shape—*FOX & Friends* had given me chances to guest host frequently. I didn't support Donald Trump because I was angling for a job in his administration. I didn't do it because I wanted to be loved by Donald Trump. I did it because I believed it was the right thing to do for America. The more I heard him, the more I studied his background and watched him perform on the national stage, the more I wanted him to be a disruptor and break every "rule"—to go in there and blow the lid off Washington, DC. I wanted every lobbyist to panic. I wanted the establishment to have no idea what was coming next. Remember, the more they panic, the closer we are to the target.

That's what we got in 2016, and that's who we have today. What happens next—especially in 2020 and beyond—is up to us.

DIVORCE, DEATH, OR DAWN FOR AMERICA?

Will America be recognizable in ten years? The stakes are almost too alarming and difficult to imagine. President Donald Trump's 2020 presidential reelection campaign and the immediate years that follow will, *once and for all*, determine whether the American experiment— the America of our founding—will die (from either internal decay or external decline), get a national divorce which will forever divide us, or decisively change course and create a new dawn for freedom-loving people. By divorce, I mean irreconcilable differences between the Left and the Right in America leading to perpetual conflict that cannot be resolved through the political process. No, I'm not calling for violence, I'm just pointing out the reality. Those are the options: death, divorce, or a new dawn. Sounds hyperbolic, I know. But it's not.

The reality of our consequential moment prompts a central question: Are Trump's election, presidency, and possible reelection the beginning of an American renewal and rebirth? Or does Trump represent the last gasp of a nation, and a generation, clinging to an idea of America that the Left has completely destroyed? This is an open question—and what 2020 is all about.

History is not on our side. The history of great republics demonstrates—time and time again—that decline, divorce, or death are likely. The average life span of republics is between 225 and 275 years. The United States is 245 years old. We're already on borrowed time, a prospect that could doom future generations—my kids, your kids, my grandkids and yours—to a future of mediocrity, dependence, and subjection to either an Orwellian government at home, evil ideologies abroad, or both; walking zombies in the land of all-powerful government.

Don't believe me? Then get "woke" fast. Underneath our noses, and at almost light speed, the Left has captured nearly every quarter of our culture—of public schools, higher education, mass media, social media, Hollywood, corporate culture, the Pentagon, and even many of our churches. Save for Americanism—which is the core of our crusade—every "ism" you can think of has been on its agenda: globalism, feminism, socialism, Islamism, elitism, secularism, multiculturalism, environmentalism, and so on. In a political sense, this all falls under the oxymoronic label "progressivism"—better labeled "leftism" *or regressivism.* As a result, the preceding decades have injected the poisons of open borders, political correctness, socialism, social justice, identity politics, radical environmentalism, gender neutrality, corporate virtue signaling, diversity worship and so on, into our cultural bloodstream. A steady cultural drumbeat of "isms" has worked—with the modern Democrat Party embracing these anti-American, leftist positions wholeheartedly.

Ronald Reagan once said, "I didn't leave the Democratic Party, the Democratic Party left me." The same can be said today of the *entire* American Left and the modern Democrat Party. America, especially after electing Donald Trump, didn't leave the Democrat Party; the Democrats left America. Unfortunately, the celebrities who promised to leave the country if Trump was elected didn't. Look at the clown car of Democrat candidates running to be the next leader of the free world!

I could point out the modest differences among Bernie Sanders, Joe Biden, Elizabeth Warren, Pete Buttigieg, Mike Bloomberg, and all the other failed Democrat candidates—but that is wasted ink at this point. In one form or another, each rejects the basic tenants of Americanism. In various shades, each supports reducing, or eliminating completely, border enforcement. Some own up to the label "socialist," the others hide their socialism behind their support of the economy-crushing Green New Deal and government takeover of health care. Each celebrates illegality, supporting driver's licenses for illegals and sanctuary cities. Each has completely caved to identity and gender politics, cowering before every suggestion of political correctness. Each would gut the military to pay for his or her trillion-dollar schemes. Each believes that God belongs in the back seat and abortions should be on demand. And your guns, they would all take them away—some just sooner rather than later.

The traditional American political paradigm—conservative versus liberals—is dead. Gone are the days when, despite our differences, political opponents disagreed on the margins of our American experiment. Today, inside our domestic political discourse, the very *idea* of America is at stake—it is up for debate and up for grabs. Modern leftists, who represent the soul of the modern Democrat Party, especially the fully indoctrinated younger generation, literally hate the foundational ideas of America. They are not reformable. They run against America, seek to destroy it, and want to remake it. Barack Obama said it himself: he wanted to *transform* America. Today's Democrats say worse. *Much* worse. They *reject* Obama for not going far enough. Obamacare, not good enough! Deporting illegal criminals, wrong! Enforcing our border, draconian! Drone killings of terrorists, culturally insensitive! "Climate change," America's fault!

For most of modern American history, although Democrats and Republicans differed on things such as taxation and welfare, they shared a common American orientation. They largely agreed on basic American ingredients such as national sovereignty, individual liberty, free-market capitalism, religious liberty, equal justice, free speech, the Second Amendment, earnest patriotism, reverence to God, and a strong national defense. Liberals and conservatives differed on size and scope of government but shared that common civic core. *No more.* The liberals are gone, replaced by naked leftists. The party of patriotic and faith-filled Democrats such as Franklin D. Roosevelt, Harry Truman, John F. Kennedy, and even Jimmy Carter, has been replaced by leftist leaders and candidates who seek open borders, universal health care, socialism, godlessness, and politically correct speech codes. And climate change, always climate change! As our president said when scrapping the globalist fantasy known as the Paris Agreement, "I was elected to represent the citizens of Pittsburgh, not Paris." Not so for Democrats.

Basic economics and human history demonstrate that if leftists take full political power, their policies will strangle freedom and prosperity. Having completely captured the culture, winning political power would complete their transformation. They seek to create an America that patriots of this country could not tolerate—and would be obligated to fight back against. Because America is not a government. Not a political party. And not even a system—or just a plot of land. As I mentioned earlier, America is an idea, an experiment in human freedom. That is all I was promised and all I want.

It pains me to say this about my fellow countrymen, but the American Left is an existential threat to freedom. I swore an oath to defend our Constitution against all enemies—foreign *and* domestic. That's why 2020 is so important. If leftists succeed in turning it into something else, then—as strident as it may seem—divorce is imminent. If they turn into King George III, find me a town square in Lexington or a bridge in Concord to stand on. I believe millions of Americans—properly prepared and organized—would do the same. Our great flag means nothing without freedom. Better to go our separate ways—a new freedom-loving country and all—than be complicit in the destruction of America. This is not a call to violence; not at all. And it's not what anybody wants. It is simply a recognition that freedom-loving Americans will not stand idly by and watch our blessed freedoms be trampled.

As Jesus Christ said in Matthew 12:25, "Every kingdom divided against itself is brought to desolation, and every city or house divided against itself will not stand." The powerful American Left, and most of Western civilization, have abandoned faith, freedom, families, and flag just as our external and internal enemies are leveraging their fake versions of each against us. We have Donald Trump right now, but should he lose in 2020, we can't call the pope to organize the faithful—because rather than leading Crusader armies as he used to, the pope is now a leftist who leads climate change rallies. We are fully divided. It's now or never; America or nobody else.

Most Americans can barely fathom any of these options, because they take our country's status as the world's most powerful and prosperous country for granted. They take our founding principles—such as human freedom, limited government, and God-given rights—for granted. Not only do most young people not understand how fragile these principles are, they instead assume that they are inevitable and self-perpetuating. Because most are no longer taught about these principles, many young Americans assume they are the rule, not the exception, in human history. Just look at a 2019 Gallup poll which showed that socialism was as popular as capitalism among young Americans. Socialism has never worked. Ever. But if capitalism is not taught, it's empty promises are soothing sounds to ignorant ears.

Too many Americans don't "live in history" as described in the previous chapter; they believe that major world events are largely complete, big wars are over, and the international system will preserve the status quo. They believe that our American experiment is "inevitable" and that we will always remain on top. The Greeks, the Romans, the French, the Brits, and many others thought the same thing. Where are they now? It's easy to cling to "norms" and "processes" that keep us on a general trajectory—but that easy path is also deadly. And what if those norms and processes have been poisoned? What if by staying on track we are booking ourselves a one-way ticket to decay, decline, and death?

But what if we fought back? What if Trump had four more years to do the same?

"He can't say that! He can't do that!" leftists shriek, on and on, about Trump. It helps them self-medicate, I suppose. Trump Derangement Syndrome is real, after all. Trump haters—mostly on the Left, but also those on the Right who unwittingly aid the Left—use fidelity to norms, processes, and establishment policies as a way to confine the disruptive movement President Trump leads and to prevent him from actually *reversing* a destructive course that benefits the connected class. At this point—245 years after our revolution—every time Republicans embrace the trappings of process, conventional wisdom, moderation, and compromise, we accelerate the death of America.

This is why 2020 matters so much. Either America embraces unapologetic and unfiltered Americanism or we elect a far-left, anti-American far worse than Barack Obama. *But* if Trump wins in 2020, it means his blunt-force, patriotic movement truly resonates with liberty-loving citizens who can create a new dawn for America. If, in the face of 90 percent negative media coverage, with the entirety of Hollywood and Silicon Valley arrayed against him—suppressing YouTube videos and banning Twitter accounts—and the Democrats launching investigations against him, Trump still wins, then our republic is redeemable.

But if Trump loses in 2020, I fear America is doomed. The Democrats—on track to nominate a radical leftist—would complete the political domination they already maintain in our culture, media, and schoolhouses. The ivory towers of the Ivy League would become the policies of Washington: speech codes instead of free speech, bye-bye Second Amendment, anti-Israel and pro-Islamist foreign policy, naked socialism, government-run everything, Common Core education for everyone, a tiny military, and abortion on demand— even postbirth. The exact opposite of what our founders risked their lives, fortunes, and sacred honor for. America would be destined to fade into irrelevance, à la western Europe. Who wants to live in a geographic America that is not actually America?

2020 VISION

Donald Trump faces every kind of resistance one can imagine, yet he can win again. If he wins, there's a good chance we'll see another conservative justice on the Supreme Court, creating the first solid conservative majority in my lifetime—and for years to come. Imagine that possibility!

This is an America first election. In 2016, Trump voters were mostly hidden. Some "converted" late in the game; some weren't sure what kind of politician he'd be. But now we know—and we know what we're up against. We've seen what he represents, and we've seen what the Left represents. It's MAGA versus ANTIFA: the red hats versus the black masks.

The goal of the Left's aggression is to intimidate us, which is precisely why we must have the courage to wear our red hats, put our bumper stickers on, go to rallies, and be unafraid to talk about our great country. This will only force the radical Left to expose itself as even more fanatical—because you're not being fanatical. You're being American. There's nothing radical about our position. For many patriots, it might have seemed radical to vote for Donald Trump in 2016, but he's a known entity now. He's not radical, he's real. And so is the Left.

Look at what the Left has done to a duly elected president since 2016. First it was Russia, Russia, Russia. Then it was racism, racism, racism. And now they are wishing for a recession, recession, recession. All of it adds up to resistance, resistance, resistance. The Left never, ever accepted the results of the 2016 election. They never will. If the Left wins in 2020, they will take it as a validation of their elitist narrative; that one deplorable hiccup was just a speed bump in the progressive trajectory of America. And although they would be wrong, they might as well be right.

The election of 2020 is a watershed moment—a chance to validate 2016, consolidate freedom-loving political power, and start to gain ground in the culture wars that have ultimately manifested in political fanaticism by the Left. We can finish what Donald Trump started and restore the course of American history.

That's where we are today: we win or the leftists win, we lose or they lose. And if we win, America can win. If the Left wins, America is going to be lost. Tell your friends, tell your spouse and kids, tell your neighbors, tell your pastor: you're proud of what Trump represents. I'm speaking especially to my former Republican establishment friends; your petty grievances are only fuel to the Left. Stop apologizing for the tweets and the tone. He's not your pastor. He's not your spouse, and he's not your counselor—he's your commander in chief. Your *crusader* in chief! He's the man we need right now, and he's crushing leftism because he loves America. Enjoy the reality show; Trump might be a performer, but he's not an actor. Get on board, or get out of the way.

"Nationalism is a betrayal of patriotism."

—French president Emmanuel Macron

"I'm a Nationalist."

—US president Donald Trump

THREE

AMERICANISM NOW, AMERICANISM FOREVER

As with his candidacy, my first reaction to Donald Trump's slogan—"America first"—was dismissal. It sounded like a smoke screen for isolationism, especially since the same slogan had been used by Charles Lindbergh and the isolationist America First Committee during World War II to argue that the United States should not get involved in that epic struggle. It was just a slogan, I believed, for a soon-to-be failed presidential candidate lacking a real foreign policy agenda. Never Trumpers today still believe this, against all evidence.

Then he won the nomination. My conversion happened, and it all made sense. For an American president awash in global crises, international demands, and potential threats, "America first" was the clarifying lens for American action. The president has a personal knack—an instinct—for internalizing the following questions when making a decision: *Does the action we are about to undertake actually strengthen or advantage America first and foremost? Or are we instead chasing an international scheme, foreign prerogative, or lost cause?* Moreover, putting America first means keeping America strong—preserving the only bastion of freedom in an increasingly contested and unfree world. "America first" might still be a controversial concept for elitists and globalists, but it makes perfect sense to patriots.

Leftists, however, have a much larger problem with putting America first: Why would you put America first if you don't believe in America? Moreover, because they believe that America is *the* source of most problems throughout the world, not only should we *not* put it first, but America should take a back seat. America "was never that great," said New York governor and establishment Lefty Andrew Cuomo. Members of the so-called squad—Comrade Cortez, Somali Omar, and Rashida Tlaib—say worse nearly every day. They literally hate America. You can't put something first if you don't believe in its goodness or even usefulness. In order to deter and defeat threats abroad—to project righteous power—you first need to make sure you preserve your righteousness and power at home. There is no America first without . . . keeping America great.

WHAT IS AMERICANISM?

Enter Americanism. Not patriotism, Republicanism, or even conservatism—just Americanism. Americanism, simply defined, is an unapologetic allegiance to the founding ideals of the United States of America. It's the opposite of leftism. Americanism is America first applied to the domestic core of our nation—to the first principles of our American experiment. In a diverse country, it is the collective American identity grounded in freedom—and the active defense of it. Why did our founders put their "lives, fortunes, and sacred honor" on the line? Not for better drug prices or debt-free college or universal pre-K; America is about much larger ideals.

If you boil it all down, our founders fought for two core—and exceptional—ideas for America's *citizens*: individual freedom and equal justice. All other aspects of Americanism stem from these. Each individual American *citizen* has God-given rights that ensure personal freedom, and each individual American *citizen* deserves to be treated equally under the law. We have a country, our country has laws, and they apply to all of her *citizens* equally. Take away these ideas—freedom, equality, and their application to citizens—and you no longer have America.

Another way to define Americanism is American nationalism— yet another phrase that would have scared me away just four years ago. The word *nationalism* has been hijacked to mean racist nativism, rabid jingoism, or ethnic nationalism—and media and academic elites point out when it has been misused in history and therefore believe it must never be used. As usual, they are wrong, and President Trump tells them straight to their face, "I am a nationalist." Because this country's nationalism is unique. American nationalism puts America first in order to preserve this nation—the only true bastion of freedom on the planet. It's a melting pot that greets newcomers with a Statue of Liberty, not a statue of Lenin. To adapt a famous phrase, I believe that "nationalism in defense of freedom is no vice"; instead, it is our highest virtue and aim, because it's all about *freedom*.

To understand Americanism—or American nationalism—you must understand the basics, which is the problem for leftists. The core principles of the United States, as spelled out in the Declaration of Independence and codified in our Constitution, are not the *cause* of the problems in this nation; they are the *solution*—to the problems we are currently facing and the problems we will face in the future. Consider the horror of slavery, Jim Crow, and the lack of basic civil rights for blacks. The United States made progress—and is still making progress—on these injustices *because* we believe in the God-given right to life, liberty, and the pursuit of happiness for *all*. Africans were not citizens, and now they are. The bright light of those historic words in the Declaration ultimately reveal injustice, empower people, and should unite us all.

Take my example from chapter one. I don't see Texas Omar and Somali Omar through the lens of their race, gender, or religion; I view them through the lens of Americanism. We the People—citizens of this great country—believe that God endowed all of His children with inalienable rights and that government cannot take those rights away. When citizens believe this—and when the selfish impulses of human nature are constrained through checks, balances, and limitations on government—we witness the most amazing explosion of progress the world has ever seen.

Consider the fact that you and I carry more technology in our hands than NASA had when it put Americans on the moon in 1969. This is what happens when you unleash the human spirit, entrepreneurship, and capitalism. In fact, you would be hard pressed to find one thing you use in your daily life that isn't a product of American invention or innovation. Try it. Your kitchen, garage, and workplace—pick a product and search online for who invented or innovated it to its modern form. I'll save you some clicks: America and Americans.

There is, and always has been, evil in America—but that doesn't make America evil. Never forget this. Anyone who understands human nature—or has studied the biblical truth of our fallen condition—knows that we are all sinners, all prone to corruption, and all inherently selfish. Rather than ignore those realities—as anyone who peddles socialism or collectivism does—our founders were students of human history and therefore provided a pathway to a more perfect union by inscribing eternal truths to be pursued, even if never perfectly manifested. *Because man is not perfectible!* Moreover, our founders created institutions that both channeled our flawed human nature productively and constrained our worst instincts for power and control. The result: the greatest amount of human freedom any government has ever produced—or tolerated.

This combination—the product of first principles, of Americanism—is what is under attack by the Left. The enemies of America aren't simply fighting for certain legislation and policy changes, although that is one of their tactics. Each government expansion—Common Core, Obamacare, and the Green New Deal, to name a few—is a permanent stain. But their real battlefield is cultural: the history they teach, the movies they make us watch, the empty gospel they preach, and the news they package for us. Subtle, and subversive, each. They want to destroy the very *idea* of America. They want to "fundamentally transform" us. They have a long-term strategy, on all fronts and right under our noses.

Americanism is not cheering for Team USA at the Olympics. It's not the White House, not our monuments, and not our national parks. It's not the movies we create or the industries we pioneer. It's not even about winning world wars and then rebuilding the countries and economies of our former enemies. Americanism is a *free* way of life.

Just a few decades ago there was little need to litigate the idea of freedom—because it was a given. Our schools taught it, politicians in both parties believed it, a plurality of the media celebrated it, and the pastors in our pulpits reinforced it. Prayer in school was allowed and encouraged. Our flag, anthem, and Pledge of Allegiance were universally revered and ubiquitous. Our movies proudly displayed patriotic themes. Hard work and discipline were expected, and dependency was shamed. Not anymore. Today those positions are outliers or outright gone. If anything, the only shaming the Left does is of American citizens who insist on those bedrock positions. Today we are forced to defend the core of American values. Our soul.

HOW GREAT REPUBLICS DIE

As I mentioned previously, the stakes for America in 2020 are stark—and in the aftermath could include a messy national divorce. But before America gets a divorce, we should get some counseling— which includes understanding how countries such as ours get to this point. Great republics such as America die when they forget who they are, become lazy and arrogant, and betray their founding ideals—seduced by ideas antithetical to what made them great in the first place. This process starts slowly but then quickly leads to self-loathing, internal suicide, all-powerful government, and eventually external subjugation. Once the core of the republic is weak, another country—not a free country—sets the terms of "freedom."

The soul of America is under a multipronged attack, and although it's easy to point the finger of blame—and I will point many—ultimately we have *all* played a part in the decline of America. When the high school refuses to allow a Bible study group on school grounds, and "we turn the other cheek," instead of standing up, we're to blame. When the local library uses taxpayer dollars to fund "drag queen story hour" and we shrug, we're to blame. When patriotic Latino restaurant owners proudly attend a Trump rally and are then boycotted by Leftists, we're to blame if we don't rally to support them. Over decades and years and in each of our spheres of influence, it is the choices of individual citizens that are the ultimate composition, or decomposition, of republics.

As I laid out in my first book, IN THE ARENA, having good leaders is important, but having good citizens is more important— citizens who are willing to work for a living, fight when necessary, raise large, patriotic families, and believe in something greater than themselves. The ingredients are easy—work, fight, forge kids, and have faith—but, as with anything in life, putting them into action is the consequential part.

In healthy republics, usually in their younger years, the religious, cultural, and civic culture reinforces these values, ensuring their perpetuation. Citizens who don't work hard are shamed, citizens who won't fight are ostracized, citizens who don't have many kids are rare, and citizens who don't believe in God are tolerated—but surrounded by faith-filled churches, families, and even schools. The next generation—including immigrant families—absorbs love of God and country almost by osmosis, ensuring a shared cultural foundation. Hence our national motto, "E pluribus unum"—literally, "Out of many, one."

President Trump has also reminded us that healthy republics guard their sovereignty. They respect their citizens enough to control territorial borders, control who is allowed into the country, expect assimilation and allegiance from new arrivals, ensure that vital industries—steel production, medical essentials, and manufacturing, for example—are not outsourced, and never cede oversight or decision making to other countries or institutions. Our dependency on China for drugs and medical supplies during the Coronavirus is a prime, recent example. For these simple principles, President Trump is attacked relentlessly—by both the Left and the establishment Right. Open borders are politically profitable for Democrats and financially profitable for the Chamber of Commerce crowd; neither group is thinking *first* about the taxpaying and law-abiding citizens of the United States.

In dying republics, the opposite occurs. Mere tolerance of fringe ideas is no longer sufficient; society must not only embrace—but celebrate—the very attitudes we used to acknowledge as unhealthy to the fabric of our culture. Think: the cancel culture and the institution of politically correct speech codes. Welfare programs growing so large that they smother incentives to work. Obama's massive food stamp expansion, which Trump is reversing. Innocent human life being sacrificed for convenience, with no expectation for personal responsibility. Partial-birth abortion on demand. Politicians and demagogues clamoring for the government to do things that individuals, private companies and charities used to do—and did quite well. Government-run *everything*.

With educational institutions completely captured by left-wing ideologues, the younger generations see almost nothing worth physically fighting for—unless it's a fantastical climate change scheme in which they get to control the solution or a fantasy that Trump supporters are "fascists." Where do you think the "Bernie bros" come from? Their efforts make them feel good about themselves, otherwise known as virtue signaling. Self-absorbed citizens also see little use for children beyond one child—who *always* wears a helmet, carries a bottle of Purel, and never eats gluten! Faith and purpose are stripped out of all institutions, including the church itself, where most denominations pick and choose which religious maxims to ignore. God is love, but sin is subjective; Heaven can be achieved on Earth, while Hell is fictional.

Finally, dying republics don't have respect for themselves—or their citizens. In fact, they're self-loathing. To a growing number of Leftists, the flag and anthem of the United States are considered racist and oppressive. They see their forefathers, and their sins, as reasons to make reparations. They try to tear down statues of Thomas Jefferson and erase George Washington's name from their universities. They clamor for open borders, call themselves global citizens, promote rampant illegality, call their political opponents racist ("Trump is racist!" has poured from the lips of every Democrat presidential contender in 2020), expose their citizens to destructive international economic currents, and reject the very ideals our founders fought a revolution to earn. Leftists are so busy reminding all of us how evil we are that they never stop to realize how wonderful we really have it in 2020—thanks to Americans of every color and class who fought for real equality and inclusion. Yet no matter what, there is always a new grievance pulling us further away from gratitude.

America is at this moment on the path to death, divorce, or dawn—and both sides know it. I'm not the only one pondering the founding principles of America. So are those on the left. Take former Democrat presidential candidate Robert Francis O'Rourke (his nanny called him "Beto"), for example. In a January 2019 *Washington Post* profile piece, he fake philosophized the following: "I think that's the question of the moment: Does this still work? Can an empire like ours with military presence in over 170 countries around the globe, with trading relationships . . . and security arrangements in every continent, can it still be managed by the same principles that were set down 230-plus years ago?"

The Constitution was ratified 231 years ago. Robert Francis wonders: Does America still work? He sees the same prognosis—but from the other side. America is dying, and we have little time left in which to heal her. By healing her, he means *transforming* her. As he questions America, he questions the Constitution and—like most leftists—ignores the Declaration of Independence. Why? It's a critically important omission. An intentional one. Let me explain.

THE CORE OF AMERICANISM: DECLARATION OR THE CONSTITUTION?

Are you a Declaration or Constitution person? It might be the most telling question of this book.

Most people today who yell about America's Constitution care very little about our Declaration of Independence, published thirteen years earlier. The Left intentionally tries to separate the documents, but the two are inextricably linked. One is utterly useless without the other. Most important, you cannot have a Constitution without a Declaration; the absence of the latter makes the former mere parchment.

The Declaration of Independence is America's soul and the Constitution is America's body, our implementation skeleton. This is not to downplay the political brilliance of the Constitution—it is the *second* most important political document ever written by man. Checks and balances, coequal branches of government, and federalism are the backbone of the American constitutional system. However, if the Constitution is not grounded in the principles of our Declaration—our soul—then the Constitution is an empty shell, a carcass of yesteryear. The Declaration lays out what we believe: laws of nature and nature's God, self-evident truths, rights endowed by a Creator, unalienable rights, "life, liberty, and the pursuit of happiness," consent of the governed, the right of the people to alter or abolish their government, and the protection of Divine Providence. Without God, truth, rights, life, liberty, and the People, America is simply not America, even with a Constitution.

The Declaration established the *principles*, and the Constitution sought the best *process* to make those principles a reality.

Unsurprisingly, leftists have a "complicated" relationship with the Constitution. They want the Constitution to "evolve" to fit *their* view of the world—a view that is the opposite of those who risked their lives to secure our freedom and the opposite of our founding principles. When leftists don't like the Constitution, it's because they no longer believe in the Declaration—because the Declaration cannot, and does not, evolve.

Leftists like the Constitution when they want to wrap themselves in the flag, which is usually right before they burn it. They see it as a "living document" that can codify policies they love and eventually restrict foundational freedoms such as *real* freedom of speech, the Second Amendment, and states' rights. They'll never acknowledge that the states actually created the federal government, not the other way around. Can you imagine a constitution written by leftists today? Instead of the 4,500-word document ratified in 1787, theirs would be a twelve-volume set containing millions of words and seeking to codify ever-changing buzzwords such as *diversity, fairness, tolerance,* and *social justice.* The European Union recently wrote its own constitution, and it's a 70,000-word maze of impenetrable bureaucratic dictates. It's not a constitution, it's a cage.

If you're exclusively a Constitution person, you probably think that something like the Second Amendment is an aberration of the eighteenth century. And that if you own a gun, maybe you should own it only because you like to hunt. Even then, you should have only *one* and use it in a three-week, government-approved time window during the year. If you're a Constitution *and* a Declaration person, you understand that the reason I have a gun is so I can protect myself *and* so my government can't impose tyranny upon me. The first step of a tyrannical government is taking away guns. Don't believe me? That's what they did in Venezuela. "Yeah, don't worry, buddy. You don't need a gun. We got ya." Bye-bye, freedom.

Anyone who understands the Declaration understands that personal freedom starts with *individuals* and their ability to defend themselves *and* defend their liberties. Establishment Republican types also use the "hunting argument" because they're scared of making the bigger case for the Second Amendment. *What? You're going to pull your gun on the government?* If my government turned on me and declared that I didn't have the freedom to protect my life, liberty, and property, you're damn right I would pull a gun on my government. No one wants to go there. But, remember, America is an ideal—not a government. When the ideal dies, the government still exists—to grow and enrich itself at the expense of individuals. This is the outcome the Left ultimately desires.

America's greatness is tied to the ideas of the Declaration. We are a nation of shared freedom ideas, values, and—yes—borders. Nations founded on identity politics, such as race or class, fail. But a nation, this nation, founded on ideals can endure—but only if we are intentional about safeguarding it. The only ideas that have no place here, that we should prevent from coming here, are antifreedom, tyrannical ideas. We cannot allow our nation to be changed by bad ideas, criminals, and cultures that are antithetical to human freedom—hence why managed immigration is so important for Americanists. As a nation, the Declaration is our soul and the Constitution is our body. If you lost your soul but are still walking around, you're a zombie.

The next time you see a "constitutional scholar" on television, online, or in a classroom, ask yourself if they're also a Declaration person. The next time you have a debate with a leftist about the Constitution, ask what they think of the Declaration and the rights endowed by our Creator. The first response will likely be befuddlement, then anger—as always. Americanism channels the Declaration, the Left wants to forget it.

Are we Declaration or Constitution people? The answer is that we are both, or we are nothing.

DEMOCRACY NOW?

On a related note central to Americanism, we need to stop calling our country a "democracy." Because it's not! It seems like semantics, but it's crucial to the crusade. James Madison warned, "Democracies have ever been spectacles of turbulence and contention; have ever been found incompatible with personal security or the rights of property; and have in general been as short in their lives as they are violent in their deaths." He's right. Hence the fact that the word *democracy* is not found in either the Declaration or the Constitution—but you'll hear the word every five minutes from Democrats, ignorant media types, and most academics.

Our founders rejected the idea of "democracy" because democracies are governed by simple majority rule. Whoever gets the most votes makes the rules—including abolishing the very rights we assume are immutable. Instead, if you believe in endowed rights—which we as Declaration people do—then pure democracy is antithetical to your thinking. A free nation requires institutional checks and balances against the impulses of the majority—a majority that, if it decides to target the minority, will eventually become tyrannical. Just look at how intolerant the so-called tolerant Left is today—it would like to apply that same fake tolerance to every part of your life. It wants you to conform, according to its politically correct rules. For now, the Constitution is in its way.

Instead, the founders chose to make our form of government a constitutional republic, meaning we elect people to represent us in government, in accordance with the road map provided by the Constitution. We do not directly vote for federal laws; our representatives do. We do not elect the president; the Electoral College does. Our representatives cannot pass any law they want; it must be in keeping with our Constitution. There are checks and balances against the tyranny of the majority. As a result, our republic inherently guarantees an individual's God-given rights, no matter the view of the majority and no matter the impulses of those with government power.

Of course, the Constitution isn't perfect; no man-made document could ever be. That's why it has been properly and constitutionally amended twenty-seven times and will surely be amended in the future—including, hopefully, by an Article 5 Amending Convention that will shrink the power of the federal government and be convened by We the People. (For more information, visit Convention of States at www.conventionofstates.com.) No matter the process, any amendment must be tethered to the unchanging, unamendable, and enlightened principles of our true founding document: the Declaration of Independence.

As I alluded to earlier, the Electoral College is a beautiful example of how our republic spreads out the influence of citizens from across the nation—so that national elections aren't controlled by elitist and leftist big-city bastions such as New York and California. Though there was no California at the time of our founding, the principle has aged gracefully. The Founders wanted to make sure that small and rural states were always included and not overwhelmed by more populous states. Hence, similarly, there are two US senators per state, giving South Carolina the same amount of say in the Senate as California.

All that said, if you're a leftist, you want "democracy" because you have already rejected the Declaration of our founding and believe that the pesky Constitution guiding our republic is merely an impediment to the immediate and radical changes you want to make. For leftists, calls for "democracy" represent a complete rejection of our system. Watch how often they use the word. They hate America, so they hate the Constitution and want to quickly amass 51 percent of the votes to change it. They are the *Democrat* Party, after all. It's why they want to abolish the Electoral College. It's why they want a national popular vote, with no voter identification required. They want to drive up the vote only in the cities and ignore the middle of the country—all without verifying who is actually voting. I wonder why that might be? It's also why many of their radical and rabid outside groups go by names such as Democracy Now! and Democracy Alliance. The left-wing *Washington Post* in the era of Trump declares, "Democracy Dies in Darkness"—which is ironic at best, given their aversion to shining their investigative spotlight on anything pertaining to Leftists. The truth is, Republics Live in History.

They might be Democrats, but we are *Republic*ans.

YOUR AMERICAN DREAM

Americanism matters because it creates the pathway for any American to achieve what we all know as the "American dream." Americanism is about empowering individuals to achieve the life they want, free from unnecessary government interference and according to equally applied laws. In short, it can be summarized as "life, liberty, and the pursuit of happiness." That said—full disclosure—I've come to loathe the modern meaning of the word "happy" as in "the pursuit of happiness" because it's become a vapid, shallow term. *What makes you happy? Are you feeling happy today?* There are lots of shallow answers to those questions these days. True happiness comes from purpose and meaning; the pursuit is up to you.

We should see "the pursuit of happiness" through the lens of the deeper, God-given opportunity to strive for a good and better life for you and your family. The American dream doesn't promise happiness—or success. It only promises you an equal shot at them, or as equal as your station and abilities afford. This opportunity isn't granted to you by government; instead, our right to pursue happiness comes from God—a divine right rooted in deep meaning, not shallow happy talk. Too many people are looking for government to change the life that God has given them and America has afforded them.

We have the right to be alive, we have the right to be free, we have the right to defend ourselves, and we have the right to go after the dreams in our hearts. We also have the right to fail—and the right to start over when we fail. In America you can dream big. In

America the poorest of the poor can rise to the highest of heights—and pass their prosperity to the next generation. In America, your last name, your race, your parents' job, and your address do not define who you are. You chart your course—up or down. In the pursuit of that dream, there are things you cannot do: you cannot restrict other people's liberty or infringe on other people's lives in the process. And yes, this includes you, government. The government is where dreams go to die.

In everyday life, the American flag is the symbol we most associate with the dream of freedom. Look at the protestors in Hong Kong or the dissidents in Venezuela. Even the protestors in Iran. They point to the American flag as their symbol of hope. Moreover, the American dream is what drives people to risk their lives to come across our borders. The only thing we ask is that people seek a legitimate path to our country—respecting our laws, learning our language, and using robust pathways to legal residence. Americanism is not racist or anti-immigrant; instead, it is raceless and pro-citizen.

The American dream is also not exclusive to our country; freedom was a human desire long before it became a destination. We always hope that other nations will embrace freedom and their people will experience the opportunities we have in America. But as we've seen, these things cannot be imposed on the world, nor can they be given away to anyone who comes across our border illegally. Leftists want open borders not because they care about immigrants but because they care about advancing their own power. Anyone who believes in the American dream cannot be for open borders. As the famous conservative economist Milton Friedman once said, "You cannot simultaneously have free immigration and a welfare state." One sells a fake dream, the other a false one. Both undercut the taxpaying citizens of America who achieved their dreams the right way.

If we actually had a wall around our welfare benefits and ensured that government assistance was only for US citizens, the idea of a walled-off border would become less of an issue—because we would probably be bringing in the type of people who are willing to work and not be dependent. Instead, we need to build a big, beautiful wall along our border because the Left has used every mechanism at its disposal to ensure that *illegal* immigrants can come to our county and steal—yes, steal—the benefits paid for by taxpayers: health care, schooling, and food stamps. Establishment politicians refuse to fix immigration or our bloated welfare system because the Left doesn't care about productive citizens; it cares only about political power. Behind every illegal immigrant and every citizen dependent on government assistance—or both, if the Left gets its way—leftists see a voter, plain and simple. Illegality and dependency are their calling cards, undercutting the American dream from those who play by the rules.

TRUMP AND AMERICANISM

Americanism is an idea, but what does it look like in practice? President Trump is showing us—every day.

First and foremost, he is unapologetic in his allegiance to America—and he fights for it like a hardened UFC fighter. It's no surprise that he loves the sport. Whereas most Republicans cater to the rigged, government-media complex, Trump punches back. In modern times, no Republican, no conservative, no American has fought harder to defend the basic pillars of what has made America a great country. As a result, the Left—and all of its media, Hollywood, and deep-state friends—hate Trump more than Lucifer himself. They attack him, slander him, impeach him, and demean him. He is supposed to fall into line like everyone else does. But he refuses. Other than his winning the 2016 election, the reason they hate him the most is that he actually fights back. Most Republicans go along to get along; President Trump never backs down—and never apologizes.

Barack Obama, on the other hand, never faced resistance from the government-media complex because he was intent on growing government in every way and welcoming the "managed" decline of America. According to him and the Left, America represents yesterday—a dead ideal founded on slavery, subjugation, and evil corporations that is wholly unworthy of modern reverence. Obama also said that there was no "magic wand" to bring back the manufacturing industries that Trump has revived. When the Left fought for "America," it was in the context of tearing down our republic in order to replace it with an antifreedom, anti-God, anticitizen agenda. Obama and the modern Left are unapologetic about one thing: apologizing for the sins of America.

President Trump understands—and defends—the founding ideals of America, chief among them that our rights come from God, not from government. His speeches emphasize this often. Government is here to get off our backs, keep the rules fair, treat everyone equally, and protect citizens. He has fought to cut taxes, reduce regulations, take on the permanent government class, protect the Second Amendment, save babies, and safeguard our borders. And although our government schools have become Common Core indoctrination camps, he seeks to revive civic ritual—yes, the military parade! These are basics, but in today's leftist-dominated culture, such stances are painted as archaic, cruel, and unnecessary. But President Trump understands what we understand: that the ideals of our founding—of our Declaration—are not outdated, they are essential.

The Left, of course, sees it the opposite way. President Trump's attacks on the "fake news" media are an attack on the First Amendment, they say. His use of Twitter to defend himself is a form of bullying. His defense of the Second Amendment is a cave to the NRA lobbyists. And his commitment to securing the border, you guessed it, is racist. In their jihad to remake America, the Left is out to crush Trump—not just because of who he is but because of what he stands for.

Finally, as President Trump says time and time again, "If you don't have borders, you don't have a country." He has fought to restore citizenship as the hallmark in a left-wing world gone borderless. Yes, America is an idea—but it is also a country. We have borders, laws, and legal citizens. President Trump believes that those things matter—just as our founders did and would today. The Left today rejects this view, spreading lawlessness with sanctuary city policies—literally telling local police not to coordinate with federal agents looking for known criminals. The result: dead citizens and endangered law enforcement. No country can survive without enforceable borders and empowered law enforcement enforcing the law equally. Make no mistake about it, President Trump is fighting for law and order, while the Left fully embraces, at best, one-sided lawfare, and at worst, lawlessness. Actually, I don't know which is worse.

Americanism has been President Trump's mantra and must be ours. Regardless of our color, gender, or class—we are Americans, dammit. We will not apologize for it. Never. And we're not Republicans or even conservatives; those small, boring, and limiting labels don't suffice anymore; they don't even come close. We are red-blooded Americans, and we know only a full investment in Americanism can save our country. The Republican Party, by default, has become the only party of America, it must embrace this fact, or we will leave it, too.

President Trump demands that we are not hyphenated Americans and we are not global citizens—we are united, American citizens. We are American nationalists. We love God, we love our freedom, we love our guns, we have natural rights (especially the unborn), we speak freely, we work hard, we fight when necessary, we love our families—and we don't expect anyone else to take care of them or us.

Thankfully, the founding principles that birthed our nation don't exist only inside our borders. They still live elsewhere in the world, and we mustn't be afraid to stand with our fellow Americanists. Americanism is alive in Israel, where Benjamin Netanyahu boldly stands against international anti-Semitism and Islamism. Americanism is alive in the hearts of Brexiters in the United Kingdom who yearn for national sovereignty. Americanism is alive in places such as Poland, which reject the globalist visions of leftist bureaucrats in old Europe. Regrettably, we have more in common with those international freedom fighters then we do with modern American Democrats. It's a sad truth to have to admit. There is a reason that members of freedom movements around the world brandish American flags, while leftists here won't stand for ours. Americanism must be lived, not just lived in. President Trump understands this and leads in this way.

WHAT AMERICANISM IS NOT

When I recently bought a new house, the first thing I did was have a commercial-sized flagpole installed in our front yard. I dug the four-foot-deep hole myself—axing (irony noted) a tree stump that needed to go. For me, the flag is the most important part of our property, just as the flag on my shoulder was the most important part of why I was in Afghanistan, Iraq, and Guantánamo Bay.

But Americanism is not only about the flag, it's about freedom. Freedom for all and freedom forever. If the flag stopped representing freedom, I would stop flying it. Americanism is not sustained by patriotism alone and is not about flying the flag; Americanism is about the perpetuation of freedom—and the flag is a representation of that. Without the principles, symbols cannot be confused with substance—and empty symbols are the worst kind.

Yet instead of understanding this connection, the Left mocks flag-waving Americans as dumb, simple, and ignorant—clinging to our God and our guns. Obama called us "bitter clingers," and Hillary put us into a "basket of deplorables." Bernie says we need a socialist revolution, counting on the witlessness of ungrateful and indoctrinated youth. Comrade Cortez says that pulling yourself up by your bootstraps is not tenable, because literally pulling oneself up by one's bootstraps is very difficult. So is "wrapping your head around something"—but enough with the analogy game. We cannot fall for leftists' ignorance, intimidation, and mischaracterization. Like the millions of other Americans who fly the flag every day, I don't give a damn about your ethnicity, race, religion, or sexuality. Eat what you want, sleep with whom you want, and pray to whomever you want. I don't care. All I ask is that you love America, just as Texas Omar and his family do. Every American deserves the blessing of individual freedom and equal justice. Even Ivy Leaguers.

I went to Princeton University as a political philosophy major. I then went to Harvard University's Kennedy School of Government. I studied governments and political philosophies up, down, and sideways—enduring the leftist, globalist bias of the Ivy League for years. The experience only made it clearer to me how special America really is—*if* you appreciate the ideas upon which she is founded—which those universities no longer teach, of course. Once you get that, our flag is the most beautiful thing you've ever seen. You want to fly it, teach it, glorify it, serve for it. And you want every parade you can get. You want to tattoo it on your arm because you realize what it represents. Our flag is—for now—the icon of freedom. The symbolism is crucial, because it reminds us what really matters.

My parents are wonderful God-fearing patriots, but they did not ram America down my throat with apple pie for dessert. They didn't have to. America is our home, and we were always proud of that. We went to the Memorial Day parade and the Fourth of July celebration in Wanamingo, Minnesota, every year, and in that tiny farming town in southern Minnesota, I'd sit on the sidewalk and take it all in. I really just wanted candy like every other kid—and to squirt my water gun. But as I waited, I watched old men in various shades of military uniforms walk slowly down the middle of Main Street. Every time they passed by, the entire town rose to their feet and applauded them. Flags waved, veterans saluted, and the fallen were honored.

Ah, these must be special people, my young mind processed. They were indeed.

Our flag must be a big deal. We must be a pretty special country. And my life experience proved that beyond a doubt.

I will happily absorb the bullets of jingoism from other people—because I want people to ask the question "Why do you love America so much?"—so I can tell them.

———————————

In this American Crusade, we need to be clear about our beliefs, our words, and our actions. The enemies of our country are very clear about theirs.

We love our country, not because it's perfect but because it's the best incarnation of both righteous and realistic values. We're patriots. We're nationalists. We're Americans. America is where freedom lives—and where freedom can fight.

But America is under siege by the scourge of leftism. Our situation is bad, very bad. We are in the fight of our lives for the soul of our country. You might be thinking "Pete, you laid this out in pretty simple terms. Us versus them. America versus the Left. Good versus evil. You're overplaying your hand. It's not that bad." Read on, and think again.

PART TWO

LEFTISM

"... the first radical known to man who rebelled against the establishment and did it so effectively that he at least won his own kingdom—Lucifer."

— Saul Alinsky, *Rules for Radicals: A Practical Primer for Realistic Radicals*

"You do not negotiate with these people; you destroy them."

—MSNBC's Elie Mystal on Trump supporters

FOUR

LEFTISM: HOW DEMOCRATS LEFT AMERICA

I was not raised in an overtly political household, but my upbringing was conservative, patriotic, and faith filled. My parents were Republicans but not activists. My dad's side of the family was conservative, my mom's more liberal. My wonderful grandmother Gwen even protested against Ronald Reagan's nuclear buildup in 1984. A few of my uncles and aunts were hippies from the 1960s but not outright ideologues—more like "peace and love" Woodstock types. The Democrats I knew—such as my grandmother—were working-class people who had a heart for the poor. Kind liberals. *Lutherans.* All were generally well disposed toward patriotism. They were liberals, not leftists. But unbeknown to them—and to me—they were the benevolent precursors of today's militant leftists.

The blasé attitude toward peace-and-love liberal hippies blinded us to a dire, future threat: they were raising radicals; militant, hate-filled babies of bong-resin boomers.

My first experience with these spawn-of-Woodstock leftists was as a freshman at Princeton University. I knew I was going to a "liberal school" but had no idea what that really meant in modern America. It didn't mean "liberal like JFK" anymore, it meant "leftist like Lenin"—even in *1999*. Instead of America being the hero of history, she was the villain. Islamist terrorists were to be "understood," not put underground. Abortion was made available at the campus hospital, as though it were no big deal. Evil was good, down was up.

Even then, though baffled, I didn't fully understand the insidious nature of the Left. *Crazy liberal Ivy League professors and misguided youths*, I thought. But this was just a preview of the coming deluge of leftist militancy. I did not yet understand how the infection of the 1960s cultural revolution had metastasized. It had spread through hippie parents who had become Marxist professors and socialist schoolteachers. Their students had taken positions in Hollywood, education, the media, churches, corporations, and even the NFL. Each new body seized by this rot was accompanied by leftist politicians who enshrined various insanities into law. Politics is a lagging indicator, so when these godless, socialist, anti-American cultural values become the policies of Democrats—as they have today—then you know the cycle is complete.

THE MIDAS TORCH

I didn't study much math at Princeton, but I do know iron-clad equations when I see them:

Leftism + *Anything* = Destruction (and Dependency, Despair, and Death).

That means Leftism + America = A dystopian future I don't want to imagine.

Leftism saturates one with the gift opposite to that of the mythical King Midas. Instead of anything touched turning to gold, it turns to shit. America has the "Midas touch," and leftists have a *torch*. Culture, religion, education, quality of life, government—leftism destroys everything it touches. The American version of leftists like to call themselves "progressives"—a name antithetical to progress. Like everything leftism espouses, even the name is a lie. Leftists are actually "regressives," hell bent on imposing their falsely utopian view of humanity on all of us; forcing us to unlearn timeless truths—not to mention ignoring our own common sense. And then we all pay their price. Their good intentions give them a free pass on reality and results. *They care more than you do, don't you know that?*

But what exactly is leftism? Before I answer that question, let's establish a few harsh realities up front. First, the Left has a very clear vision for the world; destructive, but clear. Second, leftists are able to articulate their arguments in ways that resonate with audiences. Many people sincerely believe their lies. Third, they take action on their ideas—every minute of every day. Leftists are dangerous because they are formidable. Know thy enemy, and don't underestimate them.

LIBERALS OR LEFTISTS?

Your grandfather's liberal Democrats have been replaced by leftists. The modern Democrat Party is not the party of FDR, Lyndon B. Johnson, JFK, Jimmy Carter, Bill Clinton—or even Barack Obama. Obama was a radical but knew full well that he could never win if people really understood his desire to undo America's founding. So he played into "measured" establishment preferences, such as purposefully crafting structurally unsound laws such as Obamacare that would collapse, hoping that would pave the way for full government-controlled health care later on. Radicals such as the crop of 2020 Democrat candidates dropped that strategic facade and denounce Obama's policies on a daily basis. The Bernie bros want revolution, not reform. The Democrat Party of 2020 is the party of politically correct, socially woke, socialist leftists. Its members are global citizens, not American patriots.

I've always enjoyed debating with liberals, because they also love America. Of course, we disagree on solutions to common problems, but we mostly agree on founding principles. Because of this, conservatives such as myself used to view liberals as allies of sorts: frenemies to be reckoned with but respected. Conservatives and liberals helped strike the essential balance of political discourse. They came together to solve problems, right? Wrong. That was never really true—just a lie naive conservatives and squish Republicans told ourselves. But it was a comfy lie, without existential consequences to America. No longer.

Sure, some old-school liberals still exist today. But they are a dying breed—literally and figuratively. Liberals want to grow government but can never get enough of your tax dollars to get it right. Liberals want to help the downtrodden but only end up making the problem worse. Liberals want peace but can't quite figure out how to achieve it. Liberals want more "equality" for all but only after Republicans do the heavy lifting. Liberals love America, even if they are ashamed of it. Liberals are wrong but only about the process—not the end state.

Leftists, on the other hand, are hard-core ideologues and indoctrinators. Leftists *hate* America, and they hate you. Leftists prefer to call themselves "progressives" and their cause "progress." Or "forward"—always forward. But those labels are a smoke screen. Leftism masquerades as forward progress toward solutions, but it's just revisionist propaganda. Leftism didn't end slavery. Leftism didn't give women the right to vote. Leftism didn't end segregation. Leftism certainly didn't defeat the Nazis. Check your history books. Americanism—led mostly by Republicans—did those things.

Leftism has been on the wrong side of all these issues and, until modern times, only on the fringe of the political spectrum. Look at the Democrat candidates who (dis)graced the debate stages in 2020. Each one boasts a platform that would have been unthinkable ten years ago: wide-open borders, reparations for illegal aliens, postbirth abortion, mandatory government-run health care, and socialism.

To leftists, elections are anathema to their desire for ultimate control. *Trump won? Let's abolish the Electoral College—or, better yet, impeach him!* They are unconcerned with debate or free speech. Again, anyone who thinks differently is to be targeted for annihilation. Take what they did to candidate, and then president, Donald Trump. The Left's "insurance policy" was an intelligence plot—masked as patriotic diligence—aimed at making Trump look illegitimate from the beginning. Then leftists dragged the country through three years of multiple iterations of the same fantasy. All because, to leftists, elections are an inconvenient speed bump in their quest for control.

To leftists, taxes must *always* be higher in order to pay for their outrageous social spending, programs designed to create permanent dependence on government. They do not want equality; they want to *even the social score* for four-hundred-year-old crimes of the Spanish and British. Do they want to punish the corpses? No. They want to punish anyone who has the same skin color as the perpetrators: white males with "privilege." They seek to establish their ideology as supreme over science and erase all biological facts concerning the differences between men and women. Of course, they allow an exception for radical Islam, whose practitioners are permitted to subjugate women, Jews, and apostates with impunity. It is a disgusting pandemic of delusion.

Liberals are wrong; leftists are evil. Every breath of freedom and justice we enjoy in this country was born of Americanism—the founding principles outlined in previous chapters. Most Republicans are patriotic Americans, and even some liberals stood for our values. JFK cut taxes, was pro-life, and was staunchly anticommunist! Liberals always had a conflicted yet fond relationship with America's founding because of its promise of justice, whereas leftists know where they stand: they want to erase those ideals from our schools, culture, and politics. Has your childhood school become more or less patriotic in the past twenty years? How about your community? What about your elected officials? Or, as we see across the country, are they bending to politically correct, identity-based "inclusion" standards that have no relation to love of country? Liberals fought against racism and sexism, but leftists selectively leverage difference to drive wedges between people as a means of gaining power. They want control. They demand conformity. And they hate America because America represents the opposite of control: freedom.

Ultimately, communism and socialism are leftism in action. The same thing, really. Check out a Bernie Sanders rally, and tally how many times he celebrates America. The task requires no fingers. America's sins, however: he has a fistful of those.

THE LEFTIST LIE

The founding premise of leftism is the rejection of the individual—and, more broadly, individual families. Individual souls, individual values, and individual dreams. To leftists, the individual is a data point to be aggregated into a group: black, white, gender, gay, straight, rich, poor. The collective—the "public" as a mass of categorized groups—is the focus. To leftists, instead of being an individual, you are a tool of the state, a number to be counted, or a factor in a calculation, all "for the greater good." Leftists love the terms *cooperation*, *awareness*, and *social justice*—all of which are code for "Do what we say. Now. Or else."

Leftism replaces belief in an all-knowing and loving God with belief in an enlightened and all-powerful government. To leftists, the highly educated—always Ivy League, of course—political class sets the priorities, the rights, the outcomes, and the level of equality for its . . . subjects. Americanism is defined by citizenship: empowered individuals with personal freedom and equal justice under the law. Some start ahead, some start way behind, but each runs the race without predetermined limitations. Leftism is defined by subjects— predefined data points with predetermined needs and wants and equality of outcome—at least on paper.

The founder of modern leftism was Karl Marx—hence why leftism is also known as Marxism. But you won't see many leftists wearing T-shirts with Karl's image; they like to distance themselves from his name and pretend they have a new, improved version. The fundamental theory of Marxism, published in 1875, is "From each according to his ability, to each according to his needs." From the beginning, central planning, confiscation, and redistribution have been the hallmark of leftism. Today, this language—wealth taxes, universal income, and government health care for all—is all the rage for Democrat presidential candidates.

Allow me to translate Marx. "From each" = we all pay up. "According to his ability" = if you succeed, you lose. And how sexist of Karl, "her" has ability, too! "To each" = we exist to receive, not strive. "According to his needs" = as defined by the government. The new ruling class—the people who had more power and guns at the beginning of the revolution—now set the terms of life for everyone else. Who defines my needs? How much is enough? Too much? Of course, the government decides. In a Marxist dream, life is good for the "deciders." That's why Bernie Sanders—and all the Democrat versions of him—are so passionate about achieving victory in 2020.

To fulfill this dream, each feckless Democrat candidate today—regardless of his or her ability—feels the need to give away free stuff as fast as the election cycle allows.

The entire premise of leftism is based on the godless delusion of utopia. But we live in the real world. The ideas of Marx—as manifested in countries such as the former Soviet Union, communist China, and countless other collectivist states—quickly devolved into a few privileged individuals and Mafia-like political parties wielding unchecked political, military, and economic power. The elites and well connected enrich themselves, while average people struggle to cobble together lives—waiting in breadlines without expressing a single free thought ever. If they do, they rot in prison or die. Unsurprisingly, socialist Bernie Sanders has said that breadlines are "a good thing."

The reason leftism is willing and able to sell a utopian view of the world is that it completely rejects the biblical worldview. The Left has to be godless, because government is their god. The Bible, rich in wisdom and history, tells story after story of human frailty, the search for higher purpose, and individual grace. It also lays out tenets—such as the Ten Commandments and the Sermon on the Mount—that we all fall short of but that remain timeless guideposts for our flawed lives. The Bible, especially when combined with the enlightened advances of Athens and Rome, is the foundation of Western civilization. Leftists openly reject all of this. God is too powerful to them; a threat. Instead, they peddle the counterfactual view that humankind is perfectible, if only for better social policies and more government involvement. At best, God is an afterthought confined to Sundays; at worst, He is a dangerous fiction.

As I alluded to earlier, leftism fully took root in America in the 1960s. It started in the culture, and quickly gravitated to the Supreme Court. In the early '60s, multiple rulings undercut the biblical heritage of our county. Prayer in public schools was deemed unconstitutional in 1962, as was Bible reading in 1963. Years later, displaying the Ten Commandments in classrooms was also blocked by the high court. God was ushered out of our public schools and public squares quicker than anyone realized. As a result, what had started as a cultural revolution became our country's political norm. A decade later, the sin of abortion was legalized in America and subsidized by leftists—justified by a legal ruling that even defenders of *Roe v. Wade* view as constitutionally tenuous. The results? Sixty-one million abortions and a cheapening of the value of human life to young people. The soul of our country—articulated in the Declaration of Independence—was ripped from the Constitution, right underneath our noses.

Speaking of *Roe v. Wade*, have you ever wondered why the abortion lobby—groups such as Planned Parenthood—is the most powerful interest group for leftists? The reason the so-called right to abortion is such a stalwart issue for leftists is that it represents the ultimate replacement of God by government. When America's government legally permits individuals to make the choice to take an *innocent* life, it erases the principle of God-given rights. People become all powerful; God—and his basic laws of nature—an afterthought.

Yet not one shred of human history reinforces the Left's false narrative. Simple introspection reveals that we are all prone to selfishness, pride, deception, and corruption. If you don't agree with that sentence, you are lying to yourself. Or you were never introduced to the Bible—more evidence of a Western culture adrift. Untethered from the Bible, the Left attempts to knock down the gates of Paradise through blood sacrifices of unborn babies—from late-term to full-term to postterm abortion—in unholy self-worship. They literally believe that this can usher in a perfectible kind of people to populate their institutions on Earth, thus creating a society in which no harm is ever done. Kill babies to save people. It's so stupid, it's tragic—but if you never learned otherwise, it's tempting to want to believe it.

All humans, boiled down to their basic chemistry, are essentially the same. What separates the good from the bad are the acceptance and practice of core biblical realities and ethics. Absent these guiding principles, we are left chasing chaotic notions of worldly fulfillment—or we just give in to the all-powerful grip of all-knowing, all-providing government. If we cannot govern ourselves as humble, clear-eyed individuals, we need government to show us the way. We are sheep without shepherds, blinded by arrogance.

Our challenge in America today—as during all of human history—is the transfer of timeless wisdom to the next generation. How can we teach the next generation of American citizens about our founding and biblical heritage in rudderless and godless schools? How can we sing the praises of the free market in schools that disparage profit making and personal achievement? How can we raise confident men and women in a culture that encourages them to be neither—or both? This is the blind spot leftists exploit. Lack of knowledge opens the door to ideas that sound good but are— well—horseshit. Leftism feeds on deception and lies, based on the ignorance and indoctrination of the masses. Karl Marx got this one wrong, too. Religion is not "the opioid of the masses," as he claimed; it is the *liberation* of the masses.

What is leftism? It is a lie. Always has been. Always is. Always will be.

THE AMERICAN LIE

Even more context is helpful in exposing leftism's arrival in America. President John F. Kennedy challenged the nation during his inaugural address in 1961 with the words "Ask not what your

country can do for you; ask what you can do for your country."
By today's ever-sliding standards, that Democrat would have been
labeled a radical conservative. The mantra, and challenge, of today's
leftist-controlled Democrat Party is the polar opposite: "Ask—no,
unite and demand!—what your country can do for you."

At some point, over decades of back-and-forth election cycles
and a generation of ivory-tower indoctrination—a (green) light bulb
lit up over the head of the Democrat Party. *Eureka! Why bother cam-
paigning to people as individuals and their goals when we can brand
them, group them, pit them against our enemies, and entice them into
voting for us by promising them goodies they will want in every election?*

Remember, the leftists do not see people as unique individuals.
They view people like livestock to be rounded up, divided, branded,
then corralled to the voting booth. Once divided, each subgroup is
told a different lie. Women are told that men are responsible for the
alleged "pay gap." Blacks are told that white-run corporations and
Ronald Reagan introduced crack into the inner cities so their friends
in the prison business could profit. The LGBTQ community is told
that cake bakers and churches are driving trans youth to despon-
dence. Hispanics are told that law enforcement officials will throw
their children into cages.

These are all lies. But despite being easily refutable, they remain
politically effective. Round up a large enough percentage of each of
these groups, and you'll soon have over half of the country voting
away their own freedom. Leftists understand electoral math, even if
they don't care about number one—which is you.

When a leftist politician sees a white person, he or she labels
that person with the brand of "privilege." If you're a woman, you
are defined by your so-called reproductive rights. If you're a black
person, leftists pronounce you a "victim" and campaign accordingly. The conservative activist Candace Owens, on the other hand,

exhorts black audiences, "Don't be a victim, be a victor!" and Donald Trump asked black Americans in 2016, "What do you have to lose by trying something new, like Trump? . . . What the hell do you have to lose?" Owens and Trump are Americanists, not seeing voters as black or white. They see you as an American.

But where did leftism in America really come from? When our World War II heroes came home, they had the understandable mind-set of: *I fought a World War—we beat the Nazis and Imperial Japanese—so that my kids would not have to fight and could instead live in peace and prosperity.* They came home, went to work, got married, and raised families. Their kids—the baby boomers—grew up in a world safe from leftism because their parents had defeated it. The 1950s have been called "The Golden Age of Capitalism" because—propelled by the Greatest Generation—it was a period of massive economic growth for middle-class Americans. America was back, strong and free.

Before the 1960s, the United States was largely internally insulated from leftism. In the 1960s, we had a cultural revolution of sorts against traditional hierarchies and Judeo-Christian values. As I mentioned, it included my family—and likely yours. What sparked this? There were many factors. The civil rights movement, rightly, shook our consciousness, reminding us that we still had not fully overcome the sins of slavery. Thankfully, it was Christian Republicans such as Martin Luther King, Jr., who helped us overcome this moment. The war in Vietnam was very unpopular, and that caused skepticism about the Pentagon for large swaths of American citizens. If you can't trust America's military, who can you trust? The sons and daughters of World War II veterans spat on Vietnam veterans when they came home, a telling action of the 1960s. Music, movies, and pop culture also started to push boundaries, challenging the ruling class, which they believed had failed them.

The 1970s exaggerated and enshrined these tensions, and the threat of nuke-happy Soviet communism moved back into the forefront. In the 1980s, Reagan and George H. W. Bush oversaw the implosion of the Soviet Union, and the free world breathed a sigh of relief. The first Gulf War victory in 1991 brought the parades the Vietnam vets had never gotten. A general sense of inevitability and complacency set in. *We're prosperous, we're powerful, our biggest enemy is gone.* The prevailing bipartisan theory held that China could have a peaceful rise, and the more we traded with it the more its rulers would liberalize their politics. The Islamist threat was not even on our radar at that point. There was that Iranian hostage thing, but it was a passing blip on our national consciousness. All the while, the Left pushed farther into our schools, culture, and churches.

In the 1990s, the sixties generation started to move into our institutions, getting jobs and gaining influence. Bill Clinton was doing his thing in the Oval Office, but the economy was strong and . . . *look! The internet!* Technology was omnipotent. But things were shifting under the surface that we didn't even realize, in that leftism was slowly reaching its tentacles into the public square, entertainment, and education. In the 1990s, college students continued to hear professors lecture about how unjust America was and how flawed and evil capitalism was. Worse, political correctness started to censor dialogue and expression. Al Gore crashed the party with an inconvenient truth, and the weather became a religion. Earth Day became superimportant; Veterans Day, not so much.

The national self-doubt permeated our culture to the point that when the attacks of September 11, 2001, occurred, a shocking number of so-called "elite" Americans blamed their own country as they watched the carnage unfold on live television. We were briefly united, but it would not last long. For many, patriotism was replaced by skepticism, doubt, and even self-loathing. We also had communication tools that humankind had never dreamed of, so we could express every thought, opinion, and emotion instantaneously, twenty-four hours a day. Social media had arrived.

Enter Barack Obama. All the tension and questions of the past four decades were answered in a presidential candidate. He was never a long shot. Half the country was ready for a racially diverse liberal/leftist president who wanted to "fundamentally transform" America. And he did his best to do so, traveling the world to apologize for America and declaring that America had never been exceptional. His policies were more liberal than leftist, but the culture had already moved past him. In 2011, even Superman—Mr. Truth, Justice, and the American Way—renounced his American citizenship in the comic book series. Dealing with a hypothetical showdown with Iran, Superman declared, "Truth, justice and the American way—it's not enough anymore. The world's too small. Too connected." When you've lost Superman, you know things are bad.

Fast-forward to today. You're reading this book because you can't believe what's happened to your country, and you want to know what to do about it. Whether you are a staunch Republican or even a lifelong Democrat, if you are an American patriot, you know we have lost our way.

These days, if you want to observe leftism in action, just watch House speaker Nancy Pelosi try to control Somali Omar and Comrade Cortez. Nancy says, "Not so fast, kids. You have Twitter followers, but I have votes in the House of Representatives." She may be correct at the moment, but what she's missing is the fact that politics is a lagging indicator of culture. Pelosi has "old power" because of political donations and loyalty from members of Congress who are beholden to her fund-raising prowess. She has the votes right now, but she's totally lost the soul of tomorrow. Maybe she sees the left-hand writing on the wall, which was why she staged the president's impeachment and "prayerfully" tore up the president's State of the Union speech.

Look at how leftism has captured the Democrat Party just since 2008. What's even more striking is how much territory the Left has taken since 2016. Obama was not enough. The new "cool" guy is socialist Bernie, the man who took his honeymoon in . . . the Soviet Union. Watching the Democrat "establishment" attempt to defeat socialist Bernie Sanders is the same script: bygone political power crushed by a cultural wave of leftism.

THE DELUSION

All that said, I still believe that liberals are mostly compassionate people who feel driven to help the less fortunate. They earnestly care about the people who are drowning in our society, but rather than sending them life vests, they keep throwing them anvils. Earnest "peace and love" liberals don't know that their approach doesn't work because they were never taught that collectivist policies and social welfare were the reasons for the collapse of the Soviet Union. But their leaders—the ideologues who are seeking the destruction of America—know exactly what they are doing. For hard-core leftists, the results don't matter; tearing down the traditional order is what is important. The combination of their "we care more" virtue signaling and quest for control leads them to any illogical end state necessary to eliminate us.

If you really want to help someone, what's the best way: collective planning or individual freedom? Has the soulless, detached, distracted, and overburdened government ever truly met your needs? Do you enjoy taking a number at the overcrowded DMV, or do you appreciate actual customer service? Does government tailor solutions to address the deepest yearnings of your life? Do you enjoy standing in the one-size-fits-all rope line of the post office, or is Amazon Prime next-day delivery more your style? Without a doubt, well-educated and empowered individuals, guided by the ability to pursue their hopes and dreams unimpeded by government, are better equipped to chart the course of their lives. The comparisons answer themselves, and to think otherwise is delusional.

The local city council that sets aside land for community gardens is much different from the commune that forces everyone to share, which is why every 1960s communal experiment that was tried no longer exists—because it's impossible. Everyone in a commune is flawed with his or her own desires, deceptions, and ambitions. Eventually—and it never takes long—someone wants what someone else has, and the scheme falls apart. The same applies in every situations where two or more humans are gathered. Just ask the Pilgrims: they tried communism when they first arrived at Plymouth Rock and quickly had to abandon it. America's forefathers—a group of committed, godly, hardworking people—attempted to share land, goods, and profits equally. It failed even for them, because the system, no matter how simple or complex, never works.

But despite its failing every time, leftists continue to peddle the same ahistorical sound bites. They sell a future of free stuff, friendly refugees, and UN blue helmets. Except that every piece of evidence—every one—demonstrates that *nothing* is ever free. Refugees require active assimilation, and the United Nations couldn't win a war against a kindergarten classroom, let alone communist China.

Besides defying common sense, leftism destroys the concept of individual charity and generosity. Keep in mind that the middleman between the haves and the have-nots is the government, and there's a lot of power and money to be gained in that role. It's actually a gigantic money-laundering exercise in which only a small fraction of what is taken in goes to those in need. The result is a massive enhancement of the ultrawealthy and a permanent, dependent lower class. Contrast this to the unique experiment of America, which created a massive, thriving middle class and the opportunity to defy a class system altogether. America is also the most generous country in the world, with capitalism enabling regular people to voluntarily donate large chunks of their earnings to causes they believe in. The CAF World Giving Index ranks US citizens number one in the world in personal charitable giving. This is not the case in Russia, China, and the Middle East.

Today, leftists, who believe capitalism is a failure, point to financial struggles of the middle class or "working people" as evidence that socialism would be better. They see economic illiteracy as an opportunity not to empower people to better themselves but as an opportunity to herd them and build power. Eventually this shuts down our God-given work ethic on both sides of the coin: *If you're going to give it to me for "free," why should I work for it?* And for those who do work: *If they're going to take it all away from me in taxes, why should I bust my ass to achieve more?* These are the tried-and-true, commonsense questions leftists can never answer. Try asking one sometime, just for fun.

WHO'S THE FASCIST?

"Pete, you are a fascist! You just want everyone to think like you, worship like you, and vote like you! Don't you know that extreme right-wingers like you ultimately become fascists?" If I had a dollar for every time I heard this, I could retire. But once again, the opposite of their assertions is true. Leftists are accusing me of the very thing they are.

In 1975, California governor Ronald Reagan said, "If fascism ever comes to America, it will come in the name of liberalism." At the time, I'm certain his prediction sounded ridiculous to most people—

but it has aged very well. The Gipper was always ahead of the cultural curve. Remember, he had traveled America as a spokesman for General Electric for years, meeting regular people across the country, while elites honed their theories in isolation. He was spot on, even if he did not foresee that liberals would be overtaken by leftists.

Leftists often accuse conservatives, Trump supporters, or anyone else on the right of being "fascist." They would take issue with my characterization of Mussolini's Italy, Nazi Germany, Imperial Japan, and other nationalist dictators as leftists. *They are the hard right*, they say. *They're fascists.* Yes, they are fascists—*because* they are leftists!

Just listen to the speeches of left-wingers. They don't tout the success of individuals as inspirational examples; they herd people into grievance groups and seek to control their thoughts and speech. In January 2020, a Bernie Sanders campaign staffer confided to a Project Veritas reporter that if Sanders won, there would be a need for "mass re-education." Their utopian end goal of "equality" always justifies their means—no matter what or who stands in their way. Again, let's go back to history. Adolf Hitler believed that in order for Germany to be great, he had to kill all the Jews and control the churches. Chairman Mao Zedong thought he had to forcibly relocate people from the Chinese countryside to the cities, which led to the starvation of tens of millions of people. The Soviet Union forced farmers to grow food for the collective, killed dissidents, and created a culture of control, fear, and suspicion—because the goal of "equality" was worth any individual sacrifice. Vladimir Lenin came to power under the guise of standing up for the poor and downtrodden majority, also promising the utopia of equality. He held on to power by forcing Soviet subjects to comply with his decrees, no matter how much suffering they caused. In each case, the individual was always a tool to serve the collective. And millions of people died.

Those murderous regimes were not "far right," they were leftists. Merriam-Webster defines fascism as "a political philosophy, movement, or regime . . . that exalts nation and often race *above the individual* and that stands for a centralized autocratic government headed by a dictatorial leader, *severe economic and social regimentation, and forcible suppression of opposition*." (My italics.) Not a single word of this definition meets the criteria of Americanism, especially as embodied by President Trump. In America, the nation exists to exalt individual freedom. In America, after years of fighting racism, we don't exalt any race. Our founders fought to *prevent* centralized government, with individual states retaining massive power. Our economy, by design, is not supposed to be regimented, and dissent is a hallmark of America.

Americanism is the ultimate antifascism, while leftism is the permanent gateway drug to fascism. Yet the Antifa people—they call themselves antifascists—claim that President Trump and the American Right represent the rise of so-called fascism in America. Like typical ignorant leftists, they have it completely backward. They wear masks and physically assault Trump supporters in order to shut down opposing views and advance their cause—the exact definition of fascism in pursuit of leftism. Members of the Democrat Party march with them, and leftist mayors give them space to grow. Antifa is the inevitable masked face of leftism—using intolerance to advance its one-sided view of tolerance, shutting down speech to protect only the speech it likes.

Have you ever seen an Antifa riot? I have. I've been in the middle of them—flag burning and all. On *FOX & Friends* at the Republican Convention in 2016, I asked protestors, "Tell me to my face why you hate this flag." Most could not answer my question, but one response said it all: "Fuck you and America!" Soviet flags and anarchy symbols are ever present. Left-wing activists calling themselves antifascists using fascist tactics. Make sense? Of course not, because they don't even know their own roots.

Shutting down speech is central to both leftists and fascists. Their self-appointed PC police try to shut down so-called hate speech, resulting in formal and informal speech codes in schools and workplaces. Censorship is commonplace and even celebrated in classrooms and in corporations (see: NBA). Who are the first people being banned on social media? Not intolerant jihadists or filthy leftists but outspoken conservatives. Those with the common sense to call out the real intolerance of Islamists and leftists are banned first—in the name of "respect, diversity, tolerance, and inclusion," of course. Hence why our founders had the foresight to realize that the speech that needs the most protection is the speech you don't like. Over time, with real freedom of speech in place, truly harmful and hateful expression is defeated in the marketplace of ideas. The best weapon against bad speech is more speech—not censorship. But authoritarians and leftists don't believe that free speech is the answer. After all, control is so much more efficient.

Next time you see leftists, make sure to remind them that *they* are the real fascists. That ought to get them going. And they won't know what to say.

THE LEFT MUST *REALLY* HATE VETS

The consequences of leftist rule affects all of our lives, no matter if you are a fifty-fifty American or a 100 percent American. Want an example of an undeniably good cause with almost unlimited government funding and support that has also been an epic failure? The Department of Veterans Affairs (VA) is it. The VA health care system was created with a simple and admirable goal: to provide quality, timely, and mostly free health care to US military veterans.

The VA was vastly expanded after World Wars I and II in order to meet the demand of veterans coming home. Since then, it has grown almost unimpeded. Today, it is the second largest department in the federal government, boasting nearly 400,000 employees—twice the size of the Marine Corps—and a budget of $200 billion. The VA directly runs more than 160 hospitals and thousands of smaller clinics. It's huge! America has invested in our VA, no doubt about that.

Today, there are roughly 18 million veterans in America, and roughly half of them use VA services. We spend $200 billion to serve 9 million veterans, most of whom supplement their VA health care with other forms of health care. Yet despite this massive investment, veterans still wait weeks and months for basic appointments. Medical records are a mess, technology is antiquated, and satisfaction with care is mixed at best. I talk to groups of vets often, and without fail, when I bring up the VA, those in the room burst into laughter. It's sad laughter, and we all know it; so much taxpayer money used so ineffectively.

Think about this: our country's heroes, our bravest, wait weeks and months for basic procedures and even appointments; tragically, many choose to blow their brains out in the parking lots of VA hospitals, because they feel as though no one gives a damn about them. It's a final protest against a government that has, institutionally, turned its back on them. Twenty veterans take their own lives each day.

While writing this book, I received an email from a woman whose son had been so motivated to serve his country that he had enlisted for multiple tours in Iraq. After he had come back and tried to get help from the VA, he had been put on multiple waiting lists managed by bureaucrats who, according to their VA employment contract, could never be fired for their indifference and incompetence. The young soldier ultimately killed himself. I receive emails like this all the time.

VA health care is so bad, so heartless, so dysfunctional that our nation's best—every day—take their own lives rather than endure the soulless bureaucracy built for them. Is there any better case of good intentions gone wrong? Welcome to government-run health care.

The reason this well-funded government department doesn't work is that, like all government programs, it has almost no incentive to be efficient, effective, and responsive. Veterans are numbers in a database, not customers to be catered to. The VA has no need to compete for their business, so it takes them for granted. Without competition, the VA has grown bloated and unresponsive. There is no market for VA hospitals to respond to, just more government money to grovel for.

Democrats in Congress—led by socialists such as Bernie Sanders, who was chairman of the Senate VA Committee for two years—defend the bureaucracy and status quo with a vengeance. They pump more money into the system, no matter what. Hell bent on proving that government-run health care can work, they cover up the sins of the bureaucracy and fund failed programs every year. The Democrats are content to trap veterans in VA hospitals, because they know that if veterans can choose private care—as Donald Trump has offered them—they will flee the government system. It's not a ringing endorsement for socialism. Moreover, Democrats think of the VA as a vehicle to organize VA labor unions—which represent most VA government workers—to provide for reelection security. Leftists have empowered government unions, which have, in turn, made VA employees unfireable—even if their incompetence gets veterans killed. Do you want to receive medical care in this scenario? It is absurd and frightening.

Yet Democrats want to create the same system for every single American! If our government cannot care for 9 million veterans—the people we purport to value the most—what makes any sane person think it could provide care for 330 million Americans? The Left mistrusts and dismisses the free market so much that it believes every citizen—and illegal immigrant, of course—should rely on the government to provide him or her with health care and ultimately make life-and-death decisions. Again, the lavishly funded VA can't take care of 9 million heroes, but Democrats want to bankrupt Washington, DC to take care of thirty-five times as many people? It's lunacy, but the Left believes its ideology is more important than the results actually delivered.

This is leftism at work. Every day. In every quarter of our lives. The Left wants to take over our health care, control our schools, erase our personal debts, raise our kids, and provide universal basic income. If it succeeds, its failure will become our reality.

"I have no country to fight for; my country is the earth, and I am a citizen of the world."

—Eugene Debs, five-time Socialist Party of America
presidential candidate, September 1915

"The thinking must be 'Europe first,
then each one of us.'"

—Pope Francis, August 2019

FIVE

GLOBALISM: THE WORLD'S WORST CITIZENS

What is a "global citizen"? Not sure? Just ask your nine-year-old child or twelve-year-old grandchild. Or your neighbor's teenager. They might not know precisely how to define it, but they know the answer. They've been told they are one—somewhere, by somebody or by everybody—at their public school, in cartoons, in pop culture, or at their church. Planet Earth, in need of saving and enlightenment, needs "global citizens"—don't you know? She needs humans who see past the antiquated barriers of borders, language, and culture—and as John Lennon said, all we have to do is "imagine" there are no countries or religion.

Where do you think the leftists' new mantra of "No human can be illegal" came from? The idea that crossing our border illegally is a human right, that ICE should be abolished, and that illegal immigrants should be given sanctuary? They didn't make it up; it came from the idea that we are all global citizens and therefore *deserve* whatever protections we want, no matter where and how we live. Of course, that's easy to demand in America, where rights are ubiquitous—but not so easy in places such as Iran or China. But leftists miss the fact that global citizenship is a one-way street, easily exploited by enemies of freedom. Domestic climate change zealotry is the perfect example of their hypocrisy.

Once you recognize it, the idea of global citizenship is everywhere in American society—mostly subtle, sometimes bold and blunt. It saturates the formative years of our youth. Polling shows that, more than ever, American youths self-identify as "global citizens" rather than as American citizens. Nearly *half.* If you live in a liberal area, your kids have been indoctrinated into this mind-set. Even if you live in a conservative area, your kids have been taught it. And since many of America's schools are no longer raising freethinking patriots, we are getting *parrots*—parrots who repeat the anti-American indoctrination they hear at school or see on Netflix, where Susan "Benghazi" Rice is a board member and the Obamas recently signed a huge production deal. Central to this indoctrination is the position that America is not an "exceptional" nation—that we are somehow equal to every tinhorn two-bit dictatorial shithole out there.

The citizens *of no country* believe that nations—and their borders—are outdated. The end state of this warped logic is no countries, no borders, nobody is illegal, and—magically— international cooperation and harmony will ensue. The United Nations, the European Union, or the International Criminal Court— all these institutions, as they are manifested today, are meant to break down the idea—and physical reality—of borders and citizenship. It's just another iteration of utopian delusions, completely untethered from reality. Even Obama understood this fifteen years ago, saying, "We simply cannot allow people to pour into the United States undetected, undocumented, unchecked." I can't believe I'm saying this, but where are the Obama Democrats today?

The global-citizen Democrats of today are a hodgepodge of the weak and the weird. Combine the catastrophic naivety of Neville Chamberlain with the weed-infused foreign policy savvy of Jane Fonda and voilà—a global citizen is born. This process creates social justice celebrities who skywrite open-border slogans from private jets between visits to pacifist protests, all while droning an about how carbon footprints are more evil than Al Qaeda car bombs. The tragedy is that young people pay attention to these frauds—basking in the warm glow of their virtue signaling. The more air time and social media cred we give them, the more daunting it is to stand up to their idiocy. While the global elites waste their time with this nonsense, the other side—China, Russia, Turkey, and Islamists—exploit it to advance their belligerent interests.

"WOKE" TO GLOBALISM

It wasn't until the candidacy of Donald Trump that I fully grasped the concept of globalism. Another "Trump conversion moment" hit me like a ton of bricks in 2016 when I realized an inconvenient truth: I was an accidental globalist.

I loved America—and had fought for her at the potential price of my life on the battlefield—but I hadn't seen the larger battlefield: the powerful undercurrents of influence that pushed internationalism, interdependency, and "bridge building" at any cost. From trade policy to immigration policy to foreign policy, why were corporate and political "elites" always pushing certain policies, even though they undermined American sovereignty and strength?

Because, more often than not, those elites were globalists—wrapped in a disposable flag that they were happy to remove if it suited their ideology, electoral prospects, or bottom line. Candidate

Trump cut through those entrenched viewpoints—which were held just as much by Republican "elites" as by Democrats—and he put America first. His policy positions stunned my establishment sensibilities at first but now make perfect sense. The moment that light bulb went on, I realized I had been sitting at the globalist cool kids' table and hadn't even realized it.

As I mentioned in chapter 2, for years I had been a term member of the Council on Foreign Relations (CFR), which has a "prestigious" membership including elites and emerging foreign policy types on both sides of the aisle. I had taken some hits for it during my failed Senate run years earlier but had brushed off the criticism as uninformed conspiracy theories. Then, after the emergence of candidate Trump, I finally took a harder look. It turned out that, masked in sophistication and international awareness, the CFR was actually the headquarters of anti-American globalism. Under my nose, just as under the nose of the American people, the CFR—and groups like it—advance policy positions that sell America up the river under the guise of doing what is best for America. Elites elevate feckless international institutions, outdated alliances, and anti-American solutions above the best interests of our citizens. CFR was not, and is not, America first—it puts "elite" global citizens first.

As soon as I realized I was affiliated with what can only be described as the enemy camp, I fired off a resignation email dated May 24, 2016:

To the Membership Department of the Council on Foreign Relations:

I, Peter Hegseth, hereby resign as a Term Member of the Council on Foreign Relations—effective immediately.

I do so for two primary reasons:

1. During my multiple years as a Term Member—due to deployments, geography, travel, and work obligations—I have yet to attend a single CFR event—making the payment of annual dues a poor investment.

2. However, much more *importantly*, I cannot justify financially supporting, or being affiliated with, an organization that actively and subtly advances overwhelmingly progressive, globalist, borderless, and—in many ways—anti-American views. I have always been a believer in engaging with different viewpoints—hence why I sought a 5-year temporary Term Membership in the first place. I'm a conservative who graduated from liberal colleges and am happy to debate, with comity, those with leftist perspectives—I'm a believer in pluralism and ideological tolerance, properly defined. My hope was to do the same at CFR—but that has not happened. Therefore, as I watch what is happening to our nation and the world, and the arguments CFR makes about those developments, as a patriotic American I can no longer justify supporting such an organization with my dollars and affiliation.

In the years since, I've met countless Americans who have had the same realization—especially during dozens of *FOX & Friends* diner segments, during which regular Americans have shared what I call "commonsense wisdom." Regular people get it. Why do we fund the anti-American UN? Why is Islamist Turkey a member of NATO? Is "climate change" really going to kill me in ten years? You'd think this common sense would trickle up to Washington, DC, but selling out America and American values is a very profitable business. For too many years, there was bipartisan consensus that "globalism" was inevitable and a largely good thing, and that comfy view also sounded good in sound bites and in CFR policy papers. But the reality was something far different: average Americans get *crushed*, and America *declines*.

On this issue, former president Teddy Roosevelt remains timelessly instructive—saying, "The average man who protests that his international feeling swamps his national feeling, that he does not care for his country because he cares so much for mankind, in actual practice proves himself the foe of mankind." Damn right! Once again leftism emphasizes *caring* over results and delivers destructive outcomes. He continued, "The man who says that he does not care to be a citizen of any one country, because he is a citizen of the world, *is in very fact usually an exceedingly undesirable citizen of whatever corner of the world he happens at the moment to be in*." (My italics.) Let me paraphrase in Teddy Roosevelt's terms: global citizens are 0 percent Americans.

WHAT IS GLOBALISM?

Here's the equation: Globalization + Leftism = Globalism.

I'm not against globalization, and even if I was, who could stop the technological advances in communication, commerce, and transportation that have brought our world closer together than ever? We can talk to anyone instantly, buy products from all over the world at the click of a smartphone screen, and travel to all four corners of the world faster than ever. Heck, as a small-town Baptist boy from Minnesota, I never dreamed of visiting Israel—the land of the Bible—let alone visiting frequently. I feel just as at home in Jerusalem as I do in my own neighborhood, and I can make a reservation to fly there with the click of an iPhone app. The world gets smaller each day and will only continue to get smaller.

Globalization is here to stay, but we can manage globalization without falling for "globalism." *There's a very big difference*: one is a technological reality; the other is a scheme to eliminate national sovereignty in order to centralize control over the means of production. Simply put: globalism is worldwide socialism.

The original premise of the United Nations was the idea that before countries fight with each other, their leaders should at least talk to each other. Talking is a good idea, and peaceful resolution is usually better than war. But that is not what the United Nations is today. The United Nations is now a fully globalist organization that aggressively advances an anti-American, anti-Israel, and antifreedom agenda. There's one set of rules for the United States and Israel, another for everyone else. We should just lop it off from the island of Manhattan and let it float out to sea. It would do more good out there.

Originally, the United Nations was supposed to preserve the post–World War II order, and it gave the United States a permanent seat on the powerful Security Council. There were three primary problems with that arrangement. One, communist China and communist Russia have the *very same* veto power we do—which is fundamentally unacceptable to freedom-loving people. Two, even when the UN Security Council does agree, nothing happens unless the United States takes action. And three, the United Nations overall has become the place where all the dictatorships and Islamic states come together to bash the United States, Jews, and capitalism. Name one substantial UN accomplishment in the past few decades. Last I checked, it hadn't stopped any wars or rogue nuclear programs.

The only way to prevent globalization from turning into globalism is for good and free countries to remain strong and independent. In the era of globalization, nationalism is the indispensable ingredient in blocking the spread of globalism—yet another reason why leftists hate Americanism. As long as the United States remains a sovereign superpower, the United Nations—and all other globalist organizations—cannot reign supreme. Remind me again why the

United States continues to submit to the United Nations, let alone fund it?

Thanks to the unabashedly pro-American presidency of Donald Trump, globalism has fully exposed itself here at home. It was hidden for a long time, and now it's on full display. For decades we've had a border problem, an inability to account for who comes into our country and what they do when they get here. Even Democrats such as Barack Obama and Senate majority leader Harry Reid called for border security and internal enforcement. But it was all masked by a bipartisan consensus to enact "immigration reform" that never actually did anything about the problem. If anything, immigration reforms of the past only made the problem far worse.

Then Donald Trump ran on actually securing our borders and ending the sanctioned invasion of our southern border and refugee programs. Leftists' reaction has been to pivot to the radical positions they've always believed in—but had hidden from public view. With the Left fully embracing globalism and Trump as a foil, they are calling for decriminalization of illegal border crossings, accelerated sanctuary city and state policies that shield criminal illegals, giving away "refugee" status to anyone who claims it, providing health care, driver's licenses, and college benefits to illegals, and—if they could—allowing illegal immigrants to vote. California is doing all of those things right now, as I type this. If "no human is illegal," then all of those policies make sense.

Globalists fundamentally reject citizenship, disrespecting every legal citizen taxpayer in our country. Don't believe me? As a US citizen, do you believe the mayor of a Democrat "sanctuary city" would ever shield you from federal law enforcement if you broke a federal law? Would he or she just release you—as is done with criminal illegals—and tell the feds "good luck" finding you? Of course not. The double standard is offensive—and suicidal. Globalism destroys countries, which is exactly what the leftists want. Just look at the European Union.

EUROPE SURRENDERS—AGAIN

Want a ten-year preview of what a globalized America would look like? Take a look at Europe.

It started well before the formation of the European Union. In 1985, European nations took a giant leap from globalization to globalism when they signed the Schengen Agreement. That treaty led to the creation of the Schengen Area and abolished most border checkpoints in western Europe. The countries of Europe, despite having different cultures, languages, and legislatures, decided that they would try to become the "United States of Europe." As with most leftist inventions, the stated intention seemed harmless: shared money, cheaper trade, and more tourism. *Let's eliminate borders— what could possibly go wrong?*

Did any of the geniuses in Luxembourg, where the treaty was signed, stop to think about the unintended consequences? Or was that their goal? No matter their size, countries without borders cannot protect their people—and protection is the *first and primary* reason for governments to exist. Enter the refugee crisis, which accelerated earlier this decade. Not only did borderless Europe make it easier for tourists and truckers to travel; now migrants could journey anywhere in the continent without detection. Sneak into Turkey or Greece, and you can sneak into Paris and the rest of Europe. Couple that with a globalist European Union, whose members increasingly abandoned their national identity, and you have the chaos we see today. New immigrants bring their home-country values with them—and too often, they're not the values of freedom.

It's very simple. At the same time that Christianity and Western values were being openly rejected, Europe decided to open its borders, not demand assimilation or allegiance from new arrivals, and gut their militaries to pay for their welfare states. It was the perfect recipe for decline and death. At least the Brits had enough sense to Brexit!

Even then, it might be too late for Great Britain—and it certainly is for the rest of Europe. Journalist and British citizen Douglas Murray, in his 2017 book, *The Strange Death of Europe: Immigration, Identity, Islam*, makes a bold claim and convincing case: "I mean that the civilisation we know as Europe is in the process of committing suicide and that neither Britain nor any other Western European country can avoid that fate because we all appear to suffer from the same symptoms and maladies." The maladies he cites are, you guessed it, the mass movement of third-world refugees into Europe and the fact that Europe has lost faith in its beliefs, traditions, and legitimacy. He goes on to write, "More than any other continent or culture in the world today, Europe is now deeply weighed down with guilt for its past." Sound familiar? If the sins of our past define us, then every society is doomed to fail. The question is, can countries instead build on their flawed pasts to fulfill the true manifestation of their values? Right now Europeans are choosing to burn down their continent instead of fortifying it.

In Murray's home country alone, the numbers are stark. Muslim immigration has skyrocketed in London and throughout Great Britain. Absorb this stat: according to the UK newspaper *The Independent*, the most popular boy's name in England in 2019 was Muhammad. Sorry, Oliver—but Muhammad is now number one and growing sharply. The increase in the Muslim population in England, along with Muslims' well-documented aversion to assimilation, has led to several exclusively Muslim neighborhoods—yes, "no-go zones"—in various cities and a corresponding rise in the number of Muslim elected officials, most notably Sadiq Khan, the mayor of London. Muslims make up more than 5 percent of Great Britain's population today and some say much higher—a percentage slated to *triple* in the next thirty years. This as the Christian population *shrinks* because the fertility rate of average British families stands at 1.8 kids per family, meaning fewer kids than parents. Muslim families, on the other hand, have multiples of kids (three-plus per family, on average).

Similar trends exist across Europe, especially in places such as France and Germany that have embraced unfettered immigration. Unlike the Trump administration, the European Union seems hell bent on the importation of Somali Omars, who come as quiet conquerors, instead of Texas Omars, who come to assimilate. Europe's leaders know the risk, but given the continent's rapidly declining birth rates, they cannot support their social welfare programs without outside population replacement. Immigration from *anywhere* is how leftist politicians seek to maintain their welfare states. What is a dozen dead Christmas shoppers mowed down by a truck in Germany by an Islamist if you can keep your universal health care? Or major streets shut down by Friday Muslim prayers so politicians can keep their seats? This is the evil of the globalist gambit.

THE MOSQUES OF MINNESOTA

Think this can't happen in the United States? Look no further than my home state of Minnesota. After a brutal civil war in Somalia, Minnesota opened its doors to Somali refugees. Thanks to a generous welfare state and left-wing Lutheran social services, Minnesota became a magnet for Somali refugees. Since then, more than 100,000 Somali Muslims, and likely *many* more, have made Minnesota their home. On the surface, it looks like a wonderful story of generous Americans opening their doors to suffering refugees. But the reality is much different.

Instead of embracing Minnesota and American culture, most Somali Muslims have maintained a highly insular existence. As FOX News has reported—and as I saw for myself during multiple trips to Minneapolis for *FOX & Friends*—for Somali residents in large urban neighborhoods it's possible to go about day-to-day business without ever interacting with a non-Somali. I walked the streets of "Little Mogadishu" in Minneapolis for hours, encountering Somali Muslims, many of whom have lived in Minnesota for years and most of whom did not speak English. When I asked a local Somali teenager whether his Islamic school taught about American law and the US Constitution, he looked confused and said, "Actually, I have no idea about that one." When asked if it teaches Sharia law, he quickly said, "Yes, Sharia law."

Multiple mosques in Minnesota—you guessed it—are funded by Saudi Arabia and the Muslim Brotherhood. This is not an accident, it's a campaign. Young Muslim men in these mosques have been taught that rather than having been saved by America, they are victims of American imperialism. How else can you explain the rampant Islamic radicalism emanating from the Nordic state of Minnesota? Under our noses, not only do Democrats in Minnesota allow these actions, they support them. Former Minnesota governor Mark Dayton, a Democrat, scolded Minnesota's citizens on behalf of Somali Muslim immigrants, "anybody who cannot accept your right to be here, and this is Minnesota, should find another state." In other words, Americans should leave, not refugees fostering radicalism.

After a recent trip to the Mall of America, a family member of mine explained in detail how the display outside the women's section of the Macy's department store had three female mannequins, two of which were wearing the Muslim hijab. The Mall of *America*. Speaking of the hijab, the Minnesota legislature recently afforded it a special status as well. When a new "hands-free" cell phone bill was passed—which limits Minnesota drivers' cell phone use while driving—a special exception was added: "the use of a scarf or hijab or other items of clothing to hold a device in a hands-free manner" was allowed. I can't tuck my cell phone into my baseball cap, but hijabs are kosher (offense noted). Minnesota Democrats championed the bill, but multiple squish Minnesota *Republicans* voted for it, too—saying they just want to be "inclusive."

That's the culture, but then there's terrorism. Before the rise of ISIS, there was already a problem of Somali Muslims in Minnesota going to fight with Al Shabab, the Islamist group fighting in Somalia. At first, many believed that fact was only based on a local connection to the conflict. But after the rise of ISIS in Iraq and Syria, young Muslim men in Minnesota led the charge to join the caliphate. No state in America sent more residents to join the Islamic State. How do you explain that? The truth is, Minnesota is a near-perfect reflection of Europe: blindly open, fully apologetic, willfully ignorant, and stupidly tolerant. Imams in Minnesota mosques preach intolerant radicalization, while Somali Minnesotan women face draconian religious persecution such as forced genital mutilation. Assimilation to American values is viewed as intolerant by Minnesota leftists, thereby fueling anti-Americanism.

Enter, again, Somali Omar. When, in 2015, six Somali men from Minnesota were arrested while attempting to cross into Mexico in order to join ISIS in Syria, then state representative Ilhan Omar begged the judge to show them "compassion" rather than subject them to a thirty-year sentence for treason. You read that correctly: a US representative fought for leniency in our justice system for known aspiring terrorists. Rather than condemn Islamists for giving peaceful Muslims a bad name, Somali Omar defended Islamists. She also normalized their behavior. No wonder so many people across Minnesota—and the country—loathe the woman.

Minnesota is a coming attraction of what will happen across America if we don't fight globalism and its manifestations on all fronts.

ECONOMIC TREASON?

Is Amazon an American company? How about Apple? Or Google? Or Nike? Their headquarters addresses say so, but their actions say otherwise. Today, companies founded, operating, and profiting in America are not required—or even encouraged—to demonstrate any allegiance to the free-market economy that fostered their growth. These now "multinational corporations" benefit from America's pro-business climate, then sell their souls to foreign countries while giving the middle finger to the country that gave birth to them. Worse, they embolden our enemies, China chief among them. National allegiance matters very little to far too many people on Wall Street and in Silicon Valley.

Corporate globalists want the same centralized control scheme as in the United Nations and European Union, and their strategy is the subjugation of the American worker in exchange for the cheap labor of communist China and narco-states such as Mexico. This weakens America's social fabric by putting our middle class out of work while building the ruling classes of enemy nations. Corporate globalists lobby squish Republicans and Democrats to prevent competition in this country, thus keeping their power insulated from free-market forces. This free flow of capital out of America is a serious security risk that is welcomed by Wall Street and Silicon Valley, which have financial stakes in these emerging markets. Make no mistake: corporate globalism is international socialism.

Nigel Farage, one of the leaders of the Brexit movement in Great Britain, often talks about the prerogatives of "multinational corporations," which have grown so dominant that they have become more powerful than the countries in which they reside. In some cases, the corporations actually circumvent a country's ability to defend itself from threats. Amazon, Apple, and Alphabet (Google) are the biggest examples involved in technology transfer, surveillance data, and foreign contracts that run counter to the interests and security of the United States. They literally sign contracts with foreign governments—most especially China—that enable them to circumvent US taxes and competition while enriching the most despotic regimes in the world.

The North American Free Trade Agreement (NAFTA) was also globalism disguised as "free trade"—a win-win for the Left. Like most/ all of our trade agreements forged with groups of countries, it was a losing proposition for the United States and a winner for Canada and Mexico. As the president pointed out on Twitter in 2018, "Canada charges the U.S. a 270% tariff on Dairy Products. They didn't tell you that, did they? Not fair to our farmers!" Slanted playing fields such as this are why President Trump has renegotiated—or simply with-drawn from—multilateral trade agreements (among many countries) that hurt our economy and instead entered into bilateral trade agree-ments (one country to one country) when possible. The now-spiked Trans-Pacific Partnership (TPP) would have given huge advantages to other countries, and if those countries were found to be in breach of their duties of the agreement, they could do so with impunity. Deals with no consequences for cheating are just one-sided prisons for coun-tries, such as America, that play by the rules.

The virus of globalism hasn't only infected the technology sector; iconic American institutions are bowing to globalists and communists in order to play ball—literally and figuratively. Take the National Basketball Association (NBA), for example. In October 2019, the NBA's Houston Rockets general manager, Daryl Morey, tweeted in support of anti-China, pro-freedom Hong Kong protestors: "Fight for freedom. Stand with Hong Kong." A fair sentiment in a free country, you would think. But instead, the hidden power of China came down on him and the NBA like a slam dunk. Morey quickly deleted the tweet and apologized: "I did not intend my tweet to cause any offense to Rockets fans and friends of mine in China. I was merely voicing one thought, based on one interpretation, of one complicated event. I have had a lot of opportunity since that tweet to hear and consider other perspectives."

NBA players, led by philosophers such as LeBron James, were pressured to support the Chinese, voluntarily squelching their own free speech. Those same players fought the NBA—and won—to advance their own social justice causes just a few years earlier. But when it comes to China, the NBA and Nike caved. Why? Because in 2018, the NBA's business in China was estimated at $4 billion. The sneaker business in China is even larger, with Nike alone doing more than $6 billion in Chinese sales in 2018. Many companies are afraid of the Chinese, and in the name of reaching a larger audience, they surrender the hard-earned advantages we cherish.

It is important to note that reining in out-of-control, globalist US-based corporations is not a call for government control over those entities. In fact, it is quite the opposite. Corporations such as Amazon that provide cloud services to the Chinese military should be barred from receiving contracts for the cloud services of our own intelligence agencies and military. Even better, they should be barred from doing any work that benefits the communist Chinese and their military. American companies can make widgets in China but should pay taxes in America and pledge allegiance to the country that made them rich. It is common sense. American government contracts should be awarded only to companies that demonstrate pro-American economic patriotism. Free-market proponents cannot afford to be so puritanical about this issue.

We cannot take as gospel the conservative DC think-tank nonsense about the "dangers" of tariffs as a tool for negotiation. The globalist elites handcuffed us to communist China and then called it freedom and "free trade." Fortunately, Trump has proven that tariffs are a powerful tool to put our adversaries on notice and unlock real free trade. From China to Mexico to the European Union, our partners are on notice that slanted trade deals are over and American workers and industries will be protected.

THE CHINESE DREAM

Does any sane American actually think communist China is our friend? *Anyone?* Of course not! Except for communism-loving Bernie Sanders and his "bros," commonsense Americans understand what China represents. Only the wealthy and well-connected elites who enrich themselves in China conveniently ignore the reality of Beijing. You know, Council on Foreign Relations types. Important caveat: I am not talking about farmers or other commodities producers who sell their surpluses to China; that is commonsense globalization—unless it's time to withhold those products for national security reasons. I'm talking about unpatriotic corporate greed.

Yet despite knowing this reality, our companies continue to give away American inventions and innovations, only to have them used against us. Worse, in the case of our largest geopolitical foe, communist China, we are funding the transfer. President Trump has said it directly: "China is a threat to the world in a sense, because they're building a military faster than anybody. *And, frankly, they're using U.S. money.*" (My italics.) Previous globalist trade policies have quite literally enabled China to build the fastest-growing and most technologically advanced military in the world, largely thanks to American capitalism.

Plain and simple, the Chinese economy is fake because it's not free, yet powerful—built through theft, intimidation, and the weakness of China's opponents. When it comes to intellectual property, communist China has mastered the art of the steal. If you want to do business in China, your company is forced to hand over its technology secrets—which China immediately steals. Want to do business in China? Hand over the keys. To do business in China, the communists demand that foreign companies hand over a portion of their ownership. Or, in the case of companies such as Apple and Amazon, local Chinese "partner" companies must be set up to "manage" data in China in order to comply with internal laws. I wonder who controls those Chinese companies? The most massive companies in China are *state-owned*, meaning the government controls them and can use them as it pleases—especially for its military. Contrast that with America's powerful tech companies, some of which *refuse* to support the US military and are fully "woke" islands of PC leftism. China is playing for keeps; they are playing for imaginary points awarded for corporate social activism.

China also uses American companies to squash internal dissent. When Hong Kong protestors continued to risk their lives and digitally-monitored reputations, government investigators discovered smartphone apps that the freedom fighters used to communicate and avoid police. The Communist Party–run *People's Daily* called the app "toxic software" and demanded that Apple and Google remove the apps from their stores. Those "American" companies quickly complied, leaving thousands of pro-freedom demonstrators in the dark. Get that: American companies shutting down technology for pro-American protestors—because communists asked them to.

On the military front, many of our high-tech weapons rely on "rare earth" minerals imported from China. We used to mine these minerals here in the United States, but because of environmental regulations, the costs became prohibitive. Thanks, Democrats! In May 2019, China explicitly warned the United States that it would consider disrupting the supply of these minerals. *People's Daily* published an editorial with this line: "We advise the U.S. side not to underestimate the Chinese side's ability to safeguard its development rights and interests. Don't say we didn't warn you!"

It's a massive national security issue; an emergency, really. President Trump says often, and in blunt terms, "If you can't make steel, you don't have a country." If you're dependent on other countries for the building blocks of complex construction, manufacturing, and warfare, you're screwed. Unless we can support our power grid here, generate our energy here, and build our ships, tanks, and planes here, we are beholden to other countries, unfree countries. Exporting manufacturing hurts our economy; it's another form of national suicide. Thankfully, through his pro-business policies, the president has brought back the "magic wand" of American manufacturing, and the results speak for themselves.

Thanks to naive and idiotic globalist US policies, China is actually ahead of our country in many crucial technologies: next-generation fighter jets, high-speed data transfer, long-range missiles, and the weaponization of space. For example, in 2016, China launched the Aolong-1 (Roaming Dragon–1) satellite, which featured a robotic arm capable of grabbing items in orbit. Of course the Chinese assured the world that its mission was to simply remove space debris. *Wow, forget their emissions, they're cleaning up space!* Globalists blindly repeated their propaganda. Surely the Chinese government would never use the satellite as a weapon to disable other satellites, right? This is just the tip of the iceberg of communist China's international ambitions.

Even Mickey Mouse would understand that the communist Chinese government and its economic engine are a threat and we must compel our companies to stop enabling them with American technology. We must bring the companies back home to America, coercively if necessary. They don't deserve to build foreign wealth on the backs of American freedom. You cannot trade fairly with an enemy that lies, cheats, and steals. America is strong enough and innovative enough to disengage—a move that would hurt us in the short term but ultimately send China reeling.

As America has fully embraced globalism, China has enriched and empowered itself as the ultimate antiglobalist. Our elites thought we could outsource freedom to China—but the opposite happened. The Chinese have used their wealth to consolidate communist power, spread their influence around the globe, and ultimately shape our culture. China's Belt and Road Initiative is a global development and trade effort aimed at spreading the country's influence around the world—and more than 50 countries and international institutions are involved. The Chinese are buying land, building ports, and using debt to coerce smaller countries to do their bidding. They are expanding military agreements around the globe. Do you think they are spreading peace and freedom? No, they want to control the twenty-first century.

Then there is Chinese influence in American media and universities. The Walt Disney Company and other American entertainment giants have completely sold out to China. Formally and informally, scripts and imagery are subject to government approval in China in order to gain distribution and investment there. Chinese censors demand that movie plots and Chinese characters be displayed favorably; otherwise they won't reach Chinese audiences. Dr. Strange, of Marvel Comics fame, was always mentored by a Tibetan monk; but in the 2016 movie about him, China refused to distribute the film unless that was changed. So instead his mentor was a Celtic woman. Movies such as *The Martian* and *Gravity* inserted positive imagery of China to assuage the communists, and Hollywood universally refrains from making villains of the Chinese—even though, from free expression to fossil-fuel emissions, they are *literally* the villains of our generation. In the movie *Olympus Has Fallen* the original script had the White House being attacked by Chinese commandos—until they were quietly made North Korean instead. Hollywood, long a pro-communist bastion of hypocrisy, doesn't see communist red, because its only focus is on the green.

On our shores, Confucius Institutes—Chinese "cultural centers"—have arrived in American universities at a dizzying pace; eighty-six in total, all founded in the past *fifteen years*! The Chinese government funds these centers under the guise of advancing mutual understanding and preparing students to navigate the increasingly globalized economy. Li Changchun, a Chinese government official, described the centers in more accurate terms: "The Confucius Institute is an appealing brand for expanding our culture abroad. It has made an important contribution toward improving our soft power. The 'Confucius' brand has a natural attractiveness. Using the excuse of teaching Chinese language, everything looks reasonable and logical." They're not even hiding it—because our "diverse" campuses fawn over them. Again, leftists helping fellow leftists. May I ask: Where are the "Washington" or "Lincoln" Centers in Chinese universities? You know the answer.

China has mastered the art of the globalism double standard: open up for us, but we will not open up for you. We can buy your land, but you can't buy ours. We will happily take your money, but we will never embrace your freedom. "Globalism" for China is war disguised as peace: technological war, cultural war, trade war, and military war. China has a dream—it's called the Chinese dream—and it ends with the reestablishment of the former Chinese Empire. This is why President Trump calls our trade and sovereignty policies "dumb"—because they are. If we don't stand up to communist China now, we will be standing for the Chinese anthem someday.

DUMB GLOBALISM

When I served in Afghanistan, it was under a NATO mission. I was part of the International Security Assistance Force, or ISAF. On my camouflage uniform, I wore an American flag on one shoulder and an ISAF patch on the other. The running joke of US troops in Afghanistan was that the ISAF patch actually stood for "I Saw Americans Fighting." You see, military personnel from fifty countries wore that patch—but only a handful of them actually fought. There were US troops everywhere and a smattering of British, Canadian, and Australian troops as well. Even then, the others' political limitations on the battlefield prevented them from conducting sustained combat; and in some cases, they conducted no combat at all. Americans fought, while our NATO "allies" were mostly unwilling or unable to help.

On a few occasions, I traveled through ISAF headquarters in Kabul, a beautiful, sprawling base in the midst of a third-world country. But it was all a sham. Everyone knew it was pretty much the United States's war to fight, with forty-nine straphangers. Fifty flags, one army. The Mongolians on our base had three missions daily: to drive to the chow hall for breakfast, lunch, and dinner—in Humvees we were forced to give them. They never left the wire, never fought. Other countries did less. We joked about it then, but it's deadly serious today.

NATO is not an alliance; it's a defense arrangement for Europe, paid for and underwritten by the United States. But what if the world has changed? What if European countries never rebuilt their militaries after World War II? What if the Soviet Union dissolved? What if larger enemies emerged? What if a NATO country decided to become Islamist and hold Europe hostage instead? Every one of these scenarios has occurred. What are we paying for? And how does the alliance serve America? NATO was a great idea then and is—at best—a distraction today. Little good it did when Russian president Vladamir Putin decided to grab the Crimea a few years ago. Europe cannot defend itself—and that is not our fault seventy years after World War II.

Critics will say, and I can hear them now, "You have it all wrong! The mission in Afghanistan may not have been perfect, but NATO is still very important in containing an aggressive Russia. NATO is not globalism, it's a voluntary alliance of like-minded countries." I've heard it all before. But saying those things does not make them so.

NATO was formed after World War II to provide collective security against the Soviet Union. It was a unique and special alliance that was very important. NATO played a big role in staring down the Soviet Union until it was ultimately defeated and disintegrated— for now—into Russia and a number of smaller countries. It was actually Ronald Reagan, Pope John Paul II, and British prime minister Margaret Thatcher who together brought down the Soviet Union, but who's counting? Today, NATO is a great example of dumb globalism. National security "experts" claim that NATO is indispensable. Really? To whom? Europe has already allowed itself to be invaded. *It* chose not to rebuild its militaries, happily suckling off the teat of America's willingness to actually fight and win wars.

Worse, consider Turkey, a full-fledged member of NATO since 1951. Foreign policy types back then believed that allowing it into the club would bring its government closer to the West and our Western values. It worked for a while but has fallen apart today. Instead, as with China, the opposite has occurred: President Recep Tayyip Erdoğan decided to reject the secular tradition of his institutions. He dismantled the NATO-trained army that has long maintained Turkey's secular institutions. He has ignored popular elections and openly dreams of restoring the Ottoman Empire. He's an Islamist with Islamist visions for the Middle East. Yet NATO members have pledged to defend his regime? The last time I checked, that's not what NATO was about.

Secretary of State Michael Pompeo summed it up nicely in a speech in May 2019: "America too had become unrestrained, untethered from common sense. The institutions, the institutions we built to defend the free world against the Soviet menace, had drifted from their original mission set. Indeed, some of them had become directly antagonistic to our interests, while we kept silent. We bought into trade agreements that helped hollow out our own middle class. We sacrificed American competitiveness for accolades from the UN and climate activists. And we engaged in conflicts without a clear sense of mission. No more."

Later in his speech, he added, "I am very confident, I am very confident that the Founders would have been perplexed by those moves. We had too much confidence in the international system and not enough confidence in our own nation. And we had too little courage to confront regimes squarely opposed to our interests and to our values. But I bring you good news. One man said, 'Enough.' And in 2016, you all sent him to the White House." From ending wars with no clear mission and instead killing Islamists with impunity to ending trade deals with little benefit and instead investing in American companies, Donald Trump put an exclamation point on it. *Enough!*

Static thinking in the age of globalization—and in the face of globalist forces—is a recipe for decline. We waste our resources and credibility on missions and in institutions that don't actually help us, as opposed to ones that put Americans and American interests first. The defense of Europe is not our problem; been there, done that, twice. And the Europe we saved in the mid–twentieth century is no longer the Europe of today. NATO is a relic and should be scrapped and remade in order for freedom to be truly defended. This is what Trump is fighting for.

SMART GLOBALIZATION

Remember when President Trump suggested that if people don't love America, they should go back to the countries they love so much? The media and Democrats lost their minds. But as always, the more outraged they are, the closer he is to the target. Here is the tweet from July 14, 2019:

> So interesting to see "Progressive" Democrat Congresswomen, who originally came from countries whose governments are a complete and total catastrophe, the worst, most corrupt and inept anywhere in the world (if they even have a functioning government at all), now loudly and viciously telling the people of the United States, the greatest and most powerful Nation on earth, how our government is to be run. Why don't they go back and help fix the totally broken and crime infested places from which they came. Then come back and show us how it is done. These places need your help badly, you can't leave fast enough. I'm sure that Nancy Pelosi would be very happy to quickly work out free travel arrangements!

He's right. All four of the women President Trump is referring to—Representatives Omar, Cortez, Pressley, and Tlaib—are US citizens, and all but Somali Omar are at least second-generation Americans. Obviously, America is home for them. I'm not arguing that. The tweet was mostly about Somali Omar, who had recently slammed the president. What I am asking, as is President Trump, is: Why are we keeping people in this country who, after they come here and stay here, hate this country? Somali Omar came to America as a refugee—what does that mean?

A refugee is someone who was forced to leave his or her *home* country in order to escape war, persecution, or some other disaster. No country is more welcoming—truly welcoming—to refugees than America. But being a refugee is intended to be *temporary*: another country protects you until you can return safely to your home country. Today many refugees stay indefinitely in the country they arrive in—and in the case of Somalia versus America—that is a common-sense choice. Many of them go on to achieve citizenship and embrace America. And we embrace them.

But what if they don't embrace America? In that tweet, our "See something, say something" president shouted something that regular Americans whisper every single day: "Why don't we send people who illegally cross our border back to their home countries? Why do refugees never go back even when their home country is safe? Why do so many stay in a country they openly blame for their lot in life?" Or, in the case of Somali Omar, if they think America is so bad— why not go back to Somalia and show us how freedom and security is done? That's exactly the question Trump asked, and instead of receiving an answer, he was called a racist.

I'm not talking about skin color or even religion; I'm talking about allegiance. There's no need to explain or apologize, because leftists will call us racist anyway. This is part of why Trump is the indispensable man of the moment—not only because he fights back but because he shows us how to join him in the American crusade. If people hate America, why don't they go somewhere else? If other countries are so great, why is nobody running to those places? Or if newcomers love America as much as the Left likes to claim, why aren't they signing up in droves to fight in our military? And why—in perpetuity—are Democrats fighting to keep these people in America?

The answer is simple: globalism has become yet another religion of the Left. They swear by it at all costs. People must come here.

Must stay here. Deserve to be here. And vote here; it's always about votes. But what if our country stands for values they oppose? It's a question leftists refuse to answer, because with very few exceptions, the religion of globalism has fully infected the modern Democrat Party. The litmus test for being an American has been reduced to identity boxes. Are you diverse, different—by leftists' standards, not mine—and dedicated to ensuring a Democrat majority? Our only hope (paging Obi-Wan Kenobi) is that voters, in 2020 and beyond, understand these stakes: pro-America versus anti-America.

President Trump declared these truths in a speech to the UN General Assembly on September 24, 2019. He said, "The future does not belong to globalists. . . . If you want freedom, take pride in your country. If you want democracy, hold on to your sovereignty. And if you want peace, love your nation."

If you want peace, don't fall in love with the globe; fall in love with your own country. He continued, "Wise leaders always put the good of their own people and their country first. The future does not belong to globalists. The future belongs to patriots. The future belongs to sovereign and independent nations who protect their citizens, respect their neighbors, and honor the differences that make each country special and unique."

The future belongs to patriots: patriots who fight for their country and use common sense to keep their country free.

OUR WAR

Have you ever noticed that globalists simultaneously despise America and believe that citizens of every other country have a right to live here—and would be better off here? The best measure of a country is whether people run toward it or away from it. North Korea, Venezuela, China, and the like boast populations grasping for other options. Not so the United States. People flee to us because they know what we stand for. That's even more reason to know who is coming to America.

We're in the thick of an economic, political, and cultural battle. Leftists exploit globalization into globalism, and they're gaining ground in our schools, businesses, and government. Don't be intimidated by the fake accusations of the Left; the truth is, globalism hurts America. To be antiglobalist does not mean to be racist or xenophobic. We can learn a thing or ten from President Trump in his counterattack on these issues. In the 2020 election, globalism is on the ballot: Build the wall. Raise tariffs. Learn English. Buy American. Fight back.

We have no choice but to fight, and our weapon is American nationalism. It's Americanism. The Left has tried, and succeeded on many fronts, to intimidate us into thinking that nationalism is a relic of a bygone era. *How dare you fly the flag, wear it on your hat, or ink it on your arm?* To combat globalism, we need a resurgence of patriotic display, along with vocal support for the fact that the United States is the greatest nation which has ever existed. We must overwhelm the invading forces with waves of red, white, and blue.

Because this time, unlike centuries ago, Christendom is not around to save us. In fact, it's gone globalist. "Sovereignism means being closed," the current pope said in the summer of 2019. "A country should be sovereign but not closed. Sovereignty must be defended, but relations with other countries and with the European community must also be protected and promoted." Pardon my Latin, but what the hell does that even mean?

Contrast this with the clarity of Teddy Roosevelt in a letter written just a few months after the armistice that ended the fighting in World War I. This, his last public statement, was read at an "All-American concert" under the auspices of the American Defense Society, of which he was honorary president:

There must be no sagging back in the fight for Americanism, merely because the war is over. There are plenty of persons who have already made the assertion that they believe the American people have a short memory and that they intend to revive all the foreign associations which most directly interfere with the complete Americanization of our people.

Our principle in this matter should be absolutely simple. In the first place we should insist that if the immigrant who comes here does, in good faith, become an American and assimilate himself to us, he shall be treated on an exact equality with every one else, for it is an outrage to discriminate against any such man because of creed or birthplace or origin.

But this is predicated upon the man's becoming in fact an American and nothing but an American. If he tries to keep segregated with men of his own origin and separated from the rest of America, then he isn't doing his part as an American. . . .

We have room for but one flag—the American flag—and this excludes the red flag, which symbolizes all wars against liberty and civilization, just as much as it excludes any foreign flag of a nation to which we are hostile.

We have room for but one language here, and that is the English language, for we intend to see that the crucible turns our people out as Americans, of American nationality, and not as dwellers in a polyglot boarding house; and we have room for but one soul loyalty, and that is loyalty to the American people.

Amen.

"Male and female created He them;
and blessed them."

—Genesis 5:2 (King James Version)

"There's no one way to be a man.
Men who get their periods are men.
Men who get pregnant and give birth are men.
Trans and non-binary men belong."

—Tweet from @ACLU, November 19, 2019

SIX

GENDERISM: TOXIC FEMININITY AND BETA MALES

love strong women, always have. My grandmother Gwen was a widowed single mother for much of her life, a community activist, and editor of the *Wanamingo Progress*, the small-town newspaper. My other grandmother, Edith, so I'm told, ran her kindergarten classroom like a military barracks. (Mrs. Hegseth was a legendary disciplinarian.) My mother, Penny, is an independent thinker who raised us with love and intentionality while building a small business of her own. My wife, Jennifer, is by far the strongest, smartest, and savviest woman I know, a true television professional, not to mention an amazing mother and inspirational partner.

Strong women are an equal component of the backbone of America, in our homes, communities, newsrooms, and boardrooms. Every man I know shares this view. So when I arrived in college at the turn of the century, I had zero aversion to supporting women's causes. One of those causes was a new organization founded by friends of mine. When they launched the Organization of Women

Leaders (OWL) in 2000, their mission was simple: to help women get elected to more student government positions. Even though I was affiliated with the campus conservative publication at the time (*The Princeton Tory*), it was no big deal for me to attend their kickoff event—which just happened to be a barbecue! (With cheeseburgers. Real ones, from cows. Can you imagine feminists today launching their new group by grilling red meat? *How dare they ruin the environment and offend all the plant eaters!*) So I showed up. Heck, you might even call me a founding member. *Pete for feminism!*

That was feminism as I understood it: striving for equal *opportunity*. OWL was not demanding gender quotas or poised to stage a hunger strike in the dean's office until men were kicked out of student government, they simply wanted to provide an organizational platform to help women compete more robustly for positions held mostly by men. They were more liberal, I was a conservative—but we could agree that advocacy for women leaders was a good thing.

Then worldviews collided.

The very first student body election occurred shortly afterward, pitting a conservative female against a liberal male. Neither was radical, but their political positions were clear: she was pro-life, he was pro-abortion. Guess which candidate OWL supported? The *women's* group founded to elect more *women* to student government endorsed the *man*, because the woman was a conservative. My mind was blown. How could this be? Through that experience, I realized that old-school feminism (you know, actually fighting for women's equality) was dead and leftism had taken over.

The organization's members said that their goal was to create equal opportunity for women, but what they really meant was equal opportunity for women of the Left. You see, OWL was trying to use the old lens—gender equality—to play the new game. Since twenty-first-century women are already equal to men, especially on an Ivy League campus such as Princeton, equality was not enough; conformity to the leftist narrative was the new game in town.

A future edition of my *Princeton Tory*—after I accepted the role of publisher—featured a cover image of a large tree, and on one branch was an owl—in the crosshairs of a rifle scope. The headline read "Killing Feminism: OWL Sabotages the Women's Movement." Open the front cover to the table of contents, and the owl was dead on the ground—with three sniper bullets in her (or his?) head. One of our best writers, a woman, penned a scathing yet incontrovertible article calling out OWL on its ever-growing hypocrisy and the double standards of neofeminism.

That same month, the campus daily newspaper, *The Daily Princetonian*, took note of our substantive critique, saying "Hegseth's Tory was critical of OWL, for going from an organization of leadership to one that is political and tries to speak for all campus women on issues such as reproductive rights." Even the liberals saw that we had a point, with the liberal *Nassau Weekly* noting in its April 2002 issue, "In 1970, the campus conservative movement was groundless and incoherent, and angry feminists tore it a new one. Now *the roles have gone topsy-turvy*." (My italics.) It was a backhanded compliment that we very much appreciated.

OWL's response? Anger and confusion, but—because this was before the purple-haired safe-space mobs took complete control of places such as Princeton—there was also earnest outreach. Some of the women were my friends, and they reached out to explain their position. Others lashed out via email or in the pages of the various campus publications. But ultimately, they claimed to want to understand our position. So OWL held a public event in the evening entitled "Cupcakes with Conservatives" where both sides could present our arguments. There were three of us from *The Princeton Tory*—Jennifer the thoughtful author, Brad my trusty editor in chief, and myself. There were roughly sixty ladies. Sixty versus three. I got used to those odds at Princeton. There was talking, yelling, crying . . . and cupcakes.

Nothing was solved, everyone was heard, and I was now fully "woke" to the reality of modern-day so-called feminism. I enjoyed the cheeseburgers and cupcakes, but what I saw wasn't feminism. What was it? The answer today is much worse than you think.

AM I A FEMINIST?

Have you seen those T-shirts that read, "This is what a feminist looks like"? (As seen on babies and beta males.) The slogan is stupid, but it does pose the question: What does a feminist look like today? I would consider myself a feminist, in the same way I'm an American—I believe in the original intent. Like most people in this country, I have always been for equal rights, equal justice under the law, and unlimited opportunity for women. Once again, these inalienable rights were made clear in the Declaration of Independence. The laws and Constitution eventually caught up. I want my daughters to have every opportunity in life, every door open to them.

But that is not the issue anymore. Women today attend college at higher rates than men. They win elections just as often as men (okay, maybe not the presidency, but that was Hillary's fault). They have full-blown professional sports leagues. They have access to every single job in America today. And, yes, they make the same wages as men—especially after one factors in years spent away from the workforce for childrearing, if women so choose. Women can vote for whomever they want, sleep with whomever they want, and hold any job they want. The real question is: Why aren't American feminists protesting outside the Saudi Arabian Embassy, which represents a country where women cannot travel without male guardians? Or the Iranian Embassy, which represents a country where women can be imprisoned for not wearing a head scarf? Or the headquarters of the Democratic National Committee, where women raped by Bill Clinton were publicly branded slutty liars?

So, do I consider myself a feminist? Perhaps a *twentieth-century* one. Today, American feminism has *nothing* to do with equality or women's rights. If that were the case, they would celebrate a strong immigrant woman who enjoyed a successful career and eventually became first lady of the United States. But Melania Trump has been shunned by so-called feminists. There's no need to discuss what they've done to former press secretary Sarah Huckabee Sanders; same story. Today's feminist agenda is not about women's rights; it's an agenda to change culture—including erasing the concept of gender, masculinity, and unwanted life. The so-called Women's March was a typical leftist political rally and not about women at all. It was about abortion on demand (always!), gay rights, socialist health care, and racism. The anti-Semitic radical Linda Sarsour served as its national cochair. While supposedly standing for the rights of women, she (ironically) wears the male-prescribed Islamic head scarf.

Women's rights have become, lock, stock, and barrel, all about "reproductive rights." Not abortion that is "safe, rare, and legal" but abortion on demand—meaning at any point before, during, or immediately after birth. Abortion is the heart and soul of modern feminism and the issue is front and center in our public schools. Now feminism, fully infected by leftism, has morphed into something else.

Remember the cigarette ads in the sixties and seventies that targeted women for the Virginia Slims brand? The headline read, "We make Virginia Slims especially for women because they are biologically superior to men." Women could smoke cigarettes, too, the ad told them, breaking down the stigma against women smoking. But the slogan from the ad is what everyone remembers. When it comes to feminism, all I can say is "You've come a long way, baby—or, wait, ma'am—or xe or xir or xem or xeir." No, those aren't typos, they are new gender pronouns.

So twenty years after I saw the original concept of feminism die in college, what is it? Today's feminism isn't even about women—in fact, how dare I even "label" females as women? It turns out that gender equality was not enough. Today's feminists want gender fluidity. Genderism has been born.

ENTER GENDERISM

The equation is: Feminism + Leftism = Genderism.

As our kids are now taught, your "sex" is only what you were born with—the piping between your legs. But "gender" is how you *identify* yourself. Gender, leftists claim, is a social construct impressed upon society by literature, religion, and various privileged classes (namely, white males). It's important that we understand the distinction. The number of chromosomes, or the genitals, determine one's sex. But a person's gender is what he or she decides it is. Laws and social norms therefore should conform to gender; a person's sex is irrelevant. It's batshit crazy, but this is what most "mainstream" corporations and schools have adopted as the basis for their rules and regulations. Why?

As with abortion, the leftist goal is to rip away traditional thinking in polite society, replacing God with government and replacing binary sex with multiple-choice gender. To leftists, binary gender—"male and female He created them"—is not only a thing of the past, it's homophobic, simplistic, and sexist. "Gender is fluid," they say. "What you were born with between your legs doesn't matter. All that matters is how you view yourself." This kind of talk blossomed first in radical circles, then on college campuses, and now we're asking elementary school kids to decide what gender they are. (A close friend recently found out that his school was teaching his four-year-old about "gender fluidity." He spoke up, and the school accused him of invoking "white privilege." Like a true crusader, he said "Go to hell!" to the school.)

When traditional gender roles are discarded, culture loses the commonsense—and, yes, biblical—understanding of men and women: how we interact, how men serve women, how women serve men, and the beauty of our roles and differences. This commonsense view does not mean we should be unkind to, intolerant of, or discriminatory to those who color outside the lines. Thankfully, American society has come a long way in terms of accepting people as they are. But we are now well past that, and the Left is obsessed with erasing the obvious differences between men and women—to the detriment of men, women, boys, and girls. Exit empowerment, enter exploitation. The result is not just one hundred gender choices on a Facebook profile, it is social engineering that can ruin lives.

Remember years ago when some retail stores, facing pressure from the Left, experimented with getting rid of having boys' aisles and girls' aisles? It was a real thing, and it failed. Why? Because the stores hadn't been pressuring boys to be masculine and girls to be feminine; they had simply been responding to the biological differences between boys and girls. It wasn't trickery, it was common sense. Go into almost any store in America today, and you'll see that the boys' and girls' aisles are alive and well. No matter what your "sex" is, you can shop in either aisle. When kids—including my boys—are young, they like to explore everything. I have many pictures of them in my wife's heels or their sisters' bows and many of my daughters in my army fatigues or their brothers' football uniforms. What has become unnatural is that genderists have decided that kids who cross the aisle, at the youngest of ages, are already identifying as the other gender—and must be encouraged to do so. According to leftists, boys who stay in the boys' aisle have been nurtured that way; but boys who wander to the girls' aisle—they are girls! Gender pressure is put on kids based on information they cannot possibly process, and right there, traditional genders, and gender roles, are blurred.

Take the recent case of a biologically male seven-year-old in Texas who has a mother who is raising him to be a girl and a father who believes he wants to be a boy. The parents are divorced, and the mother had custody, but the father went to court to get joint custody—and won. He feared that the mother would force an understandably confused young boy to make drastic and unnecessary life choices, such as the hormone treatment therapy she was planning and eventually gender reassignment surgery. Experts agree that predicting whether a prepubescent child will grow up to be transgender is extremely difficult, and the same played out in this case. On the first day of the following school year with his father, the boy *chose* to go as a boy. We can have no idea how his case will play out, but make no mistake that when our schools reinforce genderism, they only advance confusion that kids cannot handle. Exceptions like this case become the policy objectives of leftists, imposed on the rest of us.

What began as a long-overdue pursuit of opportunity and equal justice for women (what we used to know as feminism) has turned into gender confusion and an assault on masculinity. Consider this tweet from the ACLU on "International Men's Day" 2019: "There's no one way to be a man. Men who get their periods are men. Men who get pregnant and give birth are men. Trans and non-binary men belong." What the fuck does that even mean? Men, as you know, cannot have periods or babies—unless they are women who "identify" as men. Which means they are women. Except they are men. Get that? This absurdity creates a weird, politically correct system where everyone's walking on eggshells—except the leftists throwing the eggs. They can never be wrong, because they are rewriting the rules. We don't know the rules, but they do—and they are ramming them down our throats.

Genderism is destructive because it seeks "gendercide" against the type of men who will always fight our wars, fix our cars, build our homes, and defend our neighborhoods. Sure, women do those things, too, and that's great, but men still do the heavy lifting, literally. More than 95 percent of our firefighters are male, more than 90 percent of our construction workers are male, and more than 80 percent of our troops are male, just as more than 90 percent of our nurses are female and more than 85 percent of our public elementary school teachers are female. All of these professions are open to both men and women, with only minor caveats based on physical requirements. Under the banner of equality, natural differences are all around us—and that's okay.

For whatever reason, God created men with bigger muscles and more testosterone. Thank God women were given other natural advantages to balance that out. Nature values this beautiful balance. It's fair to say that most women don't want to see their men emasculated, just as gay men I know are not looking for emasculated men, either. The point is that, straight or gay, we all have choices in whom we seek, but if you erase the differences between men and women, you remove the choices altogether. It's quite ironic.

The percentage of people who fully support genderism is actually small, but they hold powerful positions in our schools, culture, and government. As such, they use the fear of being seen as "discriminatory" as a means to silence good people with good intentions who may otherwise differ in minimal ways about the roles of men and women. This is where common sense should take hold. Men and women are different and leverage those God-given differences. But today we're told not to even acknowledge these differences. Worse, against all common sense, we're told that we should erase gender—because certain characteristics are just not valuable to twenty-first-century leftists.

CAUTION: INTERSECTIONALITY AHEAD

Let's take it another dangerous and illogical step forward. Want a gender equation mind bender? Try this on for size: Feminism + Leftism + Racism = "Intersectionality" or Intersectional feminism. Honestly, I don't even want to dignify these terms, but they are front and center in leftist politics today. All of the 2020 Democrats have made reference to them at some point or another. If you haven't heard of "intersectionality," stay tuned—you'll soon hear it spouted with somber brows and feigned intellectual tones more and more.

Here's a recent excerpt of a definition from Wikipedia (which is sure to have changed hundreds of times since I copied it): "Intersectionality, also called intersectional feminism, is a branch of feminism asserting how all aspects of social and political identities (gender, race, class, sexuality, disability, etc) discrimination overlap or ('intersect')— for example, race with gender in the case of a black woman." This is genderism on steroids, the idea that people should add up their perceived societal slights and be elevated accordingly—or punished, in the case of able-bodied, straight, white, middle-class, Christian men. The entire concept, which separates, segregates, and discriminates on every single factor *except* what you *believe*, is the exact opposite of what Americanism and the American dream stand for.

But this political step—this newfound focus on "intersectionality"—makes complete sense given where higher education has gone. History, political science, and economics departments and degrees are being crowded out by African-American Studies departments, Native American Studies departments, Women's Studies departments, Gender Studies departments, LGBTQ Studies departments, and probably other categories I can't even imagine. Remember Lincoln's warning: "The philosophy of the schoolroom in one generation becomes the philosophy of government in the next." The same thing is happening here. Students who have been taught to see the world through the lens of their race, gender identity, economic class, country of origin, or sexual orientation have no time or inclination to be an American *first*. After all, there is no box to check for that.

Predictably, genderism has taken over our politics as well. In a recent CNN "Equality Town Hall" featuring most of the 2020 Democrat presidential candidates, a transgender black woman rudely interrupted another attendee, grabbed the microphone, and starting yelling about "the erasure of black trans people." Xe (the invented nongendered pronoun of choice of the Left) raved like a lunatic at the frightened perennial loser onstage who goes by the name of "Beto." No question was asked; it was just a live television hijacking. Of course, xe was *thanked* for the disruption by CNN moderator Don Lemon.

Imagine if a white man yelling about traditional marriage (gasp!) or gun rights (double gasp!) or the unintended consequences of "gender reassignment surgery" (full hand-to-forehead faint!) had grabbed the microphone? He would have been thrown out as fast as humanly possible and derided as a bigot and simpleton. But in this case, because the disrupter had all the right grievance qualifications—black, trans, woman, oppressed—there was no resistance. This is the race- and gender-based double standard that only grows, day by day, in elite PC society.

Another great example of this rabid double standard is taxpayer-funded schools and libraries promoting "Drag Queen Story Hour" for young children. It happens in my (former) home state of Minnesota and other states across America. Drag queens—meaning men dressed as women—read social justice books to kids. Can you imagine if taxpayer-funded schools or libraries had Baptist ministers read Bible stories to kids? That would never be allowed. If they did, we could (maybe) have a conversation about representing both sides; but alas, leftists are not interested in inclusion; they are interested only in bullying, shaming, and fearmongering us all into an ideological black hole. Yet our schools and towns accept it, and the lunacy is actively enshrined. Kids leave story time with more questions than answers—which is the point of the Left: expose and confuse kids as early as possible in the hope of squarely embedding the big lie that male and female don't exist.

If a man wants to wear makeup and women's clothing, so be it. It's a free country (for now). But I have a serious problem with taxpayer dollars going to promote it. Worse, states such as California use taxpayer money—hard-earned money from citizens—to fund gender transitions and then publicly scold states such as Iowa that don't do this. Chop off your body parts, or grow new ones; I don't care. It's your decision. But don't ask me to pay for the procedure. Again, the end state of all of these policies is gender confusion, gender fluidity, and as much intersectionality as possible—all on the taxpayer's dime.

As this cultural shift happens, still larger questions bubble to the surface: What will happen next? After we accept every inner prompting and personal life decision, what are the real impacts of genderism? Of intersectionality?

It turns out that there is growing concern about the number of people who regret choosing irreversible gender transition procedures—including exposing those under the age eighteen to surgeries and hormone treatment. The genderist lemmings have been running so fast toward the edge of crazy that no one has stopped to ask tough questions about the long-term outcomes for these people. I'm pleading for compassion here: it's cruel to allow those under the age of eighteen to make a life-altering decision such as this—taking drugs to change sex or removing body parts.

WHY IS THERE A WOMAN IN MY BATHROOM?

Let's make our own *transition*, for fun. If everyone else gets a march—a movement—where is my Men's March? What about

#HeToo? Why can't we #BelieveAllMen? *And why is there a woman in my bathroom?*

To the Left today, men and boys—who *act* like men or boys—are the problem. As they do with America, leftists choose to emphasize the negative attributes of men, rather than encouraging men to use their inborn strengths for good. A society in which men are allowed to be men and women are allowed to be women is a healthy one. Otherwise you get what we have today: the gender police, pronoun alphabet soup, weak men, unsatisfied women, and lots of angry leftists telling the rest of us that traditional gender roles are evil. Must I ask, "Can't we recognize and accept people's sexual differences without losing our minds?"

Let me be clear—I will not raise a "beta male." Ain't happening. All boys are different—some tougher, some weaker, some strong willed, and some more passive—and those differences are a good thing. But no matter what their *nature*, our *nurture* for men must include the development of the gritty virtues: toughness (physical, mental, and emotional), boldness, fortitude, and chivalry. But feminists today—and leftists generally—call that approach "toxic masculinity." In their view, not only should boys not be taught these manly virtues, they should be told that they are bad. Our culture and our government schools tell our boys to reject manly virtues and act more like, well, girls. You might call it "toxic femininity." The chauvinist "good ol' boys club" is over, or at least becoming extinct—replaced by the "I hate boys club." Remember, the Left does not want equality, it wants compliance.

This is how Western society got skinny jean–wearing metrosexuals who literally cry when Trump tweets. One of these poster children even wrote a story in Politico about how he could not get through eighty-three-year-old Ruth Bader Ginsburg's workout—it was *too hard*. I've talked a lot about the damage leftism does, but when it manifests into a thirtysomething not being able to shoulder press fifteen pounds (okay, maybe twenty), you understand the ability genderism has to turn boys into babies who blog for a living.

What everyday Americans know is that fostering the natural tendencies of their children will lead to well-rounded adults. My boys and girls have toy guns and as they get older will learn how to use real guns. They also paint, do crafts, and sing and dance like little kids (thanks to my Jenny). However, left to their own devices, the boys choose guns and the girls choose to dance. Dare I say nature? Trying to destroy that will only lead to a society in which—even at a slow boil—the lid will blow.

The arena of sports is a great example of genderism in practice— with male-dominated sports actively under assault every season. There is no richer target than tackle football. Parents are told, more and more each year, that the tackling is harmful and unnecessary. This is intentional. Sure, some of it is led by the wimpy safety police; but the reason is deeper—the Left hates the attributes of this male sport: toughness, intimidation, violence, and the ultimate locker-room environment.

For the same reason that the Left hates football, I believe that there is no better sport in America, with its true teamwork, strategy, and violence of action. Football is the closest thing to a team gladiator sport that we have in America; hence the Left would like to crush it. I could write an entire book on this dynamic. From absurd safety protocols that make the game more like flag football to scared mothers and fathers keeping their boys out of the sport to inflated fake news about brain injuries, to kneeling during the national anthem, the concerted effort to destroy football is directly related to the leftist agenda to feminize men and weaken America. To that we should say—to quote a hat made by a defiant player for my Minnesota Vikings, Andrew Sendejo—let's "Make Football Violent Again."

When I was in enemy territory, I'm damn glad that the men beside me had been initiated on the sports field into using their strengths. You should be glad, too. Football, and many other individual and team sports, builds character, resolve, grittiness, toughness, and strength— mental, emotional, and physical—along with the values one needs to succeed in the uncoddled world we live in. The world is a dangerous place. There are some really bad people who want to take our free- doms and rights—along with our stuff. When they come calling, on the battlefield or on your street, you can't call a mediator and have a listening session in a safe space. There are no cupcakes. We need mas- culine strength in society. Football really does forge freedom.

As genderism always does, it goes even further. Consider the evolution of Title IX—a picture-perfect example of leftism meeting feminism and turning into genderism. Title IX, part of the Educa- tion Amendments of 1972, sought to address gender discrimination. It read in part: "No person in the United States shall, *on the basis of sex*, be excluded from participation in, be denied the benefits of, or be subjected to discrimination under any education program or activity receiving Federal financial assistance." (My italics.)

In short, Title IX made sure that women had access to all the same educational opportunities as men—including the arena of sports. Although the law was not designed specifically to address sports, it provided a legal foundation to create a long-overdue bal- ance in men's and women's programs in high school and college sports. Sounds great, right? As long as you're clear about what "on the basis of sex" means.

You see, in 1972, biological sex—men and women—was the stan- dard. Men competed against men and women against women. Then, as the Left tried to change the biological rules and replace sex with gender, feminism was usurped. Today, genderism is used to allow bio- logical males to compete—and win—in "women's" sports. Biological females in sports such as swimming, track and field, and weight lifting have actually missed out on college scholarships because losses to these "men" have hurt their rankings. This will continue, and get worse.

What if LeBron James decided he was a female and wanted to play in the WNBA? The fully "woke" NBA could not stop him. If Michael Phelps decided he wanted to win even more gold medals in swimming and took the plunge into the woman's pool, the Olympic Committee certainly could not stop him (or her). It long ago accepted such gender transitions, so maybe we'll see him in 2024. And what if a high school female wrestler was taking testosterone to become a male and, during the doping process, won two state championships over girls? Wait, that already happened—in Texas. And in February 2020, three Connecticut teens—from three different schools—filed a lawsuit to prevent biological males from competing, and trouncing them, in track and field events. Will common sense win? It's an open question. Leftism has mutated feminism into something so unknowable that people can't even speak the truth without being shamed by the gender mob.

Tennis legend Martina Navratilova was vilified for "suggesting that transgender athletes in general are cheats" when they compete against women. She then apologized for her comments after pressure on social media. "I am certainly not advocating violence against trans people, as has been suggested. All I am trying to do is to make sure girls and women who were born female are competing on as level a playing field as possible within their sport." By the way, Navratilova is an outspoken lesbian; but that doesn't matter to the new feminists. Anyone—and I mean anyone—who stands in the way of their goals must conform or be crushed.

BATHROOM BREAK

Let's get practical for a moment in a way that helps clarify the insanity of molding and merging genders. For decades, colleges and universities have experimented with mixed-sex dorms. Some students even share bathrooms—a reality I would never, ever expose my daughters to. Have you met men in college? No, thank you.

But—as always happens—that trend has left the campus and makes its way into culture and corporations. Today, in certain restaurants and airplane lounges, there are shared bathrooms—where men and women enter together, entering individual stalls in the same bathroom. Handwashing and the like all happen together. I hate it. And if I feel that way, imagine how women feel.

Can I be blunt? (Too late to ask, I suppose.) Does a person of either sex really want to relieve him or herself in a bathroom stall next to someone of a different sex? Of course not. It's awkward as all hell and makes everyone uncomfortable. Why? At the basic level, in the bathroom, traditional gender still matters—because our physiological plumbing matters. Ninety-nine percent of people understand this. But our PC culture has told us to ignore these basic instincts and embrace insanity.

Recently, I was entering a public men's restroom and a woman in front of me accidentally almost entered the men's bathroom. As she started to push the men's room door open, I politely said, "Excuse me, ma'am, this is the men's room." She laughed, thanked me, and headed in the right direction. It was a friendly and funny interaction. Then, as I used the restroom, the "what if's" started in my mind: What if she had screamed at me and said she had a right to use the bathroom? What if she had kept walking in? What would I have said? What could I have said? Somehow I would have been the bigot—and "she" would have been the victim.

I know I'm not crazy—at least in this example. And neither are you. America cannot afford to limit the freedom, decency, and security of the 99 percent to accommodate the supposed oppression of the 1 percent. Our pursuit of happiness is a cherished freedom. But no one's pursuit cancels or supersedes my right or the rights of my family. Just because a few people want to use a different bathroom, that does not create a *right* for them. Nor does it make them oppressed. However, walk into a government school today and tell the principal that you expect boys to use the boys' bathroom and girls to use the girls' bathroom. In most school districts, your demand will be met with shock. You will be deemed intolerant—and, push it far enough, Child Protective Services might show up on your doorstep that evening.

Common sense is not so common in our government institutions. On February 5, 2019, City of Portland chief administrative officer Tom Rinehart emailed his staff about an upcoming remodeling of a municipal building, which included "all-user" restrooms but no urinals. "We will continue to have gender-specific (male and female) multistall restrooms that are readily available to any employee that prefers to use one. But, there will be no urinals in any restroom in the building. This will give us the flexibility we need for any future changes in signage." He concluded, "I am convinced that this is the right way to ensure success as your employer, *remove arbitrary barriers in our community*, and provide leadership that is reflective of our shared values." (Italics mine.)

For the record, I'm a big fan of arbitrary barriers in bathrooms. Thankfully, North Carolina is, as well. In 2016, it stood up against an Obama administration policy that muddied the waters in public restrooms across the country. North Carolina simply sought to restore common sense by requiring people to use the bathroom of their sex, not their declared gender. The mob descended on it, of course. Calls to boycott North Carolina poured in, ranging from the NCAA to Bank of America to, of course, Hollywood. And in 2019, a school district in Georgia reversed course on a similarly bizarre experiment in trans bathrooms. *Preteens and teens choosing which bathroom to use—what could possibly go wrong?*

Ladies and gentlemen, although I don't want to share my bathroom with a woman, especially one who is not my wife, that is not the point. The point is that leftists want to—and are—stripping away our rights by making us feel intolerant. I'm not intolerant, and neither are you. Freedom does not mean forced acceptance, let alone celebration, of a biological male in a women's bathroom.

MAN UP

I do not apologize for stating a simple biological truth—two genders, male and female—because there's no hatred or judgment in that statement. I am tolerant of how people want to live and how they want to identify; I just don't have to constantly alter my life so as to not offend the Left as it moves the goalpost of offenses. And I certainly don't have to apologize for being me. That is the definition of tolerance. There's no hatred here, just common sense. When we deny the most obvious facts, we hurt both boys and girls—but especially boys. America needs manly men more than ever.

Speak up, attend school board meetings, meet with your principal, talk to your kids, and equip them for gender mania. Make commonsense arguments while respecting people's privacy and right to life, liberty, and the pursuit of happiness. As parents—even though you live in an upside-down world—you still rule your home. Reject the cultural encroachment, and teach your boys to be men and your girls to be women—while nurturing their God-given strengths and unique personalities. Don't baby them. Don't emasculate them.

This is a critical battle for American crusaders. Be that parent who objects at the PTA meeting. Organize like-minded parents. If you live in a dark blue part of the country, consider homeschooling with other families. Insist on healthy feminism and healthy masculinity. Fight and win.

"Socialism is the philosophy of failure, the creed of ignorance, and the gospel of envy."

—Winston Churchill, speech May 28, 1948

"The problem with socialism is that you eventually run out of other people's money."

—British Prime Minister Margaret Thatcher

SEVEN

SOCIALISM: WILL IT WORK *THIS* TIME?

My oldest son, Gunner, was riding with me in the front seat of our Jeep on a beautiful fall day as we drove to a local park to throw a football around. Rush Limbaugh was on the radio in the background while we chatted about kid stuff. Then Rush mentioned socialism. Gunner didn't notice, but it sparked a question in my mind.

"Gunner, do you know what socialism is?" I asked.

"No," he said earnestly.

"How about capitalism?"

He thought for a moment and replied, "Isn't that when you can make a lot of money?"

"Yes, but it's more than that. Do you know about economics?"

"No," he answered again.

Gunner is nine years old and a very bright kid. I've been talking about politics, faith, patriotism, taxes, guns, government, the military, Republicans, and Democrats his whole life. He also attends a classical Christian school where he learns the Bible, American history, Latin, public speaking, English grammar, and more. He can structure a sentence better than I can. But, for whatever reason, basic economics is not something I had emphasized with him yet. But he understands math, so I started there.

"Let's say you started a business making rubber duckies (why the hell I started with rubber duckies, I have no idea), and you make one million rubber duckies. But when you go to sell your rubber duckies for $25 each, you can only sell 100,000 of them. You still have 900,000 rubber duckies left. What is your problem?"

"Maybe they cost too much!" he said. Smart kid. *Who pays $25 for a rubber duckie? Does it double as a Bluetooth speaker?*

"Could be. What else?" I quickly asked.

"Maybe the rubber duckies aren't very good. Or maybe people don't even want rubber duckies!" said Gunner as he started to get the idea.

"Exactly; could be any of those things. You could be charging too much. Maybe another company makes a better rubber duckie. Maybe rubber duckies have been replaced by remote control boats. Or maybe, you simply made too many rubber duckies in the first place." I continued, "Economics is never about just one thing, Gunner. It's complicated and includes lots of puzzle pieces that people and businesses need to figure out in order to be successful. If you make the best rubber duckie, make the right amount, advertise it properly, and sell it at the right price, then you'll be successful and make money. If you mess up one of those pieces, you will probably fail. It's exciting but also not easy."

He seemed to get it, but then I got technical: "Economics is about supply and demand, products and prices. It's about how those things interact and compete. But—as with everything in life—the government also gets involved, and that's where politics comes into play."

"Democrats want companies to pay more taxes to the government, right, Dad?"

"Bingo, Gunner," I cheered, feeling redeemed that my hours of political education had sunk in.

I jumped in to continue my rant on economics, when Gunner cut me off. "Can we not use rubber duckies anymore, Dad? Let's say I make cool cars instead."

Already a capitalist, and he doesn't even know it.

We went on to discuss free markets for another half hour, in terms he understood. We talked about different scenarios, markets, money, and regulations. After all that, I finally got to socialism. Turned out that explaining socialism was simple.

"Socialism is when you tax people who work hard and make money so the government can spread that money around to everyone else," I said.

"But what if I work harder and make more money, I get to keep more—right?" asked Gunner.

"Nope, you get to pay the government more."

"Well, that's not fair."

It's so simple that a nine-year-old can understand why socialism doesn't make sense. The problem is that most of our educational institutions today are not teaching the overwhelming merits of capitalism but instead the sanitized deceptions of socialism. Schools and politicians use a simplistic and perverse definition of fairness—they call it "economic justice"—to seduce young people to embrace socialism. Just ask Bernie.

WAS JESUS A SOCIALIST?

This book is entitled AMERICAN CRUSADE for a reason—because I believe our moment requires a holy war for the righteous cause of human freedom. But what if our holiest warrior—Jesus Christ himself—was actually a socialist? Many on the Left, who've abandoned the core tenants of faith and Christianity, like to invoke the humility, kindness, and generosity of Jesus as evidence that the only way to care for the poor is to take from the rich. *Jesus said that, right?* No, wait, that was Robin Hood.

As the Left has gone increasingly godless, you may have nonetheless seen Nancy "the Nun" Pelosi quote this verse: "To minister to the needs of God's creation is an act of worship. To ignore those needs is to dishonor the God who made us." She has used it dozens of times in major speeches and in the *Congressional Record*. It's a bold statement for someone who ignores the fact that her congressional district is drowning in feces and dirty needles. Another inconvenient fact is that those words are *nowhere* in the Bible, which she explains away by saying "I can't find it in the Bible, but I quote it all the time. . . . I keep reading and reading the Bible—I know it's there someplace." Keep looking, Nancy.

Honest people such as my late Grandmother Gwendolyn—whom I adored—would often conflate having a heart for the poor with the need for *government* to do more. Old-school Democrats were the party of the working poor, and many Christians gravitated toward their message of kindness, humility, and charity. But that was before the Democrat Party decided to embrace socialism. Is that what Jesus actually would have wanted? Was Jesus—God on Earth—actually a socialist?

The New Testament is a fantastic source of economic knowledge—most of which Jesus said himself. Besides talk of Heaven and salvation, He talked about money more than any other subject; almost one-third of His parables included the subject of money and work. Why? Because He understood that, to a disproportionate level, money and wealth have a direct link to the priorities and perspective of people. Money can control people, or it can bring freedom—but it all depends on how you view it.

Rather than weave my own response, I'd like to cite the wonderful argument made in a PragerU video entitled "Was Jesus a Socialist?" In the video, Lawrence Reed, the president of the Foundation for Economic Education, makes a devastating case that not only was Jesus not a socialist but socialism is fundamentally incompatible with Christianity.

"Socialism is the concentration of power into the hands of government elites to achieve the following purposes: central planning of the economy and the radical redistribution of wealth. Jesus never called for any of that. Nowhere in the New Testament does He advocate for the government to punish the rich—or even to use tax money to help the poor. Nor does He promote the ideas of state ownership of businesses or central planning of the economy," states Reed before citing numerous examples, two of which I'll expand on below.

Indulge me in some brief Bible reading—consider it your Bible study for today. In Matthew 25, Jesus, preaching on the Mount of Olives just outside Jerusalem, tells the Parable of the Talents:

Again, it will be like a man going on a journey, who called his servants and entrusted his wealth to them. To one he gave five bags of gold, to another two bags, and to another one bag, each according to his ability.

Then he went on his journey. The man who had received five bags of gold went at once and put his money to work and gained five bags more. So also, the one with two bags of gold gained two more. But the man who had received one bag went off, dug a hole in the ground, and hid his master's money.

After a long time the master of those servants returned and settled accounts with them. The man who had received five bags of gold brought the other five. "Master," he said, "you entrusted me with five bags of gold. See, I have gained five more." His master replied, "Well done, good and faithful servant! You have been faithful with a few things; I will put you in charge of many things. Come and share your master's happiness!"

The man with two bags of gold also came. "Master," he said, "you entrusted me with two bags of gold; see, I have gained two more." His master replied, "Well done, good and faithful servant! You have been faithful with a few things; I will put you in charge of many things. Come and share your master's happiness!"

Then the man who had received one bag of gold came. "Master," he said, "I knew that you are a hard man, harvesting where you have not sown and gathering where you have not scattered seed. So I was afraid and went out and hid your gold in the ground. See, here is what belongs to you." His master replied, "You wicked, lazy servant! So you knew that I harvest where I have not sown and gather where I have not scattered seed? Well, then, you should have put my money on deposit with the bankers, so that when I returned I would have received it back with interest.

"So take the bag of gold from him and give it to the one who has ten bags. For whoever has will be given more, and they will have an abundance. Whoever does not have, even what they have will be taken from them. And throw that worthless servant outside, into the darkness, where there will be weeping and gnashing of teeth."

Also in the Book of Matthew, Jesus offers his Parable of the Workers in the Vineyard—where He tells a story of a landowner who hired workers for his vineyard. He paid workers in the morning a certain wage (one denarius), but as the day went on, he hired more workers for the same wage—even though they worked less time. The first workers grumbled to the landowner, saying "These who were hired last worked only one hour, and you have made them equal to us who have borne the burden of the work and the heat of the day." Rather than feel their pain, Jesus relayed the message of the landowner this way:

> But he answered one of them, "I am not being unfair to you, friend. Didn't you agree to work for a denarius? Take your pay and go. I want to give the one who was hired last the same as I gave you. Don't I have the right to do what I want with my own money? Or are you envious because I am generous?"

Though these are salvation messages at their core, in them Jesus acknowledges the capitalist framework emanating from natural law, just as the Old Testament did (for more on that, see John Locke's *Two Treatises of Government*). Chief among these is the recognition of private property and voluntary entry into contracts *directly* between the boss and employee. Other themes central to a natural law/capitalist-based ethic include individual hard work, interest, return on investment, the shaming of laziness, and supply and demand. And notice what was missing—Jesus did not take from the "faithful servant" to give to the "lazy servant," nor did he instruct the workers who worked all day to collectively bargain to be paid more than the workers who worked only a few hours. He had a heart for the poor, but He also acknowledged human nature.

He also said, "Give back to Caesar what is Caesar's and to God what is God's." With that one sentence, he established the correct form of separation between church and state that has since been a pillar of the West—both politically and economically. Jesus taught that, as individuals, we should be charitable, generous, and forgiving, and care for the poor. But He never taught that the government should do those things for us; Ceasar's business was Ceasar's business. The economist Walter E. Williams frequently reminds us of the specific language of the Ten Commandments—the Law that Jesus came to fulfill. "'I'm sure that he didn't mean thou shalt not steal unless there was a majority vote in Congress."

Simply put, to help the less fortunate, reach into your own pocket, not someone else's.

Any way you slice it, socialism is fundamentally incompatible with the teachings of Jesus. So, no, Jesus was not a socialist. If anything, he was a capitalist—with a keen understanding that wealth can also be abused and the love of money is corrosive for the soul. He said, "Again I tell you, it is easier for a camel to go through the eye of a needle than for someone who is rich to enter the kingdom of God." If you allow your wealth to impede your faith, that's your problem.

GOT SOCIALISM?

The equation is: Economics + Leftism = Socialism.

Just as the inverse is: Economics + Freedom = Capitalism.

As commonly understood, socialism is both a political and an economic theory that advocates that the means of production, distribution, and exchange (meaning all business and markets) should be owned or regulated by the community as a whole or the state. By the way, so-called democratic socialism—which is how most American socialists such as Bernie Sanders define themselves—is merely socialism that you vote for. Old-school socialism comes from dictators; new-school socialism comes from Democrats; both require complete government control and the subjugation of individual citizens.

Socialism always sounds great in theory, but it never is in practice. Never. The rich always get richer and more powerful, while the rest of society gets the government-approved crumbs. There is no robust middle class and no ability for the poor to become the rich and powerful. America is full of self-made billionaires, millionaires, and presidents who came from nothing. That doesn't happen in socialist countries. Only government connections, the right last name, and cronyism breed success under socialism.

Besides a handful of small, homogeneous, isolated, and irrelevant countries, can you name one country in which socialism has ever worked? Or even so-called democratic socialism? Socialism apologists always cite countries such as Norway, Sweden, Finland, and Denmark. Their argument is so foolish. First, the combined population of these countries is roughly 26.5 million people, less than 10 percent of the United States' population and smaller than both California and Texas alone. Second, when was the last time that Norway, Sweden, Finland, or Denmark mattered in the international context? Are they known for their innovation or growth? Can they even defend themselves? And even if their half-baked version of socialism does "kind of" work, has it led to innovation, growth, or the power to defend their populations from external threats? Those countries may be running their own unsustainable and fake utopias, but they are on borrowed time. They have neither freedom nor power, which makes them irrelevant serfs floating through history.

Socialism is also cloaked as "economic justice" or "economic fairness." But what's "fair" about an entire economic system in which average people do all the work and pay someone else lots of money so that a privileged few can be rich? Sounds a lot like slavery to me. In this case, the government becomes our owner—benefiting from our labor, stealing our wealth, and never allowing us to achieve (economic) freedom. Socialism is a new form of slavery—a backward, leftist fever dream that creates a nightmare for citizens.

Yet in recent polls, over half of American millennials said they preferred socialism to capitalism, and they are quickly warming to socialist ideas. Adam Smith, the father of free-market economics, must be whirling in his grave. Do these young people even know who Adam Smith was? Or the basics of Economics 101? Of course not, because our schools no longer teach—or promote—free-market capitalism.

If you never learn why free markets, profits, and supply and demand work, it's very easy to fall for the easiest (and most deceptive) promise in political history: free stuff! As we drown in $23 trillion of debt, the socialists squeal, "Free health care!" ($53 trillion worth if you're Pocahontas.) "No more student debt! Universal basic income!" Their actual list of demands is, frighteningly, much longer and includes promises of free college, free childcare, free drugs, free abortions, and free housing. The hidden hand of capitalism is tougher to explain, whereas free stuff can win elections—especially when young voters believe that capitalism has "failed" and socialism is the savior. But the track record is clear: capitalism unleashes prosperity, while socialism enforces mediocracy and eventually requires governmental command and control—the exact opposite of what makes America special.

FRAUDS, FORMULAS, FAWNING, AND FEAR

Socialism hides—and grows—behind the success of capitalism. Consider the fraud of the modern "original gangsta" of American socialism, Senator Bernie Sanders. He's now . . . a millionaire! He became one in 2019. God bless capitalism, under which even the socialists can get rich—truly an equal-opportunity system. When asked about his snowballing net worth, Bernie—with all the charm of Bernie Madoff—shot back, "I didn't know that it was a crime to write a good book which turns out to be a best seller." That's right, it's not a crime (yet) to take a risk, create something, and reap the rewards. But don't worry, he also offered some sage, compassionate advice: "If you write a best-selling book, you can be a millionaire, too." He's a government-made millionaire, thanks to the platform his elected office gave him, but he's happy to reap the rewards of capitalism, too. (Congrats on your three homes, too, Bernie!)

Next, there are their formulas—which never add up. Here's an example. The next time you talk to a leftist—or even a liberal—ask him or her what the *real* minimum wage would be if the government raised the federal minimum wage to $15 an hour. This number was popularized by, you guessed it, Bernie Sanders (despite the fact that the minimum wage of his 2020 campaign staff was less than that amount). The leftist will reflexively answer, "Fifteen dollars!"—because for socialists, government regulation dictates free-market economics. But the real world is always much more complicated than that.

What would the real minimum wage be? Zero dollars. Because when you raise wages in a way that distorts market forces and significantly impacts profit margins, businesses cut costs. The easiest cost to cut? Low-wage workers. Those workers don't make $15, they now make $0. (As the robots enter stage left.)

But the Left says that "equality" is all that matters! And although Americans of all stripes have become more equal over time, total equality is a myth. Despite our imperfections, our nation was founded on the principles of equal opportunity and equal justice under the law. Equal opportunity is the real goal, with equal justice leveling the playing field. The Left's deceptive twist is the concept of absolute "equality"—then and now. Hence its push for "racial reparations," a concept most of the 2020 Democrats boost in some form. They believe we can pay back the slavery sins of the past in order to even out the future. But who will pay and to whom? I'm white, but I've never owned slaves, and neither has my family. Do I have to pay anyway?

Leftist policies always have unintended consequences, but those consequences could have been predicted by a fourth grader with a basic understanding of economics (I hear you, Gunner). People lose their jobs—good jobs they used to have. When your favorite burger place or grocery store is forced to double its entry-level wage, the money doesn't come from some magical warehouse. There is no vault full of Scrooge McDuck's gold. Either expenses must be cut or prices must be increased—or both. This creates two outcomes: fewer employees and higher prices, which puts more people out of work—and on government benefits. The middle class shrinks, and government grows. For those who remain employed at the higher minimum wage level, their money then won't go as far, due to the rising prices engendered by the new minimum wage. See how the socialism merry-go-round works?

Then there's the fawning. The leftist-controlled media just can't resist trying to make socialism great again. In May 2018, the magazine *Teen Vogue* published an article titled "Who Is Karl Marx: Meet the Anti-Capitalist Scholar." I ask myself the obvious questions: Why is a magazine focused on the fashion trends of teen girls doing PR for the creator of communism? Isn't the fashion industry a model of capitalism? The article paints a glowing picture of this "scholar"—it almost seems like satire—and highlights how educators use Marx's writings in the classroom.

The author concludes with "While you may not necessarily identify as a Marxist, socialist, or communist, you can still use Karl Marx's ideas to use history and class struggles to better understand how the current sociopolitical climate in America came to be. Instead of looking at President Donald Trump's victory in November 2016 as a snapshot, we can turn to the bigger picture of what previous events lead us up to the current moment." Ah, Karl Marx—the man whose ideas led to the slaughter of hundreds of millions of people—is now the leader of a global leftist therapy session!

The tactics are clear, but why the strategy of putting Marxism, communism, and socialism on a pedestal? It's all part of the Left's hope of reducing American economic might as a means to consolidate power in a single international globalist paradise. The greatest threat to these machinations, besides Donald Trump, is entrepreneurs who love America. Have you ever wondered why the public school curriculum isn't full of lessons about entrepreneurship? Have you ever heard a teachers' union threaten to strike unless capitalism was taught and more business owners were invited to share their insights with students? Kids are not taught how to make money—or even manage it. It's easier to teach dependence than independence. Today's government schools are not designed to promote individualism, let alone unleash the powers of capitalism.

Instead, students today are fed an anticapitalist view of American "injustice." What happened to the virtue of work? The American dream? The benefits of free-market competition? These have been replaced by classes such as "Adulting Is Hard," "Gender in Gaming," and "Marx for Today." That's why students leave the asylum of publicly funded education thinking that socialism is the cheat code for the game of life.

Fear is the final, and often most powerful, tool of socialists. Consider these numbers. In 2016, a study by Bankrate revealed that 63 percent of Americans did not have the funds to cover an unexpected expense of $500 to $1,000. In 2018, the Federal Reserve Board noted that 40 percent of Americans could not cover a $400 expense. These are real numbers and real life. Despite the prosperity of American-style capitalism, the financial pressures of our modern economy shape political persuasion. This sort of financial anxiety is the perfect breeding ground for socialism. When you are afraid or taught to be afraid and you believe that the current economic system is unjust, you're ripe for recruitment. Even though capitalism has brought citizens of the West more prosperity than any other group in human history, broad prosperity is taken for granted. We are so rich that people wonder, *Why can't the government give me housing, pay off my debts, provide my health care, and pay for my food, too?* That sounds attractive to the ears, but it is corrosive to the soul. All the Left wants is votes, and that's why it's selling these lies.

Why, then, doesn't the tax code incentivize savings for the near term and the long term? Why don't schools make financial literacy a requirement to graduate from high school—or even eighth grade? My God, how many adults even know how credit card interest is calculated? A financially independent and literate citizenry is frightening—to leftists. Free, secure people fight for political control. Socialism, by definition, means "I'm dependent on you, comrade."

Socialism has never worked and leads to abject misery. Socialism runs counter to human nature: the drive to create value, build, take risks, and provide for ourselves and our family. But leftists tell us—because they're so smart—that it will work this time! Meanwhile, the capitalist Trump economy raises wages, lowers unemployment rates to their lowest recorded levels, and puts American workers first.

INMATES RUN THE ASYLUM

As you know, capitalism has a conflicted relationship with unions. A century ago, when big companies would often exploit workers to work insane hours for little pay and in very unsafe conditions, it was reasonable for workers to unionize in order to negotiate more favorable terms of employment. Communists and socialists quickly leveraged this new power in numbers into a political force as a means of enshrining their anticapitalist doctrine into law. Eventually workers unionized in the only sector in which success is not tied to the quality of the product, nor the expense, nor the speed at which it should be done: the public sector. The government.

When I think of overworked and mistreated employees, government workers don't come to mind (with the possible exception of staffers for the infamously mercurial senator Amy Klobuchar. *Look out, she's throwing shit at us again!*). Even Democrat president Franklin Roosevelt—a strong supporter of private sector unions and government intervention—was adamantly against government employee unions.

"All Government employees should realize that the process of collective bargaining, as usually understood, cannot be transplanted into the public service," he wrote in August 1937. ". . . Since their own services have to do with the functioning of the Government, a strike of public employees manifests nothing less than an intent on their part to prevent or obstruct the operations of Government until their demands are satisfied. Such action, looking toward the paralysis of Government by those who have sworn to support it, is unthinkable and intolerable."

Ya think? If government employees can collectively bargain—if they can threaten to strike for more wages and benefits—they are holding taxpayers hostage. Politicians, eager to make the problem go away, quickly give away taxpayer dollars to end the standoff. Unlike in a private company, these payments don't impact the bottom line of politicians. The cycle is in perpetual motion: The government creates a government monopoly job. The government department forces taxpayers to pay for more workers—regardless of their performance. The government union then forces its members to pay dues. Then the government unions use those dues to pay politicians . . . who push for more government monopoly jobs.

All public money. Lots of power. And no accountability. As a result, in the latter part of the twentieth century, government employees unionized into a very powerful political force. And you can guess in which direction this force pulls. (Police and firefighters remain an exception to this rule, as they still work inside realms of merit and accountability.)

Teachers' unions are a great example. It's easier to get hired at Google by wearing a MAGA hat to the interview than it is to get a teacher fired. You literally cannot fire a public school teacher unless he or she is slinging meth or sleeping with a thirteen-year-old. The same goes for departments that deal in matters of life and death for our nation's best. The Department of Veterans Affairs, up until the recent commonsense actions taken by President Trump, was a cesspool of government union employees who can never be fired. It still is, but Trump is fighting this. Even when scores of American heroes are dying while waiting for health care, unionized VA employees keep their jobs. Waiting lists, drug overdoses, appointment dysfunction, and rampant suicide—and nobody held accountable.

No accountability means no excellence. Veterans and students are treated like numbers, not customers—the opposite of free-market incentives. Former president Ronald Reagan once said, "A government bureau is the nearest thing to eternal life we'll ever see on this earth!" He was correct, but I have an addendum: the closest thing to an eternal job is a government union job. You can't get fired, your pay always goes up, you get a fat pension, and your performance doesn't matter. It's the best example of socialism I've ever seen, and Democrats think every part of our economy should run this way.

WHY CAPITALISM IS AWESOME

But let's turn to the good guys. Many powerful and persuasive books have been written about the merits of capitalism. I have read many of them, even if I often preferred the *Cliff's Notes* version. (By the way, the *Cliff's Notes* publishing story is a wonderful example of American capitalism.) But the best evidence for capitalism is right in front of us. I'm not talking about space shuttles, satellite phones, and supercomputers. It is a given that almost every big aspect of the world today has been forged by American inventions, innovations, and experimentation. I'm talking about the ways in which our everyday lives have been shaped—in every way—by the inventions and innovations of American capitalism. No other country created these. No other system made them possible. Just American-style, free-market capitalism.

Consider Joe. He lives in Ohio. He works two middle-class jobs and has 2.5 kids. Thanks to American inventions (marked with *), here's a day in his life:

The air-conditioning* ran all night, keeping the room chilly, just the way Joe likes it. He woke up at 6:00 a.m. to his alarm clock* powered by electricity*. Like most of us, Joe reaches first for his smartphone*. He uses home Wi-Fi* to access the internet* to check the weather forecast* and scroll his Facebook page*. He glances at the baby monitor* before turning on the lights* and then takes a high-powered hot shower*. He brushes his teeth with toothpaste,* and he takes Lipitor* to manage his high cholesterol.

After getting dressed (no, we didn't invent clothes), he heads downstairs to make breakfast (but we did invent breakfast cereal*!). He opens the refrigerator* and pulls out

. . . whatever he wants—which nobody on Earth could do before America. He fires up the coffee maker (thanks, Germany, but we also had to save the world from you—twice). He flips some toast into the toaster* and after turning on the television*—to watch *FOX & Friends*, of course—he realizes his coffee is now cold, so he heats it up in the microwave*. He now wants his home a bit warmer while he eats, so he adjusts the thermostat*. With breakfast complete, he throws his plate into the dishwasher*.

He now realizes he's running a bit late, so he shoots an email* to his boss. Rushing out of the house, he grabs a can of soda* and some bubble gum* before jumping into his car*. He opens the garage door* before taking for granted thousands of things that make his car work—all thanks to America—from the engine* to the antilock brakes* to the airbag* to the GPS system*. He then heads off to work.

I could go on for pages and pages with asterisks. As Joe's day progresses, he and his family could benefit from any number of other American inventions, such as airplanes, ballpoint pens, computers, credit cards, cameras, escalators, fast food, flashlights, laser printers, Post-it notes, shopping carts, video games, and even zippers—just to name a few.

The point is not that American capitalism has made our nation *wealthy*, even though it has. The point is that American capitalism has made life *better*. Even the poorest people in America today have cell phones that contain more computing power than was inside the first space shuttle. The American inventions of electricity, air-conditioning, refrigeration, modern medicine, telephones, computers, and the internet *alone* have changed (and saved) the lives of billions of people—for the better. Without capitalism and the corresponding economic incentive to make a profit, America would have been just like every other country—just doing the same thing for hundreds of years and putting up with it.

In America, we improve our lives constantly and at a rapid pace. Not because we are better than other people but because our economic system unleashes the God-given human spirit. The government does not control the markets. The government does not control the means of production. The government does not control prices. The government does not determine who wins and who loses. Free-market competition creates winners and losers. And the "losers" have the opportunity to compete again—and win. The right to better yourself is inextricably linked to the right to fail. As a result, Americans are allowed to fail and succeed—and improve the lives of everyone else in the process.

America is an economic miracle, the likes of which the world has never seen. Yet socialists—ungrateful and blinded by the fruits of capitalism—want to destroy it.

THE PROS AND COMMIES

Lest we forget, American capitalism also funded the military that saved the free world from a socialist country—twice. Then American capitalism exhausted the communist Soviet Union, winning the Cold War. Today, American capitalism underwrites the most powerful and technologically advanced fighting force on the planet—challenged *only* by communist China, which subsists on tyranny, theft, and deception. American freedom is not enough; American power is a must. Freedom does not exist in a vacuum; it must be defended.

In stark contrast, here are a few things socialism and its bigger brother, communism (in all its forms) have brought us: the concentration camp, the gulag, dictatorship, censorship, mass starvation, soulless bureaucracies, and breadlines. Socialism is slavery, because it's always about power—taking rights and freedom from regular people in order to advance the wealth or ambitions of powerful people. I'll say it again, socialism is slavery.

A capitalist system is oriented toward serving citizens and creating customers. A socialist system is oriented toward controlling citizens and turning them into dependents.

Capitalism imagines, *How can individuals thrive?*

Socialism frets, *How can we keep our population alive?*

In 1985, Bernie Sanders tried to give some positive PR to breadlines: "Sometimes American journalists talk about how bad a country is, that people are lining up for food. That's a good thing! In other countries people don't line up for food. The rich get the food and the poor starve to death." Wait, so in capitalist countries you can walk into a grocery store almost anywhere and buy thirty different types of bread (maybe even with food stamps provided by our social safety net), but people lining up to beg for government-rationed bread elsewhere is a good thing? I wonder if he ever stood in a breadline while honeymooning in the former USSR? Which reminds me of this classic joke from the former Soviet Union:

A man walks into a shop and asks the clerk, "You don't have any meat?"

The clerk answers, "No, we don't have any *bread* here. The shop that doesn't have any *meat* is across the street."

The Democrat Party used to play well with capitalism. Both parties used to look for solutions to help those who "fell through the cracks" of our economy. Stuff happens. Remember that George W. Bush created the White House Office of Faith-Based and Community Initiatives because conservatives believe that government cannot, and should not, solve every problem. A healthy society depends on ordinary citizens practicing charity—and government can get out of the way to make that happen. There have always been marginalized populations that are underserved because government can't meet every need. Socialist policies tailored toward the fantasy of utopia simply destroy the mechanism by which people can rise out of poverty—and incentives for private citizens to give voluntary charitable dollars. Socialists want to replace faith-based and community empowerment with a federal-based and command economy.

As with utopias and unicorns, the Left offers fantasies instead of facts. Former president Obama famously told business owners, "You didn't build that." Comrade Cortez's Green New Deal includes "economic security" for those "unwilling to work." Bernie Sanders imagines a world without billionaires. Elizabeth Warren wants a "wealth tax" that would tax the savings of Americans, money they have already been taxed on—twice! Former presidential candidate Bill de Blasio said in 2019, "There's plenty of money in this country, it's just in the wrong hands." Democrat businessman Andrew Yang believes that the answer is a "universal basic income" and proposes giving every American adult one thousand dollars per month. We can only assume that in each of these cases the recipients will include anyone in this country—regardless of citizenship, because for leftists, the alternative would be "unjust." Remember, socialists don't care about citizenship—because they are leftists first and foremost. Karl Marx would be very proud of modern Democrats.

President Trump declared during his 2019 State of the Union address, "America will never be a socialist country." I pray that he's correct. Talking to our kids about the miracle of capitalism and the horrors of socialism will go a long way in making sure he is.

"Oh my God, when Moses is erased from the West, what is left of Western civilization?"

—Camille Paglia, feminist and university professor

"Of all the dispositions and habits, which lead to political prosperity, Religion and Morality are indispensable supports."

—President George Washington

EIGHT

SECULARISM: DEPORTING GOD FROM AMERICA

After the election of Donald Trump in 2016, one of the most powerful things to happen to our country—and to *me*—was the Christian conversion of the rapper Kanye West. Wait, the conversion of a rapper was a powerful moment in America and *my* life? Yes, it was. At first, like many others, I was skeptical of his authenticity. *Is this a PR stunt?* But when I watched Kanye live and listened to his songs, I was convinced. He loves Jesus and wants to share Him with the world. Even better, he went *all in*, not content to live a private life of faith in order to protect his iconic image. What a shot of adrenaline for the home team! *If Kanye is with us, who can be against us?* (Forgive the sacrilege.) Kanye is a changed man but not a perfect man. As often happens—throughout history and in our country— the most imperfect people become the best messengers.

One of the faith ingredients that Kanye points to is the fact that his parents raised him in the church and taught him the Bible. He made the choice—as so many of us do—to ignore much of it and chart his own course. But the foundation was there. He knew the stories, the Gospel, the Truth. Like the Prodigal Son, it just took him a while to come home. Today he sings, "God is King, we the soldiers." Amen, brother Kanye. We all have crooked paths. Sinners saved only by grace. God works in His own time, and for His purposes.

I thank my parents every day for giving me the very same foundation. Of all the priorities my parents had for the upbringing of my brothers and me, faith in Jesus Christ was front and center—Sunday mornings, Wednesday nights, and every day in between. To me, the "church" thing was mostly boring and formulaic—but it stuck. They introduced me to Jesus, and at a young age I was baptized. The worldly choices I made *after* that were on me; but no matter what, the truths of my youth have always tugged at my heart.

When I was a teenager, as fortune would have it, Billy Graham's Crusade came to town in 1999. It was one of the megaservices that Billy Graham held across America and around the world for decades, bringing millions of people to Christ. Our local church trained believers to be ambassadors, prepared to receive and pray with people who came forward to accept Christ as their savior. My parents took me with them for training, and I was at the Metrodome in Minneapolis when Billy Graham spoke—an American Crusade if I've ever seen one. I don't remember the sermon, but the scene was that of an evangelical Trump rally.

As it happened, I was living in New York City in 2005 when Billy Graham held his final Crusade. Watching him speak to a crowd of thousands outside of Shea Stadium was a cool experience. But honestly, as I had recently returned from a tour in Guantánamo Bay and would soon head to Iraq, my mind heard the words but my heart did not absorb them. Billy Graham had saved the souls of millions of Americans, and although I went to support him, I didn't realize then that it was my soul that still needed saving. The gospel message he conveyed to millions of people throughout his life saved countless souls like mine—and is the key to saving America today. Crusades work, because they don't just explain—they proclaim.

America has always proclaimed as well. Our country's official motto is "In God we trust." It's on every single piece of money our government prints. Our motto does not mean that America is perfect or that every American is a Christian. It means, simply, that as fallen humans with a sinful nature, we place our trust in a God who is bigger than we are. Politically, and perhaps more importantly, it means we know that our rights have been given to us by God, not government—and therefore cannot be taken away. Without this understanding, the entire American experiment falls apart. That is not hyperbole. If we think we ultimately control our lives, we are arrogant enough to believe that government can ultimately save us, and we become slaves to the world. But if we know that God is in control, we welcome a system that balances faith in God with the ambitions and arrogance of man, all the while protecting individual rights. This is where true freedom thrives.

SAVING A WRETCH LIKE ME

If I'm self-aware about one thing, it's the depth of my sinful nature. I'm a sinner, infected with temptation, pride, and ambition. I'm a human—an imperfect, prideful, and broken vessel. Without knowing, fearing, and recognizing God, I would be like a ship lost at sea—wrecked and sunk.

And trust me, I've almost been sunk more times than I can admit on these pages. I've seen only forty short years on this earth, and I've been divorced twice, almost gone bankrupt once, and been deployed with a bunch of "toxically" masculine dudes thrice—one tour of which included a war crimes controversy. He saved a wretch like me.

Too often, our public professions of faith do not match our personal conduct. In this sense, we are all hypocrites. We can never live up to the standards God gave us, but the point is to keep striving.

How we handle our failures, and how we react to the failures of others, says more about us than anything else. My moral failures in life have taught me to drop the self-righteous facade of my younger years and instead more freely and humbly give grace and love. It's one thing to make judgments about things of consequence; it's another to be judgmental. Huge difference.

Part of the reason that Donald Trump resonated with millions of Americans so quickly is that he didn't—and couldn't—hide his personal failings. Instead, he lived life forward. He's been bankrupt and come back. He's been on a roller-coaster ride of relationships, but he loves his kids. Instead of virtue signaling and sanitizing his image, Trump embraced his brash background—ignored the media and remained committed to the things he cared about the most. As it turns out, with God and with regular people, the reservoir of forgiveness is deep. "Let any one of you who is without sin be the first to throw a stone," said Jesus, leaving us all holding a rock in our hands, realizing we're no better.

That's why, as an imperfect husband, son, father, and public figure, I don't let the burn-him-at-the-stake criticism of me on Twitter and cable television bother me. I truly don't care, because it's not about me. I've surrendered my life, and my judgment, to God. If you don't like me, fine. If you call me names, no problem. If you want to throw stones at me, have at it. Neither my current public persona nor my past (and future) as a sinner will define whether I stand up for faith in the public square. All I know is that without faith—without belief in a power and principles greater than oneself—life is selfish, small, and scary.

At the end of every Sunday show on *FOX & Friends*, right before we end the show and as we're waving good-bye, I smile at the camera with about three seconds to go and say, "Go to church!" After a few weeks of this, my cohosts noticed and obliged me, if with a chuckle. They know I'm not perfect, and so do I. But every time I go to church, I walk away a better person. That's all I know. It's a weekly accountability session with my Creator. Sure, I space out half the time (admit it, you do too!), but there are always significant moments of connection when I'm worshipping and hearing God's Truth. Those moments are gold. More precious than gold, actually.

I don't advocate for faith because I'm a Bible-believing Christian who thinks he's better than you are. I just want the story of grace, love, and redemption to be known by every person, because it's powerful for individuals and essential for free countries. Our founders understood that belief in an almighty God would determine whether we would be able to maintain the individual moral compass required to stave off the nanny state of big government and allow us to stay free. Imperfect, faith-filled people can handle freedom, but imperfect people who ignore God's will in their life end up worshipping something far more sinister.

If future generations of Americans are not exposed to faith or the Bible—or instead grow up believing that faith is harmful—something else will fill the void; either atheists who worship human power, bureaucrats who worship government power, or strong and aggressive religions such as Islam. Being *without* God leaves us rudderless, but being *against* God leaves us defenseless—which is why today's secularism movement is incompatible with Americanism.

WHAT IS SECULARISM?

The equation is: America − God + Leftism = Secularism.

Without God, America is not America. Add leftist ideology to the mix, and secularism makes government the god.

Some people believe that secularism is merely the absence of religion in government. "Separation of church and state" is how it is commonly understood. That worn-out phrase does not comport with the real purpose of the Bill of Rights, which states, "Congress shall make no law respecting an establishment of religion, or prohibiting the free exercise thereof." We have no state-run church in America—nor should we. Americans are free to worship however they want or not worship at all. The mere absence of religion is not what I'm talking about. Secularism—as driven by the Left today—more resembles a jihad against Christians and Jews than it does a pacifist curiosity.

The Church of Secularism ultimately believes that leftism can solve the country's problems and can form their own views of right and wrong—fully untethered from history, the Bible, and God-given rights. Government is the Vatican for secularists and career politicians their saints. The Somali Omars are their inquisitors. Their God-free gospel is preached in the most elite universities in America. Blinded by their naked belief in themselves, their fatal flaw is pride. Belief in self alone is the opposite of humility, making secularists the most zealous of leftists.

Secularists seek to tear down the historical and modern connections to faith in our country, which results in unraveling the stitching Americans need to remain a free, independent, and self-sufficient people. At which point leftists happily step in and say, "Government will solve your problems."

"Separation of church and state" is the main argument secularists use to deport God from every quarter of our country. But as many Americans no longer know, the phrase "separation of church and state" does not appear in either the Declaration of Independence or the Constitution. It's leftist folklore that, after years of indoctrination, has become orthodoxy.

As I was working on this book, someone tweeted at me about this very subject. I had recently given a speech at Liberty University and said, "My rights are given to me by God, not by government." The Twitter hater replied, "There are plenty of theocratic countries that would love to have you live there. But this is America where the separation of church and state is written into our Constitution. No one is keeping you here, traitor." This imbecile isn't even aware of the original source of this deception. The "separation" myth concept comes from a letter written by Thomas Jefferson to the Danbury Baptist Church in 1801 in which he wrote that the Constitution was intended to maintain a separation, so that an establishment of a state religion would never happen—and so the right of individuals to worship freely would not be infringed by the government. That is not a wall of separation, nor is that freedom *from* religion; that is freedom *of* religion. The government can, and should, create an environment that encourages faith without imposing a particular state religion on people. Jefferson understood that, and so do we.

AMERICA'S INDISPENSABLE FAITH

Our founders were men of Christian faith steeped in Western political philosophy. After watching what happened in Europe, our founders rejected state-run religion—a far cry from rejecting religion. If anything, they understood that for a free country to work, there had to be an acknowledgment of someone bigger, smarter, and better than ourselves. People who believe that *they* are the center of their universe make terrible citizens and end up bending to, or becoming, tyrannical leaders.

Faith was an important part of personal and public life in the late 1700s, and our founding documents, along with the personal writings of Jefferson, Washington, and almost every other founding father confirm this. I'm not going to quote the founding fathers for the rest of the chapter, but suffice it to say that they didn't check their beliefs at the door when they formed our self-government. They prayed over their work and invoked the guidance and providence of God at every turn. But if you've never read their writings—or been taught only that our founders "were slave owners!"—you'll believe the secular lies the Left repeats.

Our founders may have been professing Christians, but they were also sinners—no better than you and me. As such, they understood the limits of mere mortals and the ambitions of mankind, instead creating a system grounded in individual freedom, equal justice, personal responsibility, limited government, free markets, and religious faith. In fact, in his famous farewell address in 1796, our first president, George Washington, summed up the centrality of faith very nicely: "Of all the dispositions and habits, which lead to political prosperity, Religion and Morality are indispensable supports."

Indispensable.

America was also founded on gratitude. The opposite of gratitude is entitlement—if you are not grateful, you believe that the things you have are not enough or the things you don't have should be yours. Ingratitude is corrosive to the soul and even worse to a collective citizenry. But gratitude is a humble attribute that fills an individual with an appreciation of today and the promise of tomorrow. Our founders understood this fact, which is why America's first holiday—both formally and informally—is Thanksgiving. And whom did our founders thank for our blessings? God.

In his first year as president, following a seemingly impossible victory in our War of Independence, George Washington made a Thanksgiving proclamation:

Whereas it is the duty of all Nations to acknowledge the providence of Almighty God, to obey his will, to be grateful for his benefits, and humbly to implore his protection and favor, and Whereas both Houses of Congress have by their joint Committee requested me "to recommend to the People of the United States a day of public thanks-giving and prayer to be observed by acknowledging with grateful hearts the many signal favors of Almighty God, especially by affording them an opportunity peaceably to establish a form of government for their safety and happiness."

The same sentiments can be found across the centuries in the words of our presidents. Thomas Jefferson, Abraham Lincoln, Franklin D. Roosevelt, Ronald Reagan, and Donald Trump—along with almost every president in between—have reaffirmed the centrality of faith in our nation and gratitude to God for our freedoms.

Just fifty years after our nation's founding, a French diplomat, Alexis de Tocqueville, noted in his book *Democracy in America*, published in 1835:

In the United States the sovereign authority is religious, and consequently hypocrisy must be common; but there is no country in the whole world in which the Christian religion retains a greater influence over the souls of men than in America; and there can be no greater proof of its utility, and of its conformity to human nature, than that its influence is most powerfully felt over the most enlightened and free nation of the earth.

Yes, hypocrisy is common, but it's better than abandoning faith altogether. Understanding human nature and humility = Enlightenment and freedom.

In America, there are no church and state to separate. Our founding generations viewed faith as central to freedom and then built educational institutions to teach those views. Today, we are tearing them down at our own peril.

IVY LEAGUE USED TO ♥ GOD

In my final year at Princeton, I took a course entitled "The New

Testament and Christian Origins." I was a politics major with a focus on history, and it was my first course on Christianity. The class was taught by Elaine Pagels, whose temperament is exactly as you would expect from the Ivy League—a juddering Elizabeth Warren type steeped in her own brilliance. (Obama did give her a National Humanities Medal, after all.) She is considered a "world-renowned" scholar on the Gnostic gospels—writings not included in the traditional Bible. The idea of the course was to study the "historical Jesus" by deconstructing the biblical text and piecing together a biography of Jesus using additional historical evidence, much of which removed any allusion to divinity. Professor Pagels's theory, which she confidently posited on the first day of class, set the tone: Jesus was buried in a shallow grave and eaten by dogs, because history shows us that that was what happened to a common criminal. And even if He was crucified, that proves He was associated with common criminals and there is no proof of His divinity.

That definitely was not Sunday school at First Baptist Church. I welcomed the challenge.

My final paper for the course looked at the crucifixion of Jesus in the book of Mark. Was it true? How could I prove it? The material provided throughout the course incentivized students to challenge the divinity of Christ and the writings of Mark. The internet was still in its infancy, so I headed to Firestone Library, where the biblical scholars of yesteryear were eagerly waiting for me to dust off their work. Deep in the book-stacked bowels of the Princeton library my faith was affirmed and strengthened. The historical evidence of biblical accuracy was amazing, especially when judged against other famous works our society deems sacrosanct. What did the professor think of my treatise? I wish I could remember, but I'm pretty sure there was no smiley face next to the grade on my final paper.

I went to Princeton as a Christian. Yet, as I moved through

Princeton, I wandered in my faith—constantly challenged by naysayers and skeptics. I found the real historical Jesus not in the classroom at Princeton but in my own research. By the time I got to campus in 1999, Princeton—as well as other colleges across America—had turned its back on faith. But it wasn't always that way.

The College of New Jersey, later renamed Princeton University, was founded in 1746 by Presbyterians as a center for the training of clergy. Princeton was literally founded to train Christian pastors! John Witherspoon, Princeton's sixth president, was the only active Christian minister, and the only college president, to sign the Declaration of Independence. He later signed the Articles of Confederation, supported ratification of the Constitution, and served in Congress.

Princeton's original Latin motto was "Dei sub numine viget" ("Under God's power she flourishes"). The university's English motto was introduced in 1896 by then university president Woodrow Wilson: "In the nation's service." One hundred years later, the phrase must have been deemed too nationalist sounding, and the 1996 version was globalized to "In the nation's service, and in the service of all nations." *Nope. Still not humanistic enough.* Ten years later in 2006, the motto was changed to "In the nation's service and the service of humanity."

Current Princeton president Christopher Eisgruber explained the devolution, referring to Supreme Court Justice and Princeton alumna Sonia Sotomayor: "We began as a tiny liberal arts college founded to educate young men for the Presbyterian ministry. In Wilson's era we became a research university. In Sotomayor's time, we opened our gates to a wider world, becoming at once more diverse, more international and more intellectually eminent than ever before." Translation: God is simply not diverse enough, nor international enough, and certainly not "intellectually eminent" enough for us anymore.

Similarly, Harvard University was founded by Puritans, many of whom had escaped British oppression. In 1692, the university adopted the motto "Veritas Christo et ecclesiae" ("Truth for Christ and the Church"). The university later secularized and circumcised the motto to "Truth." The institution's original "Rules and Precepts" included "Let every Student be plainly instructed, and earnestly pressed to consider well, the maine end of his life and studies is, to know God and Jesus Christ which is eternal life (John 17:3) and therefore to lay Christ in the bottome, as the only foundation of all sound knowledge and Learning. And seeing the Lord only giveth wisedome, Let every one seriously set himself by prayer in secret to seeke it of him (Prov. 2:3)."

Where is that godly charge, Harvard? It's been replaced by the Church of Secularism. Students going to schools such as Princeton and Harvard—and almost every other college in America—are never introduced to the Christian faith. And if they are, they are told it is a lie. This is intentional.

Ivy League professors make grand claims as to the rigor of their process in ascertaining the validity of religious texts. But the glaring contradiction is that such rigor is never applied to figures of the Islamic world. Imagine if kooky professor Pagels claimed that Muhammad's body had been buried in a shallow grave and eaten by dogs. Obama would have had her immediately deported to the Islamic State. Or Princeton would fire her.

Secularists today are conducting a seek-and-destroy mission against any institution that puts more faith in God than in government. This is at the direction of Karl Marx, who believed that the total destruction of all religion was necessary to achieve a proper communist society. But what is so bizarre is that the secularists today appropriate Islam for their cause, and radical Muslims such as Somali Omar revel in it. Put a cross on the House floor, and there would be a flurry of lawsuits asserting the establishment of religion. Somali Omar in the Muslim hijab, though? It's considered freedom of expression and female empowerment. The House of Representatives has literally changed the rules of the House floor for her.

It is an odd alliance, the Secularists and radical Islam, to be sure. But for the purposes of tearing down our nation's Judeo-Christian institutions, their syncretism into the Church of Secularism has given them an effective fighting position.

Faith used to be indispensable to our nation's education system; today it is invisible, confined to student groups that rarely get support from universities. The result: our nation's future citizens, voters, and leaders fall for the pathetically stupid arguments of secularists who believe that the only wall worth building is Jefferson's Wall of Separation.

Let me say again, the war to erase faith from America is not accidental; it is intentional. Because the Christian faith—and Judeo-Christian values—are the foundation of Americanism.

WE NEED ATHENS AND JERUSALEM

I first heard the term "Athens and Jerusalem" from professor Jeffrey Hart in his wonderful book *Smiling Through the Cultural Catastrophe: Toward the Revival of Higher Education*. The concept, which has been used for centuries, is a historical metaphor describing the tension and balance between Greek thought and biblical faith. Princeton and Harvard used to teach both. Athens represents an intellectual approach, while Jerusalem embodies a belief in a higher power. In practical—and governmental—application these two viewpoints sometimes contradict each other, but they also bring much-needed balance. The two traditions brought us such Western heroes as Achilles, Moses, Socrates, and Jesus. How many students today could tell you what they did and why they matter?

Our founders could answer those questions, and therefore our founding documents embrace both the form of government created by the Greeks and Romans and the essential role of Western civilization. Our founders figured out that the impulses of government almost always crush the individual, because governments are made up of fallen human beings. "Jerusalem" is the recognition that belief in something greater than yourself is the balance that an individual—and society—needs. When you combine individual freedom with a moral compass, you get what's referred to as the Protestant work ethic—an ethos that was once embraced by almost every American, regardless of race, color, or religion.

Authoritarian governments crush religion, and religious governments ultimately crush individuals. Governments that embrace the tension of both create room for people to thrive. The problem with Islam is that it's both a religion and a government, rolled into one. Christianity, unlike Islam, is not premised to be a political system. Of course, the Western world had its flings with quasitheocracies in the Middle Ages and beyond; the Church wielded a lot of power in Europe for a long time, and it became oppressive to too many people. Ultimately, as soon as freedom-loving people heard about a "new world" where they could worship freely, speak freely, assemble freely, and govern themselves, they risked their lives to flee those oppressive regimes. People still do.

THE BIBLE: AMERICA'S FOUNDATION STONE

I'm no theologian, but I'd argue that I know more about the Bible than your average Ivy League religious studies professor. One of the many themes of the Bible is freedom: freedom for Israel, freedom from slavery, freedom from sin. Our Declaration of Independence draws the pillars of life, liberty, and the pursuit of happiness from the Bible—not from Confucius, the Koran, or Buddha. Secularists view the Bible as threatening, judgmental, oppressive, and limiting. The exact opposite is true. For those who actually read the text, recurring themes of forgiveness, redemption, freedom, justice, and love stand out. They are liberating.

Abraham Lincoln wrote this about the Bible: "In regard to this Great Book, I have but to say, it is the best gift God has given to man. All the good the Saviour gave to the world was communicated through this book. But for it we could not know right from wrong. All things most desirable for man's welfare, here and hereafter, are to be found portrayed in it." Did the Bible shape President Lincoln's convictions about freedom and slavery? Absolutely it did! In his second inaugural address, which is inscribed on the Lincoln Memorial, he referred to slavery as worthy of God's judgment. Here's an excerpt:

> If we shall suppose that American slavery is one of those offenses which, in the providence of God, must needs come, but which, having continued through His appointed time, He now wills to remove, and that He gives to both North and South this terrible war as the woe due to those by whom the offense came, shall we discern therein any departure from those divine attributes which the believers in a living God always ascribe to Him? Fondly do we hope, fervently do we pray, that this mighty scourge of war may speedily pass away. Yet, if God wills that it continue . . . until every drop of blood drawn with the lash shall be paid by another drawn with the sword, as was said three thousand years ago, so still it must be said "the judgments of the Lord are true and righteous altogether."

In addition to the idea of freedom, other concepts in the New Testament ran completely against the prevailing racism and male-dominated culture of the time. The Apostle Paul wrote, in Galatians 3:28, "There is neither Jew nor Greek, there is neither bond nor free, there is neither male nor female: for ye are all one in Christ Jesus." Martin Luther King, Jr., also used his Christian faith to appeal to the equality expressed at the founding but not yet realized. The same goes for women's suffrage. In God's eyes, we are all valuable, regardless of race, nationality, or sex. Even though this was not part of culture at the time, God's truth was proclaimed, and—as usual—it was up to us to catch up.

You can't understand the Declaration of Independence unless you understand the narrative of freedom and equality written in the Bible, full stop. Look around the world; every country that has actively tried to squeeze out Christianity (and Judaism) has a terrible human rights record. That's because the Bible is nothing if not a guidebook to how to treat your fellow human beings. If you've studied Western thought (and read the previous chapter), you understand that the precepts of the New Testament don't translate into a socialist government that accumulates power "for the good of the people." It means you have a responsibility to care for your fellow man. It should be obvious that these are the best values for a society to embrace, whether you believe Jesus was the divine savior or not. Real faith brings freedom, selflessness, humility, and charity.

When you effectively put the Bible onto the banned books list, our kids miss out, and our culture misses out. Our schools have ripped the Bible out completely. Now we're taking it out of our public square, which means we've removed the central theme of Western civilization, which is also the language of America. The Exodus, Moses and the Ten Commandments, David's psalms, Solomon's proverbs, the life and teachings of Jesus, Saul's conversion on the road to Damascus— if you don't learn from those stories, you're left with an arbitrary set of lessons from someone who thinks they know better; the so-called elites in their ivory towers get to run the show. Show me a secular country, and I'll show you, eventually, an oppressive government.

Our founders would be disgusted with the secularist America

of today. Remember, way back in the twentieth century, secularists pulled the Bible and prayer out of public schools. Within a few decades, we developed a secular nation. But not merely secular—we have a society that is increasingly hostile to the expression of faith. Schools once used the Bible as a textbook. Now "Bring Your Bible to School Day" is a nonsanctioned free-speech event that happens voluntarily, once a year. Monuments that reference God and scripture—even symbols such as the cross or manger scene—have been litigated from public life by "enlightened" secular bullies. They ban the Ten Commandments (the first written laws) from courthouses and silence prayer at sporting events.

We must fight back against the evil forces of secularism. Despite their talking points (and lawsuits), their goal is not to make America a friendlier place for atheists and those of different faiths; it is to shift people's faith away from God and freedom and thereby shift people's faith toward those with government power.

President Trump has stemmed the tide of secularism, at least for now. He unabashedly supports faith and fights back against the secular currents long at work in American society. *Merry Christmas!* He has emboldened Christians, including pastors, to be more involved in politics and our culture. He has inspired Crusaders! But can he reverse the overarching trend of secularism?

DEMOCRATIC ~~SOCIALISTS~~ SECULARISTS

In August 2019, the Democratic National Committee passed a resolution embracing the values of "religiously unaffiliated" Americans as the "largest religious group within the Democratic Party." The symbolic motion had been pushed by the Secular Coalition for America, which lobbies for science nerds and atheists. The resolution read in part, "Religiously unaffiliated Americans overwhelmingly share the Democratic Party's values" and encouraged the DNC to promote "rational public policy based on sound science and universal humanistic values."

This pretty much sums up the state of the Democrat Party in 2020—including the choir of candidates running to take on President Trump. They have completely sidelined faith, especially the teachings of the Bible. Instead, they say, they are focused on science and "humanistic values." Please, someone explain to me what that means. And who defines the parameters and the outcomes?

Their sound science is just code for their religion of climate change—which is the real altar to which they bow. Meanwhile, every day they reject the science and technological innovations that shows us how babies "fearfully and wonderfully" form in the womb. Science shows them a baby, but their politics tell them something else. As for "universal humanistic values," Senator Bernie Sanders can probably preach to us on the subject. He is, after all, an avowed atheist. He shuns faith and wants the United States to fund abortions in third-world countries. Not only do leftists want "free" abortion in the United States— at any time during pregnancy and immediately after birth—they want you and me to send money to abortion clinics in other countries.

Bernie's fellow socialist Elizabeth Warren, in a rare moment when she talked about her faith, said, "My faith animates all that I do. . . . I truly do believe in the worth of every single human being." Unless you're an unborn baby, of course. She gave those remarks in 2019 at the Rainbow/PUSH [People United to Save Humanity] Coalition annual convention hosted by, you guessed it, the Left's favorite reverend: Jesse Jackson. Who knows if Senator Warren is really a woman of faith? Publicly she is whatever she needs to be at that moment to get elected, and you're not going to do well in the Democrat primary if you don't believe that women should sacrifice babies for a job promotion.

But what about the "moderate" Democrats? Well, ask the Catholic Church. In October 2019, former vice president Joe Biden was denied

Communion at a South Carolina church. Why? The priest said that a "public figure who advocates for abortion places himself or herself outside of Church teaching." Biden's response was to reiterate that he is a "practicing Catholic" who does not impose his faith on anyone else. Forgive me if I'm missing something, but isn't it possible to stand up for your faith without imposing it on others? Moreover, how can one be a practicing Catholic if he doesn't take the sacraments? Why erect a wall between yourself and Jesus? What he really means is: *I want to be president, dammit! As a Democrat I can't do that if I'm against abortion.*

The rest of the 2020 Democrat contenders also speak very little about their faith—except, that is, South Bend mayor Pete Buttigieg. Like Nancy Pelosi, he's unashamed to boldly wield his version of the Bible. He also sees the reality on the Democrat side, saying "Because my party's been so allergic to religious language, we've forgotten that people need to be made aware of their choice." Why have Democrats been so allergic? Pete says it's because of the bad name religious conservatives have given to Christianity. In reality, Democrats have pushed out faith because it's not possible to worship God and government at the same time.

The view of faith among most Democrats today is . . . silence. Silence because they either don't believe in God or don't want to talk about it. Silence because if they do talk about it, the special interest groups they depend on will slam them—and excommunicate them from the Church of Secularism. Democratic secularists believe they know better than that dusty book written thousands of years ago— yet another reason they are the party of anti-Americanism.

THE CRUSADE AGAINST SECULARISM

Defeating the Church of Secularism will require people of faith standing up boldly for their faith—in ways large and small, overt and covert. Just like Kanye! The end of this book lays out even more direct ways to fight, but here's one recent example that came from an unexpected place.

In May 2019, during a National Day of Prayer ceremony in the White House Rose Garden, Rabbi Yisroel Goldstein, who had been wounded in a shooting at his California synagogue, reflected on the horrific event: "Children [are] not growing up with values that our Founding Fathers started. Something seems fundamentally wrong when there's a generation of kids growing up doing what they're doing." Goldstein added, "We need to go back to the basics and introduce a Moment of Silence in all public schools. So that children from early childhood on can recognize that there is more good to the world, that they are valuable, there is accountability and every human being is created in God's image. If something good will come out of this terrible, terrible horrific event, let us bring back a Moment of Silence to our public school system."

Amen, Rabbi! He inspired me then, and he inspires me now. Rather than use that moment to simply bemoan the lack of God in our schools, he proposed a solution. At this moment we aren't able to get religious prayer back into schools (though maybe we will someday), but a "moment of silence" is doable. It's defensible. It's simple. And it would go a long way for our kids. (Better than the yoga, third-eye meditation crap they have replaced it with in one of my kids' public school classrooms). Even in silence, parents and kids could encourage real prayer, and the power of prayer—whether out loud or silent—is powerful.

The realm of faith provides plenty of opportunities in our families, communities, churches, and country to stand up and proclaim our faith as an exercise of our freedom and as a means to preserve it. Simply saying you're a Christian is a start. Don't be afraid! Standing for values while understanding the relationship between government and religion is another big one. And exposing the agenda of secularists—that they actually want to remove religion—is what needs to be done.

I'm not talking about self-righteously shaming others in the name of God. Some people of faith are so shrill and hateful that they even make me want to advocate for "separation." Others preach "Turn the other cheek" when it comes to government slapping you in the face. In order to defeat the secularists, we need to check our self-righteousness at the door. We are not the perfect examples of faith in society; we merely understand how important faith is in living our own lives—and understand that government does not exist to replace it or take it away.

In October 2019, in a speech at the University of Notre Dame, Attorney General William Barr declared that "religion has been under increasing attack" in the past fifty years. "The problem is not that religion is being forced on others. The problem is that irreligion and secular values are being forced on people of faith. . . . Among the militant secularists are many so-called 'progressives.' But where is the progress? We are told we are living in a post-Christian era, but what has replaced the Judeo-Christian moral system? What is it that can fill the spiritual void in the hearts of the individual person? And what is the system of values that can sustain human social life?"

We know the sobering answer: there is no other system that sustains freedom. That's why we must stand up and fight for the truth. So when you go to a school board meeting, a city council meeting, or a political rally, let your faith humble you into service and embolden you into action. Our involvement in the political arena is not motivated by a belief that we're better than anyone else, but we do believe our biblical values are the highest expression of goodness and human freedom on the planet. Be confident that faith has been, and will always be, a force for good in this country—and that when faithful Christians get involved in public life, everyone benefits. Channel your inner Kanye!

"The world is going to end in 12 years if we don't address climate change."

—Representative & Comrade Alexandria Ocasio-Cortez, 2019

"The interesting thing about the Green New Deal, is it wasn't originally a climate thing at all. . . . Because we really think of it as a how-do-you-change-the-entire-economy thing."

—Saikat Chakrabarti, then chief of staff to Comrade Cortez

NINE

ENVIRONMENTALISM: THE WAR ON WEATHER

When my youngest brother was a sophomore in high school in 2008, the entire school watched former vice president Al Gore's film *An Inconvenient Truth* to commemorate Earth Day. The film had been released a few years earlier and had sparked a great deal of debate. Al Gore had used PowerPoint graphs and provocative images to predict a climate doomsday, if urgent action was not taken.

My brother's high school was the same one I had attended a decade earlier, a suburban public school in a conservative, middle-class town. This was not New York City or San Francisco, this was small-town Minnesota. I was shocked. How could such a one-sided view (high on panic, low on science) be treated as gospel in a public school—especially in a predominantly conservative, Republican area? I wrote a scathing letter to the principal and waited for the mea culpa. It never came. Sadly, I don't know if the school showed it the next year or not. It probably did, considering that that year we elected Barack Obama.

Al Gore's film depicted much of Florida soon covered in rising ocean waters. It used scenes from Hurricane Katrina to suggest that climate change was the cause of stronger and more frequent hurricanes. "Within a decade, there will be no more snows of Kilimanjaro," Gore prophesied.

Here we are in 2020, and none of that hysteria has come true.

When Gore was confronted by scientists concerned about his "liberal" framing of their research, he dismissively replied, "I am trying to communicate the essence [of global warming] in the lay language that I understand." Translation: I'm trying to get rich off of fear; don't cramp my style.

These inconvenient facts do not matter to leftists. Al Gore has not apologized, nor will he. Because he has achieved his mission: one, to buy a 10,000 square foot home that expends twenty-one times as much energy as a typical American home; and two, to make sure he's indoctrinated kids into thinking the internal combustion engine is a greater threat to humanity than Hitler. Al Gore doesn't need to be front and center anymore, because now everyone on the left is his protégé.

In the words of leftist international superstar and 2019 *Time* magazine "Person of the Year," sixteen-year-old Greta Thunberg, inaction on climate change has "stolen [her] dreams and [her] childhood . . . We are in the beginning of a mass extinction." Do it for the kids, she shrieks. Storm the beaches of Normandy—in a zero-carbon yacht.

How does a sixteen-year-old know so much about the fate of our planet? What does she know that I don't? Leftists exalt her because she is the full manifestation of their indoctrination—and the warm reflection makes them feel good about themselves. She has been raised to believe that the world is ending tomorrow—unless we go backward. Her parents and teachers, like all those on the left, have set her on a lifelong journey of self-imposed angst and despair. The Left would like to do the same with your kids and mine. Powerful people with big spreadsheets must control our choices—and our lives. Otherwise we will all die!

CLIMATE "CHANGE"

For a moment, let's take Al Gore at his word that he is a pro-environment liberal using his platform to warn the world about pollution. On its face, it's an honorable mission. Clean water, clean air, and renewable energy sources are all good things. Count me in for those.

He is part of a long line of public figures, scientists, and writers to report on supposed changes in our climate. In 1975, an article in the "Science" section of *Newsweek* warned of "The Cooling World." A new "ice age" could be upon us, it warned, and experts suggested that humans should stock up on nonperishable food. More extreme remedies included "melting the arctic ice cap by covering it in black soot or diverting arctic rivers." As today, the experts warned that the longer politicians and planners delayed in their action against global cooling, "the more difficult they will find it to cope with climate change once the results become grim reality." Man, I sure wish we had covered the arctic in soot.

At the same time, and with much greater fervor, climate "experts" have since warned us about the eminent threat of global *warming*. In 1989, *Time* scrapped its "Person of the Year," instead declaring "Endangered Earth" the "Planet of the Year." It convened thirty-three "experts" to predict the end of mankind as we know it. In 1996, one *Newsweek* cover proclaimed, "The Hot Zone: Blizzards, Floods & Hurricanes: Blame Global Warming." Four years later, a cover of *Time* predicted the end of the polar bears (which are still not gone). In 2001, a cover of *Time* showed an egg being fried in a skillet, with the ominous title "Global Warming." The article warned of climbing temperatures, melting glaciers, and rising seas. The cover asked, "Why isn't Washington feeling the heat?" Always, the experts tell us, the politicians must act now!

A 2007 *Time* cover provided "The Global Warming Survival Guide," issuing such sage advice as "Hang up a clothes line," "Open a window," "Ride the bus," "Skip the steak," and "Move to London." Translation: turn off your dryer, give up air-conditioning, ditch your car, don't eat meat, and join the greenies in Europe. In other words, go backward. A year later, in 2008, *Time* doctored the iconic photo of the World War II flag raising at Iwo Jima to show our brave marines hoisting up a tree, declaring "How to Win the War on Global Warming."

Tellingly, in the middle of all this global warming hysteria, a 2006 *Time* cover read "Be Worried. Be Very Worried" in reference to climate. But on that cover a different term was used. It was no longer "global warming." Now the threat was described as "climate change." That wasn't the first time the phrase was used, not even close. In the years ahead, with global "cooling" no longer relevant and global "warming" data insufficient, climate "experts" had found their home—it was all "climate change." The 2019 "Special Climate Issue" of *Time* screamed "2050: How Earth Survived." The very first name listed on that cover: you guessed it . . . Al Gore.

The changing weather is the new enemy, and Al Gore is still our savior.

With the earth at a tipping point—always at a tipping point!—the left-wing media and Democrat politicians declare every piece of data as evidence of human destruction of the planet. Instead of investigating the claims, so-called journalists—climate zealots themselves—merely amplified the dire warnings. Hot, cold, rain, snow, wind, or calm—the climate is changing, they say, and we are to blame for it. *None* of their predictions came true. Those who point out their laughable track record are told to shut up and ignore their previous dire warnings. Democrat politicians, pundits on MSNBC and CNN, and radical college professors try to whip us into hysteria but are never held accountable for their misleading work and reporting. Yet this time—they insist—we must listen. We must repent for our climate sins and submit to their solutions. And always the politicians must act—now. Because the problem is always getting worse, according to leftists, the solutions must be bigger, more dramatic, and ever more draconian. The solutions needed today in order to save us by 2050, *Time* declares, are even darker than the solutions given in 1990—that were supposed to save us by 2010.

But what if that was the point?

WHAT IS ENVIRONMENTALISM?

I bet you recycle. I do, too, although sometimes I mix up the bins—the horror! You don't litter. You don't pour oil down the drain. You are careful about excessive water use and turn off the lights. Heck, you probably don't even eat steak three times a day. You and I want a clean environment and support sustainable practices in common-sense ways that apply to our lives. We are environmentally conscious and grateful for the blessing of God's green Earth.

That used to be what it meant to be an environmentalist or a conservationist. Not anymore. Today environmentalism has been hijacked. Since the Left no longer believes in God, it has to believe in something else guiding our lives from above. Enter climate change. The Left's version of environmentalism is a corrupt religion—a cult, really. It leverages science when convenient, burns heretics at the stake, and demands obedience—including penance—from the masses. Like a cult, it has prophets and shamans who interpret signs. If it rains, *climate change*. If there's a drought, *climate change*. Tornado or hurricane? You guessed it: *climate change*. Sounds like superstition from the dark ages—believing lightning strikes are a sign of Mother Earth's displeasure.

The ideological equation is simple: Conservation + Leftism = Environmentalism.

But there's more to this cult than mere superstition. Environmentalism is the highest pillar in the leftists' Church of Secularism.

This religion also needs an enemy, a Great Satan. To environmentalists, we're all the enemy, especially Americans and our evil corporations. Therefore, complete command and control are justified. Somehow we're all part of the problem, and therefore we must all be part of the solution. And the solutions, predictably, include ending oil and gas extraction, erasing borders, providing a universal basic income, providing free housing, establising more authoritarian bureaucracy—and government employees—and turning back the clock on the very technology that has elevated the global standard of living for a century. The war on the weather requires gaining universal control over every aspect of our lives: where we live, how we live, how we travel, what we eat, and what we are free to choose.

But don't take my word for it. Here's the former chief of staff for Comrade Cortez, the author of the Green New Deal: "The interesting thing about the Green New Deal, is it wasn't originally a climate thing at all. . . . Because we really think of it as a how-do-you-change-the-entire-economy thing." It's not about the climate at all! It's about a radical socialist reorientation of our lives that would make us more dependent on the government—taking the power away from individuals and placing it in the hands of unelected and unaccountable "experts" who live in Washington, Brussels, and Paris.

This cause overlaps nicely with the goals of the globalists. Climate legislation and treaties apply only to the United States and other

Western countries. So-called less developed countries such as China are not bound by these regulations. Because, as the globalists explain to us, developed countries such as America created this problem in the first place—so we should pay the price. America is the bad guy, which fits the Left's anti-American narrative perfectly. Half the products we use and wear in America were made in China—and sent here on huge, gas-guzzling ships. You can't see two hundred yards on a typically smoggy day in Beijing because of the rampant pollution. Mountains of trash are thrown into the world's rivers and oceans every day by third-world countries. But you don't see Comrade Cortez or Joe Biden protesting outside the Chinese or Indian embassy. No, it's *our* fault.

Leftists saw the media fawning and financial success of Al Gore and have continued to promote the lie of climate change for the consolidation of power and personal enrichment—all while projecting themselves as morally superior. It is the perfect means to achieve power: using doomsday fear to force people to take actions that hurt their own lives but make powerful people richer and feel good about themselves.

INDIGENOUS PEOPLE AND THE ISLAMIC STATE

Environmentalism leads the Left to some really kooky beliefs and illogical conclusions. Their cause is not just about the weather, and it's not just about control. It's also about justice. You hear it all the time: "environmental justice." Justice for whom? Justice for the middle-class folks whose tax dollars are spent on subsidies for electric cars—which can be as high as $7,500 per car? No, of course not. The word *justice* means using the climate change hoax as an excuse to redistribute wealth and empower America's enemies.

When I was at Harvard University getting a master's degree in public policy, the topic of climate change was ubiquitous. Almost every course used it as an example of the need for creative public policy solutions. It was pounded into our heads that the climate crisis was a "global commons" problem—meaning that without action from all parties involved, certain countries or people will abuse a resource to the detriment of others. Therefore, in order to solve these types of problems, common governance is needed—usually by the "international community." Invoking the common good of the global commons becomes the ultimate power play; but first, before anyone else acts, America must pay up. The "elites" call it leadership; President Trump calls it foolishness—and we should agree.

If America is a country defined by its ancient sins—which the Left believes—then climate change is the perfect vehicle by which to punish Americans. To the Left, America got rich only because of its exploitation of minorities and women. Therefore, climate change is a great vehicle for redistribution. For example, did you know that the weather affects people differently based on their skin color, gender, income, and sexual identity? Apparently, weather is not color blind or gender blind. Like Comrade Cortez, the militant leftist organization, "Youth Climate Strike"—one of the groups promoting the recent high school walkouts for climate change—does us the favor of revealing the real agenda behind climate change radicalism.

According to the "Youth Climate Strike" website as of October 2019—the website is under construction and ever changing, just like its "science"—its efforts are really all about "An equitable transition for marginalized communities that will be most impacted by climate change" to include "communities of color, impoverished communities, disabled communities, and LGBTQ+ communities." Its goal with climate efforts is to "Remove entrenched racial, regional, ability, and gender-based barriers to income and wealth" and "create a public bank to finance a transition for the benefit of all Americans."

Got that? There it is, socialists to the core. Create a "public bank" to take money from taxpaying citizens—none of whom ever owned slaves or discriminated against anyone—and redistribute it to classes of people the leftists deem marginalized. It gets better. They call for ensuring climate change remedies that "Respect Indigenous women, Indigenous queer and trans women, women of color, and queer and trans people of color and protect them from assault, sexual violence, and trafficking." Understand? Me, neither. They continue by demanding that we must "Acknowledge the term 'climate refugee' and welcome all climate refugees including: war refugees, communal/gang violence refugees, and natural disaster refugees."

It's a leftist grievance list that never ends. They continue by calling for "Compulsory comprehensive education on the impacts of climate change and the importance of climate justice throughout grades K-8" because it's the "ideal age" when kids are the most impressionable and susceptible to a worldview of fear. Just ask Greta. It's a lot to digest, and—as you can see—none of it is about the climate. Before you dismiss this organization as a fringe group, consider that tens of thousands of American high schoolers walked out of class in their #ClimateStrike—and were applauded by the media, leftist politicians, and Democrat presidential candidates.

The group also calls for "100% renewable energy by 2030." No plan is necessary. Just demand it and make it so. Because if the world is going to end in twelve years, we might as well ditch our planes, trains, and automobiles anyway. Everything and anything is justified when mobilizing kids to fight a fear-based war against the weather.

Another common refrain of leftists is that ISIS—the Islamic State—arose because of—yep, you guessed it—climate change. Instead of recognizing the morally bankrupt and evil ideology of Islamists, preached in mosques and madrassas across the Middle East, the Left and their friends in the media prefer to blame the rise of radicals on warmer weather. A headline from *National Geographic* in November 2017 sums up their argument nicely: "Climate

Change and Water Woes Drove ISIS Recruiting in Iraq." That particular article was written from Samarra, Iraq—the very town where I served in 2006. I know of what I speak.

According to their logic, when the temperature goes up and farming is more difficult, it drives otherwise peace-loving Muslims to grab an AK-47 and fight for a caliphate. Of course, on-the-ground grievances can make anyone more desperate—that's a fact of life. But rather than placing the blame where it belongs—corrupt local government, lack of economic development because of dictators, or intimidation by Islamist hard-liners—the Left goes to the enemy it understands: the weather. The arrogance of leftists leads them to believe that American-led climate change leads to economic refugees who find their purpose, magically, in blowing themselves up.

Did you know that the weather has never vacillated in the Middle East before? That there have been no previous droughts or famines? Forgive the sarcasm, but it's merited here. A simple Google search reveals that the Middle East, like the rest of the globe, has seen irregular weather patterns for millennia. Just like the Left's false predictions of the past, the hubris of modern leftists leads them to believe that warmer weather or lack of rain—for a season or two—must be the result of man-made climate change. As such, otherwise secular, peace-loving Muslims would be tending to their sheep if not for the coal plants in middle America.

If you believe that, I have a ticket on a SpaceX rocket to Mars to sell you.

AMERICA THE BEAUTIFUL

Our national parks, the clean water we drink, and the miraculous level of sanitation our communities enjoy are all the result of those who valued good stewardship of the environment—and we should be thankful for that. Republican president Theodore Roosevelt was a brilliant example of this commitment. Roosevelt reserved more than 230 million acres of land for public enjoyment. He designated the first national wildlife refuge, presided over the creation of the National Forest Service, and signed the Antiquities Act of 1906, giving presidents the authority to protect cultural and natural landmarks. He personally oversaw the establishment of five national parks. Teddy was a lover of the environment, a true conservationist.

Roosevelt called his predecessor—and fellow Republican—President Ulysses S. Grant the "Father of the National Parks." In 1872, Grant established our first national park, Yellowstone. Many other Republican presidents took innovative and forward-thinking steps to protect our environment. Hell, Richard Nixon even created the Environmental Protection Agency (EPA). Preserving clean air, clean water, and untouched lands has a long tradition in America. We love the environment, and it shows. No country on Earth has so many people and so much industry, yet an environmental landscape as clean, protected, and pristine as America's.

In fact, in July 2019, the Trump White House published statistics on energy and the environment that so-called environmentalists should have applauded. From 1970 to 2018, the combined emissions of the most common air pollutants, including CO_2, fell by 74 percent while the economy grew by more than 275 percent. Sounds damn good to me—pollution down, economy up. One factor leftists *always* miss is innovation. The free market creates solutions to problems that prognosticators can never predict and never factor in; hence, predictions about the future based on current assumptions are always wrong. The climate predictions of the Left are not science, they are science fiction. The free market gets a vote and is way more powerful than climate data spreadsheets. Today we drive faster, more affordable, and more powerful cars that require less gas and produce cleaner emissions. American charities are using emerging technologies to help third-world countries process waste and turn it into energy. Government didn't do these things; innovation did.

Oh yeah, and the United States is ranked number one in the world for access to clean drinking water; and of the top ten countries, the United States has by far the largest population. Clean water for all people, of all backgrounds, is a luxury we take for granted. And when we get it wrong, as in Flint, Michigan, the world finds out about it and action is spurred. As it should be.

In July 2019, President Trump affirmed, "My Administration is committed to being effective stewards of our environment while encouraging opportunities for American workers and their families." America has always led the way in business innovation, economic growth, *and* environmental stewardship. We can do all of these things—unlike some other countries.

SHITHOLE COUNTRIES?

Go anywhere around the world and look at environmental conditions. Billions of people live in environmental catastrophes; I've seen those places myself. Hundreds of millions of humans live in areas with unclean water in cities that send industrial waste and raw sewage directly into rivers and oceans. This includes many parts of China, by the way. Why can't you drink the water in those places? It's because those countries don't have the free-market system and empowered population that bring prosperity—and ultimately create higher standards of living for every resident. In those countries, the leaders are not accountable to the people.

Instead of taking the eco-friendly aspects of Americanism to the developing world, environmentalists want to place more restrictions on this country while giving the biggest polluters a pass. In 2017, President Trump pulled the United States out of the climate scheme dumpster fire known as the Paris Agreement. "I was elected to represent the citizens of Pittsburgh, not Paris," he said. The uproar from elites was immediate and frenzied. But what few pointed out was that the Obama-era agreement allowed China to continue increasing its harmful emissions through the year 2030. Both China and India were allowed to increase the amount of energy produced by coal, while the United States faced immediate restrictions on doing so. Pardon me if I'm against destroying our country while giving the worst polluting countries a free pass, all in the name of "saving the planet."

If we really are all "global citizens" why don't climate clamorers hold other filth-emitting countries accountable? If it really is a "global commons" problem, wouldn't the entire world need to get on board to save Mother Earth? Why do certain countries get a pass? Because, to the Left, America is the real guilty party because we figured out how to power our cars, fly our planes, and grow our food in more advanced ways before anyone else. America is evil because America was first—and is the best. If you've been taught that America's success is also the cause of every problem in the world, indicting our country makes perfect sense. Of course, those same rules don't apply to the elites who peddle them—they get a free pass, or at least carbon credits to assuage their fake guilt over the use of their private jets. Al Gore may be the pope of environmentalism, but he still has a larger carbon footprint than Godzilla.

PREDICTIONS AND PROPAGANDA

As I mentioned earlier, you've heard the dire predictions from politicians—but what about the scientists?

"Unless we are extremely lucky, everybody will disappear in a cloud of blue steam in twenty years," said "population biologist" Dr. Paul R. Ehrlich in an interview in the *New York Times*. The following year, he predicted that the oceans would be as dead as Lake Erie in less than a decade.

NASA scientist Dr. S. I. Rasool was quoted in a *Washington Times* article as saying that continued use of fossil fuels would clog the atmosphere with enough dust that the sun's rays would be diminished in the next "five to ten" years and "such a temperature decrease could be sufficient to trigger an ice age."

Everybody is going to disappear in twenty years! No more Lake Erie in ten years! An ice age is coming! And it's all our fault!

It's scary stuff. Except when it's revealed that these quotes are from 1969, 1970, and 1971, respectively. The same predictions have been made in the decades since and are still being made today. If anything, the predictions have gotten more dire, but they have also become more vague. "Scientists" are sick of being called out for how wrong they are, so their predictions have gotten louder but the evidence they tout has gotten more ambiguous—the perfect recipe for fear-based control.

What is one to make of their "science"? Were their numbers wrong? Were their models wrong? Or is it something else? The funny thing about numbers is, once you get past $2 + 2 = 4$, it's pretty easy to make numbers tell the story you *want* them to tell. This is why I don't buy—for one second—the arguments used by environmentalists: "99 percent of climate scientists agree that climate change is happening." If that were the case, their models would truly be predictive of the coming catastrophe. Instead, the science before our eyes—the decades upon decades during which scientists have gotten it wrong—is what matters most to me. The "scientists" have cried wolf one too many times to be taken at their word; or maybe they just cannot admit the amount of arrogance required to assume that you can predict future weather patterns based on finite scientific models. There are too many factors, too many fudged numbers; frankly, too much blind faith in bad science.

Let's address the climate elephant in the room—the one with the rectal thermometer that nobody wants to check. I see that some glaciers are melting. And I hear that the Antarctic ice is growing. Some places are warmer, others are colder. I want to have the best environment and climate possible. But I don't see "the data" on global warming that everyone is clucking about. Where can I find "the science"? At the United Nations? Yeah, right, I trust those guys—they don't have an agenda at all! It's a sincere question, and we should ask more such questions more often.

The antithesis of science is bending the results, the numbers, to meet a predetermined outcome. Science, at its most basic, is defined as "systematic knowledge of the physical or material world gained through observation and experimentation." Scientists make hypotheses, gather data, run experiments, and observe them. Based on that, they can draw empirical conclusions or develop informed theories. Instead, international scientists have convinced themselves that climate change *must* be happening—and mankind *must* be causing it. Therefore, they have cooked the books in their favor, ignoring the fact that all of their previous hypotheses and observations have turned out to be false.

Not to mention that scientists also—always—skew their observations to modern times. Recorded temperatures go back only to the mid–nineteenth century, so that is understandable. Even then, the numbers can be fudged. Through a process known as "homogenization," historical temperature data are manipulated to make it appear that ever-warming trends exist, when records of the temperature of certain places over time show no such warming at all. The expert "scientists" never discuss this when they make their apocalyptic predictions. Nor do they ever mention that, according to Marc Morano, the founder of Climate Depot, "in the geologic history of the Earth, we are in the coldest 10 percent of the geologic history of the Earth. In other words, 90 percent of our Earth's history was too warm to have ice at either pole." The earth warms, the earth cools—it has for millions of years. But that is an inconvenient truth for leftist environmentalists.

The inability to spin the numbers is why globalists and environmentalists give the microphone to celebrities and sixteen-year-olds at the United Nations instead of scientists. The numbers don't work, but emotion does. Could this also be the reason environmentalists have tweaked their language over the decades—migrating from "global cooling" to "global warming" to "climate change" to "climate justice"?

It's all propaganda—and their movement is rife with hypocrisy. In 2019, the Green Party in Canada photoshopped an image of its leader, Elizabeth May, not to make her look better—but to change the cup in her hand. Originally, she held a paper cup and plastic straw. Oh, the horror! But after a few mouse clicks, she held a reusable cup and metal straw. When asked about the trickery, May said she was "completely shocked," adding "I walk the talk every day." I'm sure she does—but she probably doesn't actually walk to work every day.

As I was writing this, a *New York Times* headline blazed across my screen: "Climate Change Is Accelerating, Bringing World 'Dangerously Close' to Irreversible Change." Wildfires, droughts, floods, heat waves, melting glaciers, and thawing permafrost are headed our way. Scientists call it the "climate feedback loop." "The only solution is to get rid of fossil fuels in power production, industry and transportation," says the secretary general of the World Meteorological Organization. Some guy with a title that sounds like a villain in a James Bond film is telling me we must get rid of . . . everything.

As the propaganda gets louder and louder, the "solutions" peddled by politicians get grander and grander. More control. More restrictions. Less common sense. In the end, modern leftist environmentalists end up proposing socialist solutions that will tear down America—and capitalism—and grant unlimited power and money to international bodies and governments but don't actually help the environment.

2020 AND THE GREEN NEW DISASTER

A few years ago, one Texas town tried to actually practice what environmental activists preach. It applied for, and secured, a $1 million grant from Bloomberg Philanthropies, a nonprofit created by former New York City mayor and presidential candidate Michael Bloomberg. The small municipality of Georgetown, Texas, began a transition to solar energy for its utilities. Within a year, the program cost $7 million. After raising property taxes, the city council finally voted to scrap the deal and return the initial funds. I'm guessing the high school there didn't participate in a "Climate Strike" walkout last year.

Am I happy the experiment failed? Yes, because it was stupid. But I'm not here to nag every little municipality that does stupid things. Should we be surprised that it went up in the smoke of $7 million? Nope. The fact is, people want lights that turn on and reasonable bills to pay. Climate schemes, large and small, make people feel good about themselves—especially the people who come up with the schemes. But good intentions are not good enough. Eventually somebody has to pay for them, and those folks in Texas were fed up.

That was at the local level. Federal schemes have met similar fates. Remember the Obama administration's $535 million loan guarantee from the Department of Energy to the soon-to-be-defunct solar company Solyndra? In the name of "green energy" and economic stimulus, hard-earned taxpayer dollars went to a deceptive company in a failing industry, all so Democrats could tout a green new future.

Solyndra, although the most famous case, was far from unique—billions of dollars have been spent on green energy that would have been better spent in the furnace of a coal plant.

But that's nothing, because every 2020 Democrat presidential candidate would leave Obama's climate plan in the dust. No overarching climate scheme has yet passed at the federal level, but it remains priority number one for leftists. I mentioned the Green New Deal earlier. The name itself demonstrates how big the leftists want it to be—they want it to be our generation's New Deal, minus the Great Depression. FDR's New Deal played a part in helping America cope with economic collapse; Comrade Cortez's Green New Deal would lead to it.

But the Green New Deal is not a fringe idea; it has been endorsed by *every* major Democrat presidential candidate in 2020. What have they signed on to? After making epically unreasonable demands for renewable energy and eliminating greenhouse gases, the Green New Deal goes much further. Here are just a few of its promises (the italics are mine):

Guaranteeing a job with a family-sustaining wage, adequate family and medical leave, paid vacations, and retirement security to all people of the United States.

Providing all people of the United States with (i) high-quality health care; (ii) affordable, safe, and *adequate housing*; (iii) economic security; and (iv) access to clean water, clean air, healthy and affordable food, and nature.

Upgrading *all existing buildings* in the United States and building new buildings to achieve maximal energy efficiency, water efficiency, safety, affordability, comfort, and durability, including through electrification.

Working collaboratively with *farmers and ranchers* in the United States to eliminate pollution and greenhouse gas emissions from the agricultural sector as much as is technologically feasible.

The Green New Deal would be a Green New Disaster for America. It is the ultimate socialist Trojan horse. Democratic socialists—under the guise of caring for the environment—want to give everyone a job, give everyone a house, upgrade *every* building in America, and stop cows from farting. You cannot make this stuff up. It is the most radical proposal ever advanced in our country—costing trillions of dollars and millions of jobs. And for what? Not for the environment. China and India would keep polluting, and America would grow weaker by the day. Leftists want to cut off our nose while the rest of the world stuffs its face.

PESKY PEOPLE

The other core philosophical reasoning behind environmentalism is this: Mother Earth needs fewer humans. We should have fewer babies, because those babies will only make the problem worse and will probably die an apocalyptic death anyway.

According to Bloomberg News, 11,000 "experts" at "The Alliance of World Scientists" (more Bond villains) in 2019 agreed "there needs to be far fewer humans on the planet." People produce things. People create things. And people consume things. Without those pesky people, we could all frolic in green pastures forever.

Hollywood agrees. The most popular action movies in Hollywood over the past two years—*Avengers: Infinity War* and *Avengers: Endgame*—not so subtly make the depopulation case. The villain, Thanos, is introduced as a conflicted environmental truth teller hell bent on erasing half of Earth's population in order to save the planet and the rest of humanity. The movie triggered a flurry of media coverage, including headlines like this one from *Forbes*: "The Science of 'Avengers: Endgame' Proves Thanos Did Nothing Wrong." You read that right; in the name of climate change, killing half the earth's population can be a good thing. As of this writing, *Avengers: Endgame* is the highest-grossing film of all time. Not a bad way to introduce an idea.

I could cite examples like this all day long, because the environmentalists are dead serious. They see human life as the problem. When you devalue human beings, you open the door to all sorts of cultural catastrophes. Abortion becomes a "good" thing—a solution. So do euthanasia and assisted suicide. When the crisis is so urgent, all solutions are deemed acceptable. Dead people or unborn people become assets—not liabilities. Mothers and fathers are told to feel guilty for having kids—and those kids are told not to have kids of their own. It's a sad state of affairs and evil psychology.

There's only one big problem: China and Islamists will never abide by this rubbish. They're playing for real-world domination.

But as courageous American Crusaders, we can do something about it. Environmentalists want to brainwash our kids, establish emotional faux science in our educational institutions, and change— decimate—the entire economy. They used to repeat the mantra "Think globally, act locally." But now it's "Govern globally, control locally." Leftists act on the global stage—a stage they own—and ram their false religion down our throats at home. Our only hope in this American Crusade is to do our own version of "act locally."

Think twice about buying products made in China, and take time to find American-made products. If you're going to protest, do it outside the Chinese Embassy. Let's embarrass the Chinese rather than emasculate ourselves.

Help normalize the idea of expanding nuclear power! France, Japan, and other countries figured this out a long time ago. Our nuclear power plants are aging and not being repaired or replaced. If we invest in the next generation of nuclear power plants—which are much safer and much more efficient than earlier models—we can improve the environment and not bankrupt our country. It's so obvious, it's absurd.

Find out what your school is teaching with regard to climate science. Is it science at all? What are the teachers saying? Has your school forsaken science and bowed to environmentalism? You'll be surprised what's going on in classrooms and how straightforward it is to make a difference.

American Crusaders care about the environment, we always have—but we haven't done a very good job expressing that in the public debate. Historically, we've carried the mantle of protecting God's green Earth. Despite that fact, we've been labeled as heartless polluters. That's a lie. If you're for free-market capitalism, you're for the environment. If you're for secure borders, you're for the environment.

But if you really do believe the seas are rising due to you driving your car, just look at the Obamas. They just purchased oceanfront property on Martha's Vineyard. If they're not worried, you shouldn't be, either.

"Political correctness is tyranny with manners."

—Actor Charlton Heston, 1999

"You might say the road to Hell is paved
with Ivy League degrees."

—Economist Thomas Sowell, 2012

TEN

ELITISM: THE POISON OF POLITICAL CORRECTNESS

"**P**ete, this is Vice President–Elect Mike Pence's office. Do you have a moment to speak with him?" said the voice on the other side of the phone. I was on an Amtrak train in November 2016, rumbling along, going into and out of cell phone coverage.

"Um, yeah. I mean, yes! Of course," I muttered quietly.

After about ten seconds, the vice president-elect joined the call. Following brief formalities, he informed me that the president-elect would like to meet with me soon at Trump Tower, because I was under consideration for the role of secretary of the Department of Veterans Affairs. I was surprised but not shocked. I had been heavily involved—along with my former organization Concerned Veterans for America—in fighting for serious reform at the VA for years. I'd also highlighted the issue regularly on FOX News. But still, as a younger guy with no formal government experience, I didn't know what to expect. Either way, I was grateful for the opportunity to meet the president-elect for the first time and discuss a topic near and dear to my heart.

As I've noted, I had been a vocal critic of Donald Trump before my "conversion" moment in 2016. Despite that, candidate Trump had noticed my advocacy for veterans. The president later told me that my segments on FOX News had helped inform him on veterans' issues and inspired him to make fighting for veterans a central part of his campaign. Of course there were—and are—many other voices championing our veterans and military, but I have to admit, his comment was gratifying. As an advocate, all you can hope for is that powerful people notice your efforts and become willing to champion them. We found a champion in Donald Trump.

Within a week, I was walking toward the front doors of Trump Tower on a rainy day in New York City. I knew the media were piled up inside—and I knew better than to speak with them. Instead, I did my best to not look awkward as I walked in with my umbrella in one hand and my group's *Fixing Veterans Health Care* report in the other. My friends—and my future wife—were watching on television back at FOX News, as the lobby of Trump Tower had become the epicenter of cable news coverage. The president-elect was holding court, meeting with his future staff and cabinet. I tried to play it cool, but inside I was nervous as all hell.

I rode up the gold-plated elevator to the twenty-sixth floor and was shown to a seat in the waiting area. A flurry of staff buzzed around the office, including Kellyanne Conway and Reince Priebus. People were coming and going from the elevators and into the offices, side conversations happening all around. This lobby, this office, was the new center of gravity in American politics. Before I had time to go from nervous to petrified, a young woman walked in and broke the silence with "Hello, Pete. The president-elect will see you now."

A week ago, I was just riding a train. Today, I'm meeting the new president.

I followed her to an open door, where she paused to let me enter first. Standing just inside the doorway was Reince Priebus, and around the corner, seated behind his desk, was Donald Trump. I'd seen the setting in photographs before: the desk, the stacks of magazines, the windows behind him. It was familiar but totally surreal. The president-elect stood up. I walked forward to shake his hand, but before I even got close enough for a handshake, Trump said without hesitation, "Pete, at the beginning you were very bad to me. Very bad. I mean baaad."

He wasn't joking. "Oh, you're right, Mr. President-Elect . . ." was all I could get out.

"Just bad," he continued. "You know, at the beginning, who were you for?"

There was no reason to mince words now. He had me dead to rights. "Well, Mr. President, I was for Rubio, because he was great on vets issues and—"

"Oh, that's right, Little Marco. You were with Little Marco." With amusement, Trump turned to Reince and Steve Bannon, who had also entered the room, and said, "Little Marco. Lyin' Ted. Crooked Hillary. Weren't they grreat!"

I shook the president-elect's hand, laughing. Then I chimed in, saying "I have to tell you, Mr. President, my favorite nickname is Pocahontas."

He laughed heartily and said, "A lot of people tell me that. *A lot.*"

Then for the next two minutes, before we jumped into veterans' topics, President-Elect Trump delivered a detailed indictment of how Elizabeth Warren had used a falsified racial background to game the system for her own personal privilege at the expense of those she pretends to care about. She had used her supposed minority status to leverage an elite professorship in the Ivy League, perpetuating a selfish fraud. "I'm a marketer," Trump explained as he outlined his choice of the nickname Pocahontas. Instead of making a lengthy case about her arrogant misappropriation, he cut to the chase with a nickname that revealed her blatant hypocrisy.

It was classic Trump, just as months earlier when on a FOX News program then presumptive GOP nominee Trump was asked if he "regretted calling [Warren] Pocahontas?" He replied, "I do regret calling her Pocahontas, because I think it's a tremendous insult to Pocahontas. So, to Pocahontas, I would like to apologize to you."

With politically incorrect comments like these, President Trump upended the game the elites have played for decades. He cuts through the equivocation, hesitation, and polite talk average Americans have been forced to use—while fighting back against a corrupt elite class who, under the banner of political correctness, have imposed a de facto speech code that they weaponize to dictate what is acceptable and what is not. By setting the terms of the debate, you tilt the debate in your direction: from the Ivy League, where the rules are written, to the schools, where they are engrained, to the media that weaponizes them to the politicians who leverage them.

This is why President Trump's use of the nickname "Pocahontas" for Senator Elizabeth Warren is so important. He is not being racist or even mean-spirited; instead, he is using the power of free speech—of marketing—to point out her hypocrisy. And, by extension, the hypocrisy and never-ending double standards of the Left. They want him, and us, to stop using this tactic because it is so effective, not because they are offended. We must learn the difference, or we will lose.

This is why political correctness is the ultimate poison to freedom. It sets the terms and never—ever—in favor of traditional values, conservatives, free speech, Christianity, or Americanism. This is why Trump's war on political correctness is one of the most important, and defining, aspects of his presidency. It's a big reason why the so-called elites hate him so much.

For decades, establishment Republican leaders have played by the politically correct rules of the Left, placating ivory-tower and media elites. The establishment would have counseled elected officials to use a more "civil" tone regarding Warren's claims—instead issuing carefully worded press releases or staging self-serving press conferences. But they would never have called her Pocahontas. They would never have questioned her motives or sincerity with a nickname. Tell me: Which strategy works better? The point of this opening story—in addition to the fact that I never got the VA secretary job—is that American Crusaders must courageously ignore the rules that PC culture seeks to impose.

Leftists don't want civility. They want control.

And when, for fear of a ticket from the PC police, you bend—even a syllable—you give them power. But, like Trump, when you laugh at—and mock—their hypocritical and intellectually dishonest arguments, you regain control. Imagine if millions of us continued to follow President Trump's lead and ditched political correctness altogether? What if we stopped playing by their rules? They would lose their control and their power.

ENLIGHTENMENT FOR DUMMIES

Our nation's elites love to use fancy words, not to enlighten but to make the world a dumber place. They pontificate about complex theories such as "intersectionality" and "cultural appropriation." It doesn't matter if their theories make sense; the complexity of those theories is what makes them correct. They are the "elites." They are sophisticated. They are smarter than you are. They think deeper than you do. They factor in more variables than you do. And they eat a great deal more kale and sustainable foods than you do. Their entire existence is predicated on the assumption that they are better than you are. I've met them. Trust me, they are not.

Every society has elites, but with the rise of Trump, their true ugliness in America has been exposed. The elite media hate Trump—and, by extension, everyone who supports him—with the fire of a thousand suns. Every newsroom in Manhattan and Los Angeles, save for FOX News, is full of *only* left-wing elites. They go to the same "journalism" schools (elites call it "J School"), live in the same gated communities, attend the same clubs, and vote the same way. They call themselves journalists, but they are full-on ideologues. And a new "elite" class—the tech oligarchy in Silicon Valley—uses its social media power to empower a social justice mob that hates America with the ongoing passion of college activists. They also actively silence conservative, or un-PC, voices—something I learned firsthand myself.

In decades past, America's elites were different. They were liberals—but not leftists. Even if they wanted higher taxes and a larger welfare state, old-school liberals loved America. Today, they loathe America. Our elites assert that America is the problem—and they drive that message home in almost every streaming service, website, social media platform, newscast, movie, and textbook. Even though social media have widened the conversation, with President Trump's Twitter feed changing the game completely, they impose their worldview on those platforms as well. Social media elites have the power to ban accounts, ostracize individuals, censor speech, hide content, steer traffic, and ruin lives. Predictably, the consequences of these actions overwhelmingly happen to conservatives.

In December 2019, a Saudi Arabian military pilot attacked and killed three brave American aviators on a navy base in Pensacola, Florida. I was hosting *FOX & Friends* when the early reports came out. It soon became clear that it had been an Islamist terror attack, especially after tweets were uncovered showing the attacker supported Osama bin Laden, Al Qaeda, and the Muslim Brotherhood. One of those tweets had been sent just minutes before the attack had occurred. After my Saturday show, I took a screenshot of the terrorist's tweet that clearly demonstrated his Islamist motivations.

Thinking nothing of it—and especially because such information was newsworthy—I tweeted out a photo of the terrorist's mini-manifesto, saying "This is Islamist terror. No reason to ever mince words. Saudi Arabia must be held to account."

Eight hours later, Twitter locked my account. It demanded that I delete the tweet, or my account would be removed. I had guarded Islamists in Guantánamo Bay, Cuba. Led a platoon in Iraq fighting Al Qaeda terrorists. And pulled American bodies out of a troop carrier in Afghanistan after a suicide car bombing. Now, for sharing the motivations of an Islamist terrorist, I was banned from Twitter.

Why?

Because Twitter—like every other institution that so-called elites control—is a cesspool of social justice enforcement that has created virtual protected classes. You can be as vile and untruthful as you want about conservatives or Trump supporters or Christians or Jews, as the terrorist was, but you are not allowed to speak ill of Islam, Islamists, or other self-proclaimed protected classes. The elites—none of whom have actually faced Islamist terrorism or ever engaged with real Islamist ideology—have decided that any criticism of Islam or Islamism is Islamophobic. The same goes for many other leftist-protected "ism" classes.

The elites control the speech, because they want to control us.

WHAT IS ELITISM?

How do you spot an elitist? Have you ever met someone who was the least informed about human nature but the most adamant about his or her ideology? You've met either a millennial or an elitist. Or both.

The equation is: Arrogance + Leftism = Elitism.

Every era of human society has had people with more money or higher status—the "upper class" if you will. They go to better schools, build better investment portfolios, vacation in better places, and seem to have better opportunities than the rest of us. That is not what I'm talking about. Elitism is more than the concept of power and wealth, it's the elites' belief that they are *better* than you and I—and that they should lead us. Their arrogance, combined with self-induced leftist indoctrination, makes them elitists. They are smart; you are ignorant. They are powerful; you don't matter. They are sophisticated and evolved; you are deplorable. Of course, the ultimate irony of their thinking is that the elites are actually the ones whose frontal lobes have atrophied.

As my favorite philosopher, Bazooka Joe, once said, "Keep an open mind, but not so open that your brain falls out." Yes, I read that proverb on a bubblegum wrapper, and it stuck with me. Elitists are so drunk on themselves that they prefer to toss out the wisdom of the ages in favor of the latest leftist grievance or fad. It's far easier to be angry about what you don't have then grateful for what you do have. The elites of the past were simply arrogant people who were also liberals. They used their status to rocket to the top of America's social structure and used their power to keep themselves there. Today's elites are using their status to tear apart America's social fabric.

Words are also important here. Being "elite," in the purest sense of the word, is not a bad thing. There are elite athletes, elite musicians, and elite mathematicians. There is nothing wrong with being among the best; America was founded on the idea of a meritocracy. But *elitism* is the complete opposite of what it means to excel. Elitism is premised on the arrogant belief that a chosen few people know better than you do; add this to the leftism that dominates their cultural and educational spheres of power, and you get very arrogant people who know very little about the country and system that made them "elite" in the first place. At best, some elitists are ignorant Americans using their power and privilege to prop up fellow anti-American elitists in order to maintain their status; at worst, most elitists are anti-Americans using their power and privilege to tear down America's moral and economic might, knowing they'll be just fine either way.

Note that being a leftist elite does not necessarily denote having any sort of *actual* talent. Often, people we see as our "betters" are not smarter or richer than we are. It's merely a social designation that people obtain if they attend the correct schools, shop at Whole Foods, read the *New York Times*, drive a Tesla, and have a Peloton bike gathering dust in their high-rise condo. They would trade their yippy little dogs for a ticket to the World Economic Forum in Davos. They would still be friends with Jeffrey Epstein if he hadn't been killed in jail.

What unites all manner of leftist elites are power, privilege, and status. They have power, want more of it, wield it to benefit themselves, and advance whatever causes their fellow leftists believe are important at the moment. Today, those beliefs center largely on tearing down the very country that enabled their rise. Their privilege leads them to believe that they play by their own set of rules, rules written by their friends in power. And their status—oh, their status—means everything to them. Who they know, where they summer, and whom they live next to is *very* important to them. They give awards to one another to validate one another. Anyone who challenges those three status symbols is public enemy number one— which is why they hate Donald Trump so much.

Elitists hate Trump as much as they used to love Barack Obama— because Obama came from their groupthink. As a candidate, he declared of conservative Americans, "It's not surprising, then, they get bitter, they cling to guns or religion or antipathy toward people who aren't like them or anti-immigrant sentiment or anti-trade sentiment as a way to explain their frustrations." Then he appointed elites from various think tanks, universities, and news publications to his administration. This action was the holy grail to people such as *New York Times* columnist Paul Krugman, the guy known for claiming that the internet wasn't going to be a driving economic factor and that Trump's election would lead to economic depression. Under Obama, elitists had infiltrated every corner of our government, even spying on candidate and president Trump to undermine his presidency. They called their Russia hoax an act of patriotism. The only time leftists invoke patriotism is when they are tearing down the very country they purport to love.

But if you question Barack Obama, the elites call you a racist. If you question Hillary Clinton, the elites call you antiwoman. And if you question radical Islam, the elites ban you. That's because, for modern elitists, the most powerful weapon they wield is political correctness.

POLITICAL CORRECTNESS

Ever wonder what elitists dream about? It's a scary question, I know. But the dream can be summed up in two words: power and control. Elitism is really the passive-aggressive term for authoritarianism.

Political correctness is a perfect example of their daydream becoming a nightmare for the rest of us. Imagine setting the terms of every debate in your favor, *free speech be damned*. Someone decides what words are good and bad, what ideas are best and worst, and who is right and wrong. What a time-saver. Since the 1960s, so-called elite universities, newspapers, media, entertainment, and leftist-infused corporations have effectively established the ground rules. That's what they want to do, anyway. And they're succeeding.

President Trump represents the ultimate rejection of political correctness, hence their hatred for him. If anyone could be labeled an "elite," it's Donald Trump. His education, résumé, connections, and portfolio check all the boxes. Yet he rails against the self-proclaimed elite, mocking their self-importance and impotence. Trump has an uncommon touch with salt-of-the-earth Americans because he genuinely *respects* them. He would rather speak honestly and plainly than censor himself with the PC guidebook. Trump has become our first line of offense against political correctness, because he's (a) a billionaire, (b) president of the United States, and (c) never gave a rat's ass about playing the game. Think his words are racist, homophobic, or sexist? He doesn't care, because he knows he's none of those things.

His unfiltered trashing of PC "rules" creates a clear path for the rest of us to express our opinions freely and not care how our motives are judged by leftists. And he arrived just in time. We've gotten to the point where speaking our minds and questioning the prevailing culture is uncomfortable; we are forced to whisper commonsense truths to each other even though the majority of the population feels the same way. Every single day, lovers of America, common sense, and Western civilization are shamed into silence and verbal conformity because of the "woke" PC police. Once they label you, there is no department to go to in order to get the label removed. The label doesn't have to be true, and the Left doesn't even need to prove it.

Before the candidacy and presidency of Donald Trump, American culture was on the cusp of being almost fully controlled by elite-imposed political correctness. Did you feel afraid to speak up about your faith or your patriotic politics? Scared to be shunned by the powers that be? Many of us did and didn't know how to fight back. Trump paved the way back to free speech, liberating millions of patriots in the process. It might be his single greatest accomplishment.

Consider this take from the lifelong Democrat and Ivy League professor Alan Dershowitz: "People on the 'woke' hard-left seem so self-righteous about their monopoly over Truth (with a capital T) that many of them see no reason to allow dissenting, politically incorrect, views to be expressed. Such incorrect views, they claim, make them feel 'unsafe.' They can feel safe only if views they share are allowed to be expressed. Feeling unsafe is the new trigger word for demanding censorship."

Later in the piece, he continued, "For many 'wokers,' freedom of speech is nothing more than a weapon of the privileged used to subjugate the unprivileged. It [is] a bourgeois concept that emanates from an anachronistic white, male constitution that is irrelevant to the contemporary world. Free speech for me—the underprivileged—but not for thee—the privileged. That is what the 'wokers' want. Affirmative action for speech!" And they are moving full speed ahead with their speech reparations scheme.

If you control a nation's language, you control the nation. Of course, leftists don't begin their efforts to control speech by publishing lists of banned words and approved phrases. Well, sometimes they do; look at the student handbooks at most universities in America, and you can see their speech codes! The Left, instead, starts more subtly with controlling sentiment.

> *"Of course I'm not racist, and I certainly don't want to offend those who've experienced racism, so I'll mindlessly comply with the new and ever-changing language rules."*
>
> *"I'm inclusive—really, I promise—and happy to adopt the new and ever-changing pronoun rules."*
>
> *"They tell me 'diversity is our strength,' whatever that means, so I'll mindlessly comply with quotas—um, sorry—I mean diversity and sensitivity hiring guidelines."*

"I won't question, because I'd like to keep my job and my social credit score."

Ironically, the people who are the *least* racist, *most* inclusive, and *most* diverse are the ones targeted the most by the PC police. Have you ever been to a Trump rally? I've been to dozens. The crowd is the most diverse—meaning all races and political backgrounds—that you will see in American politics. Yet the media never report it; worse, they lie about it. The undercover "thought police," as described in George Orwell's *1984*, use the levers of power to limit speech, label opponents, and intimidate people into conformity. These leftist elitists populate media conglomerates, schools, human resources departments, and nonprofits such as the Clinton and Ford Foundations. The rest of us, left with no recourse, either comply with their demands or risk being alienated, ostracized, or fired.

As I travel the country, I cannot tell you how many people come up to me and say, "I love this president and hate what the Left is doing to our country, but I can't say anything. If I do, I will lose business. I will lose friends. And I will ultimately lose my job." The overwhelming sentiment of corporate America today is fully "woke" and politically correct, with HR departments teeming with "diversity coordinators" and "tolerance workshops." Those places are not free-speech zones, they are PC enforcement zones. Leftists are free to say whatever they want—because they've defined the parameters of what is acceptable!

They have also been very good at subtly infusing their preferred characterization into the American lexicon. Take the term "African American," for example. How and why has that become the politically correct word for Americans who are black? It's not even accurate half the time, with many blacks in America coming from places other than Africa yet regularly referred to as African American. The term was largely invented—and certainly popularized—by the leftist Jesse Jackson in the 1980s. Why? You guessed it, to further separate us. Never forget that the success of the Left is dependent on division.

I learned about this from black friends of mine. They said, "Stop using 'African American.' I'm an American! An American who happens to be black." So now I say "black American," because it removes the hyphen that is so very unnecessary. I'm an American who is white; I'm not a Norwegian American. But if you live in the politically correct universe where everyone has a grievance and everyone has a label, you create the hyphens and monikers that divide people. The elites start the trend and then ram it down our throats. Do you think that out of the blue, people just started thinking "I want to be called African American"? Or Asian American? Or Native American? No, it is all elitist phraseology intended to divide us. Because once we are divided, we can be controlled. It's time to unhyphenate America!

The same goes for phrases such as "illegal alien." It's a legal term, long used. But it sounded too harsh to globalist elites. So first they demanded that the phrase "illegal alien" become "illegal immigrant." Then it had to be "undocumented immigrant." Then it was "undocumented worker." Now those people are "undocumented persons" or "economic migrants." It's all wording designed to fit the latest leftist globalist mantra: no person can be illegal. They change the words in order to get their way.

PETE THE ELITE?

Why do I get so fired up about elitism? Because I've been inside the belly of the elite beast—within its walls of power and in its classrooms. And I'll admit that their "elite" status was a major reason I studied at both Princeton and Harvard. I was following their playbook for success: If you want to be elite, you go to the right institutions. If you want power, live where the world changers gather—or at least where the privileged kids of the world changers gather—and you might get a seat at the table. If you're going to play the elite game, you need to check the elite boxes.

But I had no real concept of that strange old world. I showed up at Princeton, and my first roommate was a great kid who had graduated from an elite boarding school: Phillips Exeter Academy, which is basically the Harvard of high schools. (See how I'm still brainwashed by elitism to use Harvard as the standard?) If I had understood the subculture of boarding schools—the tutors, test prep, and credential building that are routine in those circles—I probably would've been so intimidated that I would have never applied to Princeton in the first place. But somehow I snuck in—mostly because I could shoot the hell out of a three-point shot on the basketball court.

At Princeton, there are also elites circles *inside* the elite circles. Princeton doesn't really have fraternities; instead it has "eating clubs." It's the same thing, really, just with a fancier name. Eating clubs were where we ate our meals and partied. We paid dues—or our parents paid our dues—and other people cleaned up after us. I belonged to Cap and Gown, which, when I was there, was mostly athletes. It was considered a good club, with good parties. But others were more "elite"—especially the Ivy Club. I once decided to just walk into the Ivy Club, which was where all the Manhattan blue bloods congregated. I immediately sensed that I was not welcome. They looked at me sideways, like *What are you doing here? You clearly don't belong here—you need status to be in here.* I'll never forget it, because I had never encountered anything like it before. It was a glimpse of how blacks must have felt during segregation; elitism, like racism, segregates the societal haves from the have-nots. After four years of Princeton liberal indoctrination, I have no doubt that most of those elite Ivy Club kids are now lock-stock-and-barrel elitists.

As I first observed at Princeton and later at Harvard and briefly on Wall Street, elitism is a shallow existence and certainly antithetical to American-style meritocracy—save for Bear Stearns, which was an awesomely aggressive, politically incorrect investment bank. *May it rest in peace.* Once you're in the elite club, your life's goal is to stay in the club, rise within the club, and continue in the good graces of the club. If everyone plays along, cheered on by the prevailing culture, the dutiful elites find that their credentials and connections open more doors for them: big mahogany doors in ivory towers, government buildings, and media boardrooms. It's in those places that elitists do the real damage to our country, because they bring their leftist, globalist worldview with them into their positions of power. They're smarter than everyone else, know that government is the solution to every problem, and believe America is . . . dumb.

The best thing that ever happened to me, other than how I was raised, was joining the military. Fresh out of Princeton, I deployed for a year to Guantánamo Bay, Cuba, with the New Jersey Army National Guard. We guarded Islamist assholes for a year. It was long, boring duty. But as a platoon leader, I got to know the lives of my men intimately. They were hardworking, God-fearing, America-loving, middle-class men. Like the guys I grew up with in Minnesota. They loved their country, their families, and beer. I went from partying with millionaires at Princeton to sleeping in a tin can with hundredaires at Gitmo. And thank God I did.

I went on two more overseas deployments with soldiers from every corner of our country, the best America has to offer. I also met Muslims from far-flung places, many of whom remain dear friends today. I met troops from fellow NATO countries and saw their strengths and weaknesses. When I came home, I ran two nationwide veterans' organizations, traveling across the entire country on tour buses, meeting every cross section of America. I was literally on the road all year, working my ass off to build a movement of veterans and military families. You might call it "community organizing," veteran style.

Today, I have the amazing fortune of still traveling the country, this time on national television. Since even before President Trump's election, I had the assignment as one of *FOX & Friends'* "diner correspondents." Every few weeks I travel across the country—mostly to small towns and suburbs—to visit breakfast diners, talking to the everyday Americans who are the backbone of our country. On camera, but mostly off camera, we talk about life, culture, economics, and, of course, politics. No other program in America brings the voice of average voters—and their commonsense wisdom—to the ears of other American citizens.

I would argue, without hyperbole, that for the past decade, I've spent as much time on the road—talking genuinely to unfiltered fellow Americans—as any other person in America. I've met people from all walks of life, all races, and all ideologies. At rallies, in diners, at meet-and-greets, at speeches, at debates, at conferences, in town halls—and in the halls of Congress. I've been to all fifty states and every major airport in America many times over.

I can say, without hesitation, that those men and women—the soldiers, the workers, the farmers, the mothers, the activists, the police—are the real "elites" of America. They are the forgotten men and women. They have been called deplorables, clingers, and racists. They are none of those things. They are the elites. As he often does, President Donald Trump characterized them best at one of his rallies: "You're the great people. You're the smartest people. They talk about the elite. You ever see the elite? They're not elite. You are the elite."

Amen. If the so-called elites of our country—from Princeton and Harvard and Wall Street and Silicon Valley and Hollywood—would ever take the time to meet the American people, they might actually like them. Maybe that's what they're afraid of. By meeting authentic, everyday Americans they would lose the self-appointed moral high ground they wag their fingers from. I've met the elite of the elite, and I didn't like what I saw. Now we have a chance to empower the real elite—which is what Donald Trump is doing every day.

WHEN THEY LOST BARACK . . .

Oddly, when it comes to politically correct elitism, American Crusaders can agree with the recent words of former president Barack Obama. In 2019, he offered the following comments in a not-so-veiled criticism of the lineup of Democrat presidential candidates:

> I do get a sense sometimes now among certain young people, and this is accelerated by social media, there is this sense sometimes of: "the way of me making change is to be as judgmental as possible about other people and that's enough."
>
> Like, if I tweet or hashtag about how you didn't do something right or used the wrong verb, then I can sit back and feel pretty good about myself, cause, "Man, you see how woke I was. I called you out."
>
> That's not activism. That's not bringing about change. If all you're doing is casting stones, you're probably not going to get that far.

Wow, when you've lost Barack Obama, maybe you've gone a tad too far. Obama wanted to "fundamentally transform" America, and even he thinks that the modern Left is too "woke."

As we wage our fight against elitism and the elitists' bludgeon of political correctness, keep Obama's criticism in mind. As I've demonstrated in previous chapters, leftists have lost their minds. They are so out of touch with common sense and basic values that they've made it much easier for you to defend those values. They are going to yell at you. They're going to tweet at you. And they are going to hashtag you. But it's all noise. When you have the courage to persevere, you will see that the PC police really have no clothes on at all. There are no police, there is just pressure. It's a mob but a fake one.

The real mob—call us the silent majority or, as Trump has put it, the "angry majority"—is standing behind you. As an American Crusader, your charge is to stand up for America and the timeless truths that built her. Defending the Declaration, capitalism, and free speech is not that hard when you're debating lunatics. Great republics like ours require good citizens—the real elites. There is never a reason to cower to a title or a Twitter handle. Truth is truth, and we still have the First Amendment in this country. Join forces with your fellow crusaders, and use your voice—because elitists hate that you still have that power.

"[Democrats don't need] any more black faces that don't want to be a black voice."

—Representative Ayanna Pressley (D-Mass.), 2019

"Our diversity is our strength."

—Chief of the National Guard Bureau Joseph Lengyel, 2017

ELEVEN

MULTICULTURALISM: E PLURIBUS RACISM

What year was America founded? 1776, right?

Not according to the *New York Times*. It has declared the real founding of America to be . . . 1619. Why? In announcing "The 1619 Project," it explained, "The 1619 Project is a major initiative from The New York Times Magazine that began in August 2019, the 400th anniversary of the beginning of American slavery. It aims to reframe the country's history by placing the consequences of slavery and the contributions of black Americans at the very center of our national narrative."

They don't even hide their agenda anymore: to "reframe the country's history" and make the year 1619 our "true founding." So the day a group of slaves came ashore the English colony of Jamestown is the date of our *real* founding? Yep, that's what the vaunted *New York Times* wants Americans to believe. The goal of the Left is to make every American believe that racism runs in the very DNA of this country. It's a never-ending cycle of barfing up nonsense, then lapping it back up like a sick dog.

But wait, do you own slaves? Did your father? Your grandfather? No. Neither did mine. So why am I racist? What part of my birth must I atone for? Why does 1619 define me, or anyone else, more than 1776 does? Or 1865? Would the *New York Times* suggest that blacks in America should look to 1619 and whites to 1776? Separate but equal?

If we are all defined by our deepest sins, then we will all join Qasem Soleimani in Hell: you, me, and everyone at the *New York Times*. But we are not. Thank God.

As American Crusaders, you know that this nation was founded as an unprecedented experiment in self-governance, based on the *timeless and God-given* principles of freedom, equality, and opportunity. We also know that we have always been far from flawless. Slavery is a sin atoned for by a bloody civil war that ended it. Our flawed history has been a heroic march toward equal freedom, setting an example to the entire world—and serving as a lighthouse to which people of *all* cultures have flocked.

Now the *New York Times* tells us that we need to go backward and stay mired in guilt over the crimes of the British and Spanish. Did the authors of "The 1619 Project" fight in the Civil War to emancipate black Americans? Nope. I'm also not British nor Spanish, and I'm not two hundred years old. Yet leftists try to shame us into atoning for sins of the past as if they were ours. We can improve America for all people without hanging the title of racism around every person because of his or her race. Doesn't that sound ass backward?

I attended Infantry Officer Basic Training after college, four months in the sweltering heat of Georgia with a bunch of men I'd never met before. Then I spent one year with infantry grunts in Guantánamo Bay and Iraq and another in Afghanistan with a bunch of knucklehead patriots—of all backgrounds. When you have a clear mission, you strip away the superficial identities and get to know real people. You don't care about the color of anyone's skin or how much money he has in the bank—all that matters is the content of a man's character. When the bullets are flying and the job needs to be done, there is no black, brown, or white; there is only red, white, and blue.

No wonder our elites despise the military so much. When you put the mission first, it's our *unity* that makes us stronger—not our differences. If we think of America as our mission, the same should apply to how we see superficial attributes such as race. During my time as a platoon leader in Cuba, six of the guys in my platoon were Hispanic, legal noncitizens, and I fought like hell during the entire deployment to shepherd their citizenship packets. The military is a common pathway to legal citizenship. I didn't give a shit about the color of their skin; they *earned* citizenship, unlike border hoppers. They wanted to be on Team America and had done it the right way, which is all that matters.

But the Left wants the exact opposite. How the hell did we get to a point where elites tell us that seeing *more* race is better than moving *beyond* race? Once again, it's intentional. It takes a kernel of truth, infects it with leftism, and then poisons our society with solutions that are actually problems.

MELTING THE MELTING POT

The Left hates to hear this, but it's true: America has always been a melting pot. Sure, some of the melting has taken generations. But fundamentally, Americans have come to embrace cultures from around the world. Our system is built to absorb people who are willing to work hard, seek freedom, respect the law, and pursue the American dream. Our first immigrants were from European cultures: British,

French, Spanish and then Italian, Irish, Scandinavian, and German. And America grew. Our rallying cry was "We're all Americans!"

Of course, the immigrants included hundreds of thousands of black Africans brought to our nation under horrific conditions and sold into slavery. They were not an equal part of our nation, not at all. They were bought and sold, subjugated, and then—after they were freed—treated worse than second-class citizens. Slavery and segregation were a sin and a stain; there's no other way to put it. But that was then, and this is now. There are no black slaves in America today, just as there are no slave owners. Today, our country has a thriving black community—just as it has a growing Hispanic community—who are just as American as members of the Daughters or Sons of the Revolution.

This melting pot is what has made America successful. The very fact that we melt, that we leave behind our former lands and former allegiances, is what has allowed the American experiment to not only survive but thrive. In America today—on election day and every day in between—the great-great-grandchildren of slaves, the great-great-grandchildren of slave owners, and the great-great-grandchildren of citizens of every nation on Earth go to the same ballot box. Yes, we have sins of the past—but it is only the forgiveness of those sins, not the relitigation of them, that sets us apart. By the way, without Christianity's influence on American culture—particularly Jesus' emphasis on seeking and granting forgiveness—we would not have survived our rocky journey together.

America has always been multicultural, but in order for America to work in practice, allegiance to our nation and her ideals must be held in higher regard than racial or cultural identity. We pledge allegiance to the Declaration and Constitution of our country, not to the ethnicities of America. That unity has always brought tremendous achievement—in society, justice, technology, military might, and prosperity. This country has always welcomed people to bring their own culture, their own appetites, and their own dreams. But there is no room for you to bring your own laws or competing allegiances.

Today, the rallying cry of the Left is "We're all immigrants first—and Americans second." In a small sense, the leftists are correct. According to a 2019 report from the Center for Immigration Studies, based on US Census Bureau data, a "record 67.3 million Americans speak foreign language at home, over 50% in 90 big cities," and "In nine states, one in four residents now speaks a language other than English at home." At one level, this is very alarming. Shared language, the English language, is the language of America—of her culture, civic arena, and business.

But those numbers aren't dissimilar to the mix of foreign languages that came here in the 1700s and 1800s. All new immigrants come with their existing languages, cultures, and traditions. America has been enriched—especially our pallets—by throwing these ingredients into the melting pot. Look at a map of any US state, and you'll see town and city names that pay homage to immigrants' former homes yet have melted into "One Nation under God, indivisible." Take a few municipalities in Pennsylvania, for example: Alexandria, Athens, New Lebanon, Nazareth, Catasaugua, Corsica, Bethlehem, Berlin, Eau Claire, Emmaus, Etna, Hamburg, and York—living tributes to old worlds.

But America's promise comes with one gigantic caveat: new immigrants must seek to assimilate and pledge allegiance to the United States of America. Assimilation and allegiance; without those ingredients, we melt down our melting pot and destroy what holds us together.

What's alarming today is that the Left *encourages* new immigrants not to assimilate. The problem is not that immigrants speak different languages when they first arrive, it's that the Left wants to keep it that way. Worse, leftists believe that destroying the melting pot is the key to their own future political power. They open our borders, celebrate illegality, encourage segregation, incentivize government dependence, preach racial reparations, and teach new immigrants that this country is a bad place. Rather than seeing legal immigration as a pathway to strengthening America, they use it to tear down America—and reintroduce raw racism in the process.

MULTICULTURAL VERSUS MULTICULTURALISM

Being multicultural is a by-product of the premise of America. Human beings of all backgrounds—excepting those poisoned by certain ideologies—aspire to life, liberty, and the pursuit of their dreams. This does not happen because Washington, DC, has a "Bureau of Diversity" with enforcement quotas. How has America helped break down the cultural and racial barriers that otherwise separate us? Not just through common shared values but also through a common English language. If we can't speak with one another—especially with those with whom we have differences—we quite literally cannot survive as a nation.

Again, let's apply some common sense. I think about my experience in Iraq and Afghanistan, trying to work with locals without having a shared language. I can't have the same level of relationship with someone with whom I have to communicate through an interpreter. Shared language, like shared values, creates connection. But the Left has no interest in promoting English as a *first* language, because that would make it more difficult to divide people. Especially the new Left. Take, for example, the so-called moderate Amy Klobuchar. In 2007, Klobuchar was one of seventeen Senate Democrats to vote *for* an amendment that would make English the official language of the United States. Then in February 2020, facing pressure from the Left, she disavowed that position—on the basis of "diversity," of course.

Language is powerful. It sets people free. It allows them to achieve. Not only is English the language of America; it is the language of our commerce, our politics, and our media. It is the language of equal opportunity, just as it is the language of our common civic discourse. Citizens who don't learn English will always be at a disadvantage, which puts America at a disadvantage.

I'm a fifth-generation Norwegian. I don't speak a word of Norwegian, but my grandparents did, and my great-grandparents spoke primarily Norwegian. Over time, we became part of the melting pot, and now I have no allegiance to Norway. Sorry, Grandma. Sure, I'm somewhat fond of our traditions, and my parents would like to travel to Norway someday. But I'm not really interested. In just three generations, our family's allegiance fully immigrated to the United States. Traditions from "the old country," as millions of immigrants refer to their ancestral homes, have shaped this country in beautiful ways. But although we might have fond memories of those celebrations, foods, and languages, we live in the *new* country—because it's simply better.

I live in New Jersey, and Italian Americans are everywhere. I mean everywhere! To my untrained mind, they all seem to have the same haircuts (high and tight), fashion sense (track suits are alive and well), and bombastic tone (yelling is whispering). They make amazing Italian American food (duh) and look at me sideways if I don't pronounce their favorite dish or cheese correctly. Let's just say that Italian culture has made its mark here. But, more important, at the end of the day their hearts bleed red, white, and blue—not red, white, and green. The Italians who came to this country are amazing American patriots.

During World War II, US citizens of Italian descent were not tempted to go to Italy and fight for Benito Mussolini. They might have missed the olive groves, but there was no way in hell they'd give up the American dream or risk their lives to defend the new dictator of their old country. If anything, they were thrilled to see their former country free of fascism and took pride in beating the Axis power. This was the original incarnation of "America first"; before it was about trade policy, it was about putting our shared national identity over personal history or genetics. This reality was part of my Trump conversion moment in 2016—watching Mexican-born youths protest Trump's visit to southern California while waving Mexican flags. If you love Mexico so much, then go back there. If you want to be an American, it's time to ditch the flag of the away team and wave the Stars and Stripes.

In contrast to the idea of a multicultural society, *multiculturalism* is not a melting pot—it's a cafeteria tray with an endless number of separate compartments and separate communities with separate grievances. It encourages enclaves, native languages, and tolerance of anti-American ideas such as socialism. Yet, ironically, it is the newly arriving immigrants fleeing socialist countries who are the most passionate about fighting against it.

Multiculturalism ultimately divides us, because it tries to elevate other cultures above the cultural identity of America. When you label, separate, or hyphenate, you create "others"—an "us" and a "them." As Christopher Harris of Unhyphenated America so astutely points out, labels only create more racial discord in our nation. Thanks to multiculturalism, more and more people identify with labels related to ancestry, race, and religion rather than as Americans, and that's just fine with leftists.

I don't refer to myself as a white American or Norwegian American, although those could be factual descriptions. I'm repeatedly told that it's easier for me because I'm a white male—and I should recognize my "white privilege." I acknowledge that other races and backgrounds have had different experiences in this country. But the question remains: at what point will the goal become to drop all the labels and fully embrace our citizenship in the greatest country on Earth? If our nation is to survive, there is room for only one allegiance, as Teddy Roosevelt pointed out a century ago:

> In the first place we should insist that if the immigrant who comes here in good faith becomes an American and assimilates himself to us, he shall be treated on an exact equality with every one else, for it is an outrage to discriminate against any such man because of creed or birthplace, or origin.
>
> But this is predicated upon the man's becoming in fact an American and nothing but an American. . . .
>
> There can be no divided allegiance here. Any man who says he is an American, but something else also, isn't an American at all. . . .
>
> We have room for but one language here, and that is the English language . . . and we have room for but one soul loyalty, and that is loyalty to the American people.

Teddy perfectly described the difference between a multicultural country and the obsession with multiculturalism. Being multicultural is a reality, an opportunity for anyone to come here *legally* and invest in America. Multiculturalism is a fantasy, the belief that you can maintain a great and free country while encouraging people to label and segregate themselves by race and national origin. The first is special; the second is suicidal.

E PLURIBUS RACISM

If being multicultural is not a mere fact but instead a goal, what happens? What shall we call those who publicly categorize people based on their ethnicity or skin color? Let me think of the term.

Wait, I know! *Racists.* The repeated emphasis on color over character reduces people to their color, lumping individuals into categories—and treating everyone in that group the same way. Sound familiar? Sounds a lot more like 1619 than 2020.

The equation for this chapter is simple: Multiculturalism + Leftism = Racism.

Or, E pluribus racism.

Our nation's motto reads "E pluribus unum," Latin for "Out of many, one." It is a message of unity, and the Left has flipped it on its head. Instead they say, "Out of many, many." You came from many places, and you shall continue to be defined by those places.

This definition is different from the other "ism" equations laid out in this book because there's a fine line between being multicultural and the destructive cult of identity that is multiculturalism. We need to be brutally honest about what's taking place in our American culture: leftist racial reverse engineering.

Leftists have repeated the mantra until no one questions it anymore. "Diversity is our strength." Really? How so? I've heard leftists and human resources officers say it, but it never makes sense. Even the US military—led by politically correct Pentagon creatures who were promoted rapidly under Barack Obama—has said that "diversity is our strength," to the glee of the Left. With every utterance, we all get dumber. It's just not true.

Multiculturalism is a worship of identity. But its end goal is not only institutionalized racism—it's permanent division in this country, which gives the Left an opportunity to grow in political power. We worship Colin Kaepernick as a martyr. He gets richer. Those he pretends to kneel for aren't helped. And the flag is trampled upon. All of the noise the multiculturalists make about race, really isn't about race at all. In July 2019, the African American cis-gender congressperson Ayanna Pressley said the Democrat Party doesn't need "any more black faces that don't want to be a black voice." Here's the translation: "Your skin color should determine your outlook on life and political affiliation. Fall into line or be silent. Know your place." And she has other hyphenated allies.

In a November 2019 editorial, Ruben Navarrette, Jr.—who writes about "ethnicity and national origin" for the *Washington Post* and *USA Today*—offered his insight into multiculturalism while talking about supporters of President Trump. Warning: if you're triggered by racism—or stupidity—skip this excerpt.

> As a Mexican-American Never Trumper, I wanted to under-
> stand these people. Besides, as a journalist who is trained
> to talk to strangers, the idea of Latinos who support Trump
> sounded plenty strange to me.
>
> So, I went out and interviewed a couple dozen Latinos
> for Trump.
>
> What I found is that, in many cases, these folks are *not
> really Latino at all*. They're "post-Latino." They see them-
> selves as Americans. They're ambivalent about their her-
> itage, relatives, ancestors. They don't take offense when
> Trump insults Mexican immigrants because—even for
> Mexican-Americans—they see the people he's talking about
> as another species. [My italics.]

Ruben—let's call him "Rube" for short—evidently can't fathom the idea that people with a certain ancestry are free to have their own unique worldview—and see themselves as Americans first. Further, after exhaustive research with "a couple dozen" people, he found that supporting Trump actually changed their DNA—from Latino to Deplorable. Like Ayanna, Rube doesn't need any more Latino faces that don't want to be a Latino (read: Democrat) voice.

In trying to be fully "woke" multiculturalists, leftists such as Ayanna and Rube weaponize their own forms of racism in an attempt to herd minorities into their assigned racial pens. If you are black and conservative, you're not black! If you're a Latino who supports Trump, you're not Latino! To them, your racial identity should be your primary identity—and should predetermine your political outlook. What do they want—all Republicans to be white and all Democrats to be black or Latino or whatever? Apparently so. The idea of freethinking and American identity is a speed bump for them, not the goal. Therefore, they—not you—are the racists.

WHITE PRIVILEGE?

Multiculturalism always leads to racism. And racism is evil. To be honest, there are many other subjects I would rather write about. Who wants to talk about racism? We fought wars to move past it, and we have worked very hard to eradicate it. Race is, quite honestly, the last lens through which I characterize other people. But if you love this country, you can't ignore the issue.

So first let me address this question: if white privilege is such a "privilege," why didn't candidate Barack Obama promote the fact that he was half *white*? Why did Elizabeth Warren claim to be an Indian in matters related to career advancement? Why does Robert Francis O'Rourke take on a Hispanic nickname to garner votes? The answer reveals itself: because in today's leftist, politically correct America, the new ultimate privilege is *not* to be white and *not* to be a man. All things equal in corporate America today, if you have a white male applicant and a black female applicant, who gets the job? We know who the elites demand we hire, which is—in fact—racism.

That said, does racial discrimination still exist in America? Of course. Every society has racism. But there comes a point where emphasizing race in every instance has the opposite, unintended consequence. White people—and white men especially—start to look around and wonder: *Why am I the bad guy? I'm not racist and I've never been racist, yet I'm repeatedly told that I'm the problem. I have a high school degree, limited job prospects, and massive credit card debt—yet I have white privilege?* To the elites, America's sins can never be atoned for and America is never diverse enough. White men have been the problem and will always be the problem, we are told.

Saritha Prabhu, a self-described "brown, female immigrant" and columnist for *USA Today*, just came right out and said it in a 2018 column: "Today's Democratic Party is predicated on having and expressing open hostility toward white citizens." She's 100 percent correct. Leftist pundits and politicians in America today have free rein to tell white men to "get off the stage" or "move aside." Imagine, just imagine if a white person dared say that to anyone else? You can't, because you wouldn't.

In the December 2019 Democrat presidential debate, two white candidates tried to outdo each other in the multicultural circus. Pete Buttigieg promised "reparations" for illegal immigrants who were detained at our southern border. 1/1024th Native American Elizabeth Warren pledged, if elected, to hold an annual powwow in the White House Rose Garden to honor victims of murder. Not all murder victims, just "transgender women" and "people of color." As the 2020 field of Democrat contenders faded to white—and old— Bernie, Biden, and Bloomberg tripped all over one another in a pander dance for every "diverse" microconstituency.

Blatant racist rhetoric like this—alongside experiments such as racial "reparations," a cornucopia of public benefits for illegal immigrants, and race-based hiring preferences—are part of what drove certain young men to carry tiki torches in public, in Charlottesville in August 2017. If you're like me, the images of them were jarring. Scary, really. Hundreds of white men—without hoods but still invoking imagery of the Klan—demanding to be heard. It was truly sad to see.

There were also protestors in Charlottesville who felt that tearing down Confederate statues was reactionary and a dangerous path for our country—erasing history rather than confronting it. Those people have a right to be heard, and, as he has a knack of doing, President Trump heard them. As the president said after Charlottesville—while unequivocally condemning white supremacy, white nationalism, and neo-Nazis after the attacks—there are at least two sides to every debate.

Often overlooked, President Trump made a larger argument after Charlottesville, saying to a reporter, "George Washington was a slave owner. Was George Washington a slave owner? So will George Washington now lose his status? Are we going to take down—excuse me—are we going to take down statues to George Washington? How about Thomas Jefferson? What do you think of Thomas Jefferson? You like him? Good. Are we going to take down the statue? 'Cause he was a major slave owner. Are we going to take down his statue? You're changing history; you're changing culture."

Donald Trump is not a racist. He condemned all forms of racism. Always has. But Donald Trump understands people—black, brown, and white. He is willing to look at their grievances through the lens of Americanism and speak truths that make leftists shriek. He took a bold stand and, once again, motivated me.

I hosted *FOX & Friends* that weekend. The president's comments following the violence—which were completely mischaracterized—triggered a massive conversation about race in America. Rather than parrot the easy groupthink of self-righteous, one-sided condemnation, I decided it was precisely the time to speak inconvenient truths.

After airing a clip of the president speaking, I said, "I think the president nailed it. He condemned in the strongest possible terms hatred and bigotry on all sides as opposed to immediately picking a side out of the gate. And then this line to me is so important. He said, 'We are all Americans first.' And you hear the slogan 'America first,' but what does that mean if you are America first? It means you're not a racial identity first. You're not a class first. You're not a gender first. You're not a sexual orientation first. You're not another country first. It's not multiculturalism first. It's America first. And if we see ourselves through that lens, then it unites us as opposed to dividing us, which, frankly, the Left and others have done for so long by saying, 'No, I see you as a gender or a race or a class,' and the Balkanization creates division. We love our country. We love our God. We love our flag. And we are proud of our country. That to me is a unifying message that people should be drawn to, as opposed to criticize."

Moments later, I went after the even deeper—and more difficult—reality: "You can call [racism] out but still also listen, say, on Black Lives Matter, to the grievances of young African American males in urban cores who feel like they are looked at differently by police. That discussion still should be had. Just like young white men who feel like 'Hey, I'm treated differently in this country than I feel like I should be. I've become a second-class citizen. They tell me I have white privilege.' None of that justifies racial preferences or violence at all. But there's always a grievance underneath it that's worth talking about. And we should never live in such a politically correct culture that we can't at least have a conversation. There's a reason those people were out there. Some of it is outright racism and needs to be condemned. A lot of it, though, is I feel like my country is slipping away and just because I talk about nationalism—not white nationalism—doesn't mean I'm talking in code that I'm a racist."

The next day, just as they do to the president, the headlines were predictable: "FOX & Friends Sunday Defends White Supremacist

Charlottesville Protestors." And there you have it. When you make perfectly legitimate points that are not politically correct or conventional leftist thinking, you are called a racist. And the racist feedback loop, fueled by leftists, continues. Violence is not the answer; but just as Black Lives Matter has a right to voice its view, so do white people who feel that the deck is today stacked against them. The common thread of the entire conversation is the poison of identity politics.

That same weekend on *FOX & Friends*, my friend the professor Carol Swain, herself a black female, came on to discuss Charlottesville. Having literally written the book about white identity politics, her answer about the anger of white men was spot on: "These are people who are aggrieved over affirmative action, immigration, minority crime, and just what they see as discrimination against white people. If we want to come together, we need to move away from identity politics and multiculturalism and focus on the American national identity. That's the only way we're going to be able to get beyond this."

That goes for white people, black people, Hispanic people, all people. When you tell a certain group—in this case white men—that they have privileges they've never actually had or experienced while elevating other people based on their racial identity, you only push them further into their own corners of racial identity. You fuel identity politics. The same goes when you perpetually tell minority groups that they are still oppressed. Too many minorities in this country are being taught that because previous generations of minorities faced real discrimination, they remain oppressed. As Candace Owens—a future leader in this country who also happens to be black—says often, "Stop being a victim and start being a victor."

If you tell people that they're automatically privileged if they are white, which is both not true and the definition of racism, your stereotyping infuriates them and makes them point fingers at the other side. Likewise, if you tell people that they're automatically oppressed if they're black, your racial stereotyping infuriates them and makes them point fingers at the other side. Racism begets racism, all of which is bad for America.

CRUSADING AGAINST MULTICULTURALISM

Let's cut the bullshit; diversity is *not* our strength.

Our strength is our founding, our military, our prosperity, and the average ordinary Americans—of all backgrounds—who make the country work. Everything the Left does aims to weaken these attributes, and it does it by spouting the lie that people are still being treated unfairly—fifty-five years after the Republican-written Civil Rights Act and despite decades of affirmative action programs. Diversity can be a strength, for example, a diversity of nuclear weapons for various types of conflicts—tactical, ICBM, thermonuclear, and so on—but I digress. More often than not, diversity initiatives are just redistribution schemes and a way to control public discourse. In a country with First Amendment protections, it's like putting all of us on a vegan diet and then banning vegetables. It is a diet of identity politics, revisionist history, and name-calling that makes us weaker.

Here's a message to the *New York Times* 1619 crowd: It's okay that America was founded by a bunch of white guys. It's okay that white Europeans expanded America. And it's okay that forty-four of our forty-five presidents were white and one was half white. These are all facts that cannot be erased—despite the fact that you've torn down more historical monuments than the Islamic State has. What is not okay is using a revisionist, moral rearview mirror to condemn this country to death. The United States has made great progress on human equality over time—greater than any nation the world has ever known. Our past is there to learn from and build upon, and we cannot tolerate it being used as an anti-American bludgeon.

If multiculturalism made a nation better, I'd be all for it. If more focus on racial differences made a community less racist, I'd lead the march. But it doesn't.

Once again I ask, if other countries have it all figured out, why aren't all the disgusted and ungrateful leftists packing up to move somewhere else? Because, in the back of their minds, they know America is the most diverse, most free, and most equal country on Earth. Compare it to Heaven, and it has serious warts. Compare it to Afghanistan, China, France, Germany, Russia, Saudi Arabia, and [insert any country here], and it outshines them all.

Yet when you share these truths, you will be attacked. To that I say, yet again, follow the leadership of President Trump—*especially* after a tragic day such as the one in Charlottesville. Wussing out means to pander, to simplify, and to equivocate in order to "get along" with the Left—the people who have targeted you for annihilation. Those are precisely the moments to expose their radical ideologies that actually divide us further. Courage only really counts when the consequences are real.

Don't be afraid to be an equal opportunity insulter. We've all found ourselves where the PC voice inside our head says, *You can't say that because she's black.* Or *Because I'm white [or whatever], I can't make that comment.* That voice inside your head was put there by leftists who want to police your speech and keep us divided. Just as Trump eviscerated his white political rivals during the 2016 election, he has eviscerated his political rivals of all shades during his presidency. He takes on Maxine Waters's idiocy and Ilhan Omar's radicalism just as he takes on Bernie Sanders's socialism and Joe Biden's sleepiness. Black, white; male, female—he is an equal opportunity offender.

That is the exact *opposite* of racism. Our goal is to treat people equally based on the content of their ideas, not their skin tone or gender.

Twenty years ago, in a speech about race and bias, President George W. Bush introduced the phrase "the soft bigotry of low expectations." This dynamic still exists in America today, kept alive by multiculturalists. They tell us that certain races, genders, and demographics merit certain treatment precisely because of their categorization. This bigotry tells certain groups of people that their individual traits—their minds, souls, and hearts—are not what matters. Instead, the Left tells them that it is the attribute they cannot change—their race—that defines them.

This mind-set is corrosive, and it is evil. We fought wars to free ourselves, and others, from it. Now the Left is doing it to us. The only answer to this bigotry is the simplest answer: the content of our character is what matters, and our unity as Americans is our strength.

It's simple; do what you've always done—judge people based on who they are, not what they look like. If you find yourself debating leftists, call them racists first—before they call you one—and make them defend their undefendable bigotry.

"Muhammad was the tenth most popular name for newborn boys in the United States in 2019 and the most popular boy's name in England."

—According to BabyCenter

"Of course Islam will rule the world someday— the prophet [Muhammad] foretold it."

—Esmatullah, my interpreter in Afghanistan

TWELVE

ISLAMISM: THE MOST DANGEROUS "ISM"

Esmatullah was one of our interpreters during my Afghanistan deployment. He and I would talk for hours on end, often late into the evening. We became friends and were honest with each other. "Esmat," as I called him, was *not* a "radical" and not an "Islamist." He was an ordinary young Muslim from the capitol city of Kabul with ordinary life ambitions—including marrying a young girl his family forbade him to spend time with. We talked a lot about that. He wanted a normal life but was surrounded by war. Every day he rode home on his motorcycle, making sure to take a different route each time because the Taliban was watching everybody—and he knew it. With his salary, he took care of his parents and siblings. Esmat was a good kid; I trusted him.

During one of those conversations, Esmat said, very matter-of-factly, "Of course Islam will rule the world someday—the prophet [Muhammad] foretold it. We are having ten kids, and you are having one." Regular Muslims like him believe that Islam's destiny is to control the world—and by having many children, they are contributing to that cause. It's why he wanted to get married: to raise a family. He spoke with a tone of inevitability. It wasn't laced with threats of violence or subjugation, just his view of destiny. He was an average, ordinary Afghan kid repeating what he had learned in his madrassa (Islamic school) and mosque—not much different from what the other 2 billion Muslims are taught.

Esmat is a Muslim, not an Islamist. To him it's a big difference, but in the larger scheme, the distinction becomes less important. As the influence of Islam grows, Islamists use the earnestness of fellow Muslims to advance their more radical view. And they have help.

There is a reason I chose this topic to close out the "leftism" section: because no "ism" benefits more from leftism than Islamism does. And no "ism" is more dangerous to freedom than Islamism is. Derived directly from Islam, the life of Muhammad, and the writings of the Quran, Islamism is the most coherent, most evangelical, and most aggressive worldview on Planet Earth today. Allow me to say this again, to make sure it soaks in: Islamism is *the most coherent, most evangelical, and most aggressive ideology in the world today.*

In my first book, IN THE ARENA, I wrote at length about the threat of Islamism. Most Americans, especially leftists, live with a romanticized Lawrence of Arabia view of Islam and Islamism. Islam is a "religion of peace" to be embraced by the tolerant West, they say. This mantra is pounded into our head in school and then repeated ad nauseam in the herd mentality culture and politically correct news media. The "Islam = Peace" narrative is a naive and cowardly worldview, because the alternative is confronting the reality of a threat that's almost too scary to fathom. For most of America's history, we've had the convenience and good fortune to shield ourselves from the impact of Islamism; it was on other continents, endangering other people, far from our shores.

Then two towers fell in Manhattan, and an entire generation of Americans—including myself—went to war and got a front-row seat to the reality of Islamism.

I've spent a fair amount of time in the Muslim and Arab world, certainly more than most Americans. I've patrolled the battlefield both against and with Muslims. I've spent hours in deep religious, philosophical conversations with Muslims from all walks of life—rank-and-file religious and nonreligious types, Western-educated professionals, imams from both radical and "moderate" mosques, and every type of Sunni and Shia Muslim in between. I fully understand the distinction between "peaceful" Muslims and Islamist Muslims. I have many dear friends who are Muslim—including Texas Omar, his family, and colleagues at FOX News. They are wonderful people, working and fighting—in their mind—to save a religion besieged by radicals. I don't agree with that assessment, but they love America, so I respect them greatly.

But they are under siege. Next to the communist Chinese and their global ambitions, Islamism is the most dangerous threat to freedom in the world. It cannot be negotiated with, coexisted with, or understood; it must be exposed, marginalized, and crushed. Just like the Christian crusaders who pushed back the Muslim hordes in the twelfth century, American Crusaders will need to muster the same courage against Islamists today.

WHAT IS ISLAMISM?

Regardless of how peaceful moderates advance their narrative, radical Muslims—Islamists—exploit nearly every aspect of mainstream Islam to advance their cause. Moderate Muslims are battling not just the Islamists but also the bulk of Islamic theology, history, and traditions. They've been losing the fight to make Islam great again for 1,300 years, as evidenced by the fact that it is so easy for the Islamists to leverage "moderate" Islam to advance their cause. The logical conclusion: the real heart of Islam is much closer to Islamists than to moderates—which is a huge problem and should be a loud, five-times-per-day wake-up call.

When appropriate, I am careful to separate individual moderate Muslims from the radical elements. Other times, the words *Muslim* and *radical* can be used interchangeably. This underscores the difficult reality that Muslim "moderates"—who are large in number—are either complicit in Islamism's expansion or impotent to reverse it. As a result, Islam—the fastest-growing religion in the world—is almost entirely captured and leveraged by Islamists who believe that their mission is the same as their founder's. Muhammad led armies, enslaved or killed his opponents, and sought to conquer everyone else. Modern Islamists, of course, have the same goal.

Islam is a religion practiced by billions. Islam*ism* is defined as the belief in the imposition of Islam on others, both violently and nonviolently, that is practiced by hundreds of millions. Even if you take a low estimate of the percentage of Muslims in the world who can fairly be characterized as Islamist (roughly 25 percent), we are still talking about a population greater than that of the entire United States. That is not a tiny fringe movement. But no matter how carefully we try to make distinctions, Islam and Islamism are two branches of the same theological tree. Islamism is a widespread interpretation of Islam that draws on the text of the Muslims' holy book, the Quran, which tells the story of a leader who, empowered by his god, spread the Islamic faith by subjugation and the sword. This is a fact, whether it makes you uncomfortable or not.

You can already hear the PC call-to-prayer police through the media's loudspeakers: "Islam is a religion of peace!" Do not bow to that call.

Yes, millions of those who identify as Muslims are peaceful. Obligatory disclaimer made. But, no, Islam is not a religion of peace, and it never has been. Islam is neither a religion of peace nor a religion of violence; it is a religion of submission. The word *Islam* itself translates into English as "submission"—submission to god (Allah), submission to god's Book (the Quran), and submission to the life and teachings of god's prophet, Muhammad (told in the Hadith). To those who follow the religion rigorously, the text of the Quran and the teachings of Muhammad are infallible, inflexible, and unquestionable—making the *text* of Islam the real challenge. Almost every single Muslim child grows up listening to, and learning to read from, the Quran. Contrast this with our secular American schools—in which the Bible is nowhere to be found—and you'll understand why Muslims' worldview is more coherent than ours.

If the Islamic holy books, the Quran and the Hadith, are reordered and read chronologically, the text starts with peaceful passages and evolves toward violent passages—mirroring the life of Muhammad. As he accumulated devotees, power, and a conquering army, his approach to spreading his new faith changed: he captured Mecca through persuasion but took Medina by the sword. In both scenarios—peaceful and violent—the outcome was the same: non-Muslims paid a second-class-citizen tax, converted to Islam, or were killed. Whichever way, they submitted.

Prior to the life and teachings of Jesus and the New Testament, many of these same things could have been said of the Bible and Christianity. The God of the Old Testament was violent, vengeful, and very judgmental. But a key distinction makes these two Abrahamic religions very different. The Quran has no "New Testament," meaning that the painful reformation such as the one Christianity eventually emerged from—peace over violence, equality over slavery, and state separate from church—is a long way off for Islam. Or, as I see it, not possible at all.

Making matters even more complicated, Islam is not just a religion but also a system of governance—based on Sharia law in various forms—a judicial and penal system, and a cultural way of life for devout Muslims; meaning that Islamism, as well as mainstream political Islam, cannot peacefully coexist with any other system of government. Again, millions of Muslims have joined modernity and choose to live peacefully; but they do so by disregarding intolerant and violent quranic passages that are no less authoritative today than they were a thousand years ago. Islamists choose to interpret the Quran as it is written, not as modernity tries to edit it; and when they demand an "Islamic state," they mean it. They celebrate holy death, even invite it; meanwhile, Westerners cling desperately to increasingly secular and shallow lives.

America is not at war with Islam, but we are always at war with Islamists. Al Qaeda, the Islamic State, the Taliban, Iran, and the likes are the latest manifestations of an Islamist movement that has no plans to "coexist." They seek land, they seek power, they seek demographic and political advantages, and they actively seek the military means—especially nuclear weapons—to bring the West to its knees. The longer Americans live with the delusion that Islam is a religion of peace—especially as the demographics of Europe and the United States continue to change—the more difficult our task. Islam has been at war with its enemies—meaning all "infidels"—since it was founded, and it will never stop.

Saudi Arabian oil money funds radical, anti-Western Islamic schools (madrassas) and mosques across the Muslim world, in

Europe, and even here in the United States. Groups such as the Muslim Brotherhood and the Council on American-Islamic Relations (CAIR) have advanced the radical mission of Islamism for decades. In the past two years alone, more than one hundred members of Congress—including Ilhan Omar, Adam Schiff, Rashida Tlaib, Elizabeth Warren, and Amy Klobuchar—have signed letters endorsing CAIR. Socialist Bernie Sanders, a favorite among Muslim Americans due to his support for Palestinian causes and distaste for Israel, addressed the Islamic Society of Northern America Convention in August 2019, the largest such gathering in America. Leaders of CAIR speak very highly of Bernie because his hard-core leftism provides the best gateway for their Islamism.

Leftists in America, eager to whore themselves out for foreign causes if the price is right, embrace Islamists as members of their "diversity" and interfaith coalitions. Many radical Muslim leaders exploit these relationships as opportunities to spread their extreme ideology, and eventually—sooner rather than later—will attempt to slip Islamic law into our government. They will start small, in local municipalities, and get bolder over time. They've done it time and time again throughout history. If Islamists are one thing, they are consistent and patient.

This equation is simple: Islam + Leftism enables Islamism. (Otherwise known as the Red-Green Alliance. Red for Leftism, Green for Islam).

Islamists will not conquer Europe—and attempt to conquer America—militarily; they will first do so demographically, then culturally with the help of sycophantic leftists, and then politically. Here is the reality: we must never ridicule Islamism; we should respect its clear vision, efficient power structure, leveraging of human nature, and unrelenting aggression. As I said, Islamism is the most coherent, aggressive, evangelical, and threatening worldview on the planet.

The Chinese communists seek to rule the world, but their ideology is based on a political framework for gaining power. Islamists have a book, a tradition, a leader, and a narrative that has held steady for 1,300 years. At the same time, we must boldly speak the truth about how Islamism crushes the cry of the human spirit for freedom. There is a reason Islamism is our enemy.

THE ISM OF ISMS

Islamists have two immediate advantages over their opponents in the Western world. The first is their aggression and militancy. Islamists—and even mainstream Muslims—use aggressive tactics to exploit American "tolerance" as utter weakness in order to achieve accommodations that would never otherwise be tolerated. I'm not talking about on the battlefield, I'm talking about in our classrooms, city councils, and social media. Simply put, their sheer insistence, the specter of violence, and their passionate beliefs lead many average citizens to retreat on demands for assimilation to American principles, a reality we have seen powerfully in Minnesota among a large Somali refugee population. Muslims insist, insist, and insist— making "others" feel as though they are under the gun or somehow wrong. "Bigots!" the leftists cry. For fear of public reprisal and cries of "intolerance" against anyone who questions their religious demands, most Americans simply cave in to a stubbornly insular Muslim community.

The aggression of Islamists accelerates their second advantage: the weakness of their opponents. As Islamism has exploded around the globe, the Left has systematically destroyed the very institutions needed to fight it. You can't fight a coherent ideology with incoherence. You can't defeat militancy with coexistence. You certainly cannot defeat aggressive evangelism with passive ambivalence. Though still vastly outnumbered in America and the West, Islamists very strategically leverage the leftist "isms" to their advantage. Just as the ancient Greeks used the Trojan horse to infiltrate Troy, Islamists use our ignorance and good nature against us. They use our leftist "isms" to trick us into opening our cultural gates—and leftists are their willing gatekeepers. Here are a few examples.

Globalists tell us that borders don't matter; that anyone, from anywhere, with any ideology, has an equal right to live in America, Europe, and the West. "These are peace-loving citizens of the world. Let them in," they say. Not only do they balk at Muslim immigration bans or moratoriums, they celebrate Muslim immigration. Of course, Islamists happily exploit this view to seed the West with as many Muslims as possible. Suddenly, years later—thanks to their very high birth rates relative to native populations and their strategically insular culture—the sons and daughters of those migrants and refugees multiply in greater numbers than do native citizens. Islamists, first peacefully and then militantly, expand their influence within this otherwise "peaceful" cycle. Name one modern European country that has opened its borders that has not seen this happen? Time's up. The answer is: none.

While American elites ponder what gender pronouns to use and whether it's ethical to have children anymore, feminists and *genderists* whisper, "Look at those majestic hijabs." The West confuses our kids about whether they are boys or girls but embrace the highly misogynist culture that exists within mainstream Islam. Leftists tell us we must embrace backward Islamist thinking because Muslims are diverse and different. In the meantime, Islamists in the West still force youth marriages, practice female genital mutilation, and execute homosexuals. Genderists look the other way, too busy condemning North Carolina for asking boys to use the boy's bathroom.

Socialism, in the form of government handouts, lures Islamists eager to advance their ideology at the expense of the government. Just as in Europe, the majority of Muslim refugees who come to America rely heavily on government paychecks. A 2015 Center for Immigration Studies report found that "The cost of resettlement includes heavy welfare use by Middle Eastern refugees; 91 percent receive food stamps and 68 percent receive cash assistance." The average cost of each Middle Eastern refugee resettled in the United States: $64,370 in the first five years, or $257,481 per household. We are literally paying Muslims to stay in our country without working. If even one Muslim on government benefits becomes an Islamist, that is a failure. As we saw during the rise of ISIS as young men flocked from America and Europe to join its ranks, we now know that we have a *massive* failure on our hands. But the Left thinks America, not the Islamists, is the problem.

Unsurprisingly, and ironically, *secularism* is a huge enabler of Islamism. As our culture ditches God, two distinct consequences occur: First, we become less equipped to defend our faith. We don't know Jesus, the Bible, and our values. We stand for nothing and therefore fall for anything. Second, secularism in America hates only two religions: Christianity and Judaism. Islam, on the other hand, is not to be criticized. While our Judeo-Christian roots as a nation must be ripped out of every inch of public life, Islam is given a free pass. Secularists will not criticize Islamists, because—as leftists have dictated—Islam is considered a protected "diversity" class. To secularists, the religious views of Muslims are personal and private—which remains that way only until they are in charge. At which point, religious freedom fades away.

Of course, *elitists* are the worst. Their think tanks and universities are riddled with so-called experts who tell the rest of us the lies, over and over again, that "Islam is a religion of peace" and "diversity is our strength." The country of Qatar donates millions to powerful DC think tanks such as the Brookings Institution, funding "experts" who won't dare cross their donors. We must not only tolerate Islam and Islamists—we must *celebrate* them, we are told. Leftists impose speech codes, written and unwritten, about what can be said about Islam—and then dare the rest of us to defy the PC police. Any criticism of Islam is deemed "hate speech" (see: Canada and Europe), and they tie themselves in knots explaining away Islamist terrorism as rooted in economics, politics, and even climate change. Elitists are first apologists, and then enablers, of Islamists.

Multiculturalism, you will recall, is the worship of identity. If someone looks different, sounds different, and prays differently—he or she is to be celebrated. Because, to multiculturalists, the celebration of diversity is skin deep. Multiculturalists do not care if new arrivals to the United States actually love this country. Moreover, they believe their own electoral prospects are enhanced by bringing in groups of people who are dissatisfied with America and, if given the option, unlikely to assimilate. Yet again, radical Muslims fit these criteria perfectly. Moreover, politically correct politicians welcome groups such as CAIR to the table, just as they might welcome the AFL-CIO. They refuse to face the fact that CAIR represents a radical ideology because, well, diversity.

Not to be out done in absurdity, even *environmentalists* enable Islamists by providing them fodder for propaganda. America and the West are always the evildoers, according to environmentalists, and Islamists seize on that lie. Even Osama bin Laden told his followers to urge the world to "put its efforts into attempting to reduce the release of [greenhouse] gases. The choice is with whoever is continuing to assault us. This is a struggle between two of the largest cultures on Earth, and it is in the shadow of catastrophic climatic conditions, and it would help to avoid that by relaying a true picture of the struggle." On this, environmentalists and Osama agree.

Leftists are sedated—and distracted—by their grab bag of "isms," while Islamism takes advantage of this sedation to implement their version of end-times theology. Leftists wittingly and unwittingly roll out a wide red carpet for Islamists, believing that even if they are wrong about Islam, it will never impact them. They might be right, but only in that the Islamists will come for them last.

What the Left cannot understand is that Islamism today—like the Islamism of the past—remains violent and aggressive because those attributes are in its DNA. Islamism cannot thrive without violence and conflict, unless and until it has subjugated every "nonbeliever" or "infidel" in its path. Islamists attacked us on 9/11, have infiltrated Europe, and are making inroads in America. Likewise, Christians around the globe are being slaughtered, persecuted, and forced to flee their homes—thanks to Islamists. Here we are again, just like the time right after Muhammad, when peaceful Christians around the world were without an army.

THE THREAT THAT NEVER DIES

Ever since Muhammad was powerful enough to build his first army, Islam has been spread by the sword. The entire Middle East once had flourishing Jewish and Christian populations. *Swoosh!* Gone. North Africa had vibrant Christian roots. Gone. As the eleventh century unfolded, Europeans found themselves increasingly tormented, surrounded, and invaded by Islamists. Spain even became a Muslim stronghold. Then Europeans decided to push back. Enter the crusaders. Exit the Islamists—for a few hundred years.

Even America has a long history with Islamism. As my friend and *FOX & Friends* colleague Brian Kilmeade wrote about in his best seller *Thomas Jefferson and the Tripoli Pirates: The Forgotten*

War That Changed American History, in the late 1700s, America's merchant ships were under attack by Muslim pirates from North Africa who routinely captured our sailors and held them as slaves. Thomas Jefferson and John Adams were told by diplomats that the attackers believed that "it was written in the Quran, that all Nations who should not have acknowledged their authority were sinners, that it was their right and duty to make war upon whoever they could find and to make Slaves of all they could take as prisoners, and that every Mussulman who should be slain in battle was sure to go to Paradise." Just as Europe finally saw the threat clearly and waged a crusade, America had a similar revelation. Adams said, "We ought not to fight them at all unless We determine to fight them forever." He was right on all fronts. The United States fought them then and did prevail—and we are still fighting them today.

Today, Islam and Islamism are back, knocking down the door of Europe. But this time, at least for now, the Islamists' tactics are different.

In Islamist circles, there's a principle known as *hegira*. This term refers to the nonviolent capture of a non-Muslim country. Hegira is a cultural, physical, psychological, political, and eventually religious takeover. History is replete with examples of this; and because history is not over, it's happening in the most inconceivable places right now. Take the United Kingdom, for example. Radical mosques and schools are allowed to operate. Religious police control certain sections of many towns. Sharia councils dot the underground landscape. Pervasive political correctness prevents dissent against disastrous policies such as open borders and nonassimilation. Take the British cities of London, Birmingham, Leeds, Blackburn, Sheffield, Oxford, Luton, Oldham, and Rochdale. What do they all have in common? They have all had Muslim mayors.

The British were invaded, and they didn't even know it. In one generation—absent radical policy change—the United Kingdom will be neither *united* nor a Western *kingdom*. The United Kingdom is done for.

The same can be said across Europe, especially following the disastrous open-borders, pro-migrant policies of the past few decades. Countries such as Germany, France, Norway, Sweden, and the Netherlands threw open their doors to Muslim "refugees" and will never be the same because of it. Like the United Kingdom, each of those countries now contains countless crime-ridden "refugee" neighborhoods, including de facto no-go zones where police fear to tread. Radical mosques exist in their cities, and Western traditions are openly contested. Rape has skyrocketed, as notions of "honor" and misogyny clash with modernity. These "tolerant" countries opened up their borders and their welfare states, while doing nothing to assimilate Muslims into themselves—as if they could have anyway.

Islamists in Europe and around the globe seek to exploit the growing number of Muslims in their midst in order to challenge the existing order. Political and radical Islam is growing in Europe precisely for the reason my friend Esmat explained: simple demographic math, their most powerful tool. Quivering European beta-male politicians talk about the need for new immigration policies and assimilation requirements but prove incapable of delivering security and safety for their citizens.

Today, Europe is *sort of* waking up to the fact that it has been invaded again—culturally and demographically. According to the Pew Research Center, the Muslim population in Europe, *excluding Turkey*, was estimated at 30 million in 1990, at 44 million in 2010, and is expected to grow to 58 million by 2030. The number is growing while birth rates among native Europeans have all dropped. Many European countries would have declining populations if not for Muslim immigration. Combine these factors over time, and this is what you get: in 2019, the most popular name in England for newborn boys was Muhammad.

Could the same thing happen in America? Of course. With enough leftism and enough time, anything is possible for Islamists. As I have reported on extensively at FOX News, certain cities in my home state of Minnesota have started to look much different thanks to overwhelming and intentional Muslim immigration. What started with good intentions (see: Somali Omar in chapter 1) and peaceful refugees eventually evolved into insular communities, internationally funded mosques, welfare fraud, culture clashes, and radicalization. Then, as Muslims' birth rates have grown—alongside their political influence—local "tolerant" populations have made concessions. Critics are called racists, crimes are hidden from the public, and the European cycle has begun. Similar trends are happening in other states, including Michigan and New York.

Thankfully, we are behind the trends of Europe. Our two oceans, barriers to refugee invasions, and traditional Christian fabric have insulated us well, but we are losing them—quickly. American leftists insist on pursuing the very same policies that led to the cultural invasion in Europe. The unholy alliance between leftists and Islamists means that open borders, nonassimilation, the erosion of national allegiance, and toleration of the intolerable has left the door open for Islamists to establish a foothold in our country. In November 2019, twenty-six Muslim candidates won elected office in the United States. Muhammad is now a top ten boys' name in America—what will it be in 2030?

BUILD THAT (CULTURAL) WALL

As usual, President Trump has been—and continues to be—willing to say and do the things most American political leaders would never have the guts to do. In December 2015, candidate Donald Trump called for "a total and complete shutdown of Muslims entering the United States until our country's representatives can figure out what the hell is going on!" He was right then and, once in office, tried to implement a more tailored ban from certain countries with large populations of Islamists. It was tied up in the courts until going into partial effect. With a win in the courts, he now plans to expand it. The result: it's 2020, and half the country, more than half of elected officials, and almost everyone in the media still have no idea what the hell is going on. Except for President Trump, our leaders still don't take the threat of Islamism seriously.

Though our country might be falling short in preventing the internal spread of Islamism, some countries do see the danger—and have taken bold measures. Countries such as Japan, Australia, Poland, Hungary, and Israel all have built some form of immigration policy wall against the cultural invasion of Islamism. In their own ways, leaders and citizens of those countries withstand the barrage of false guilt from the Left because they understand that Islam itself is not compatible with Western forms of government. Those countries want to stay free, so they are fighting like hell to block Islam's spread. In this age, it's incredibly difficult to remain clear-eyed about the fact that some ideas for society are better than others. And that is where the real fight lives.

There is an unholy war on truth and intellectual honesty going on in the West. The Left does not want the real story of Islam and Islamism told. It wants to glorify it and embolden it by brushing its shortfalls under a Persian rug and highlighting a sanitized version of its better qualities—all of which perpetuates the politically correct lie about Islam that it is a religion of peace. That's why we're here—to tell it like it is and keep telling it. And, when necessary, as American Crusaders, to fight back against it with history, facts, and the truth.

I'm against Islamism because I'm for freedom. If you support women's rights, instead of wearing a pink hijab in front of the White House, you'd protest in front of the Saudi Embassy—or pretty much any Muslim country's embassy. Take your pick; there are no protesters there at the moment even though women are widely, openly, and brutally subjugated throughout the Muslim world. If you support gay rights, instead of harassing conservatives, you'd protest outside the Iranian Embassy—where they claim that there are zero homosexuals in Iran because it's illegal to be gay. The examples write themselves, as does the leftist hypocrisy.

Areas of the world ruled by Islamists are the most unjust and the most backward. They suppress free commerce, free thought, and free speech. The result is a way of life and a way of thinking that most Americans can't imagine. What you have is what you'll always have. What your family has is what you'll have—and no more. Your future is defined by your father, your name, or your tribe, unless you're an oil sheik. And it will always be that way. Your sons will plow the same field and run the same shop. There is no pursuit of happiness.

I don't say this to ridicule fellow human beings. I simply point out the truth, because what Islamism does saddens and sickens me. The Middle East used to be a center of science, math, and the arts. While it's been kicking around in the same dirt for generations, the United States has sent people to the moon—and back. That, among countless other modern miracles, is what the human spirit unleashes when it's free—not enslaved.

Once again, citizens of this country cannot naively hope that oceans will hold back the cultural invasion. The invasion is not just at our shore, it's in your community and schools. Arming yourself with facts is not against the law, and neither is speaking those facts to those in your community. Protecting American culture is not racist. Questioning the fruits of Islam is not Islamophobic. Demanding assimilation is not xenophobic. Condemning Islamism and its cruel worldview is not only right, it's essential for freedom's survival.

OUR CRUSADE MOMENT

Our present moment is much like the eleventh century. We don't *want* to fight, but, like our fellow Christians one thousand years ago, we must. We need an American Crusade. We Christians—alongside our Jewish friends and their remarkable army in Israel—need to pick up the sword of unapologetic Americanism and defend ourselves. We must push Islamism back—culturally, politically, geographically, and in the case of evils such as the Islamic State, militarily.

The first step in this crusade is to have the courage to be intellectually honest about the enemy. Islamists haven't stopped and they will not stop, unless we fight back. So-called tolerance smells like surrender to Islamists, because it is. Jesus did tell us to turn the other cheek, but I'm pretty sure he wasn't advising a secretary of defense at the time. People can slap me on Twitter because of my faith, and I will turn my head and smile. But bring a sword onto my property, into my community, and threaten my culture and country, and I'll turn on you with every weapon at my disposal.

Leftism has made us passive. We can't even imagine, as people did a thousand years ago, raising a sword and carrying a shield with a cross—or an American flag—on it. But there are millions of Islamists who believe they are in a war with us and are willing to die for that belief. They teach their kids that suicide bombers are heroic. They are willing to kill for what they believe. Christian communities in the Middle East are dying by the sword. Christian nations in

Europe are dying a death by a thousand cultural cuts. At what point do we face reality and deal with the fact that American and Christian culture is under attack and the outcome is far from certain?

America is the greatest country on Earth, but today—because of what leftists are doing to us—we are not even close to Islam in our coherence or resolve. Islamism may be many things, but it is not weak.

PART THREE

THE FIGHT

"The philosophy of the schoolroom in one generation becomes the philosophy of government in the next."

—President Abraham Lincoln

"Israel has hypnotized the world, may Allah awaken the people and help them see the evil doings of Israel."

—Representative Ilhan "Somali" Omar

THIRTEEN

THE FRONT LINES: EDUCATION AND ISRAEL

Take a moment to consider the overwhelming evidence laid out in this book, and before our eyes, of ongoing and effective leftist depravity. As an honest, sensible patriot, ask yourself if this is a threat that can be ignored, managed, or negotiated with. Was winning an election in 2016 enough to ensure the perpetuation of a free and prosperous America? Or will winning another in 2020 be?

In your hearts, you know the answer. And you know our time is now. This part of the book is vital because it lays out the strategy we must employ in order to defeat America's internal enemies. Though they are important and amusing, "owning the libs" on social media, donating to candidates, and voting are not enough. As American Crusaders who want to fight and win, where should we start?

Allow me to suggest a three-word answer: education, education, education.

It's never too early or too late to make education your focus. It's something you can impact right where you are. No age is unreachable; no school, principal, or teacher is untouchable; and no arena is too small.

The reason that invading the realm of education sounds too simple is that it is. We spend so much time focused on outrage *du jour* that we overlook the very battle that can be most transformative for future generations. Yes, I'm talking about education in the classroom but not just that venue; I'm also talking about education in our homes, in our culture, and in our churches.

America wins when its story is taught—because it is based on truth, common sense, and human nature.

The story of America, when told, is a beautiful, blessed, and undeniably good story of human freedom—a miracle, really. The stories of the Bible, when told, provide timeless insight into human nature, moral values, and real miracles. And the story of free enterprise, when told, reminds people that the economic prosperity we enjoy did not magically appear; it is grounded in time-tested, tangible principles. We know these things are true. We learned them and love them. But entire generations of Americans are growing up without ever being introduced to these stories. The stories *must* be told, and that job is up to us.

Electoral miracles such as what happened in 2016 are not enough to stave off the purposefully programmed ignorance that government schools are feeding future voters. A handful of patriotic, but hugely outnumbered, teachers is not enough, either. As long as the Left controls educational institutions, the indoctrination will continue. When students are actually introduced to the truth—of Christ, country, and commerce—they recognize it and are drawn to it. People are not stupid; they are quite intuitive and thirsty for truth. But if they are never taught, they can be deceived.

We should have seen this coming. President Ronald Reagan wanted to abolish the newly formed Department of Education. Why? At a first and superficial glance, it sounds as though Reagan—or anyone else who considered the idea—was *against* education. The liberals whined, "Reagan hates kids!" But the reality was the exact opposite. Reagan understood the long game of the Left. He realized that when we "federalize" education, we weaponize it—and we put that weapon into the hands of pro-government elitists. Whatever "good intentions" led to the creation of the Department of Education and countless other state and federal bureaucracies created "for the children" would eventually be fully infected by leftism. That has happened.

In this American Crusade, issue number one must be education. Education is literally the front line. We are in a daily battle for the minds, souls, and hearts of future and current generations. Children, teenagers, high schoolers, college kids, and young adults all require an aggressive and intentional focus on education—and, for some, reeducation. We need to share the common sense that will unclog their brains, share the faith that fortifies their souls, and share the stories of human flourishing that fill their wallets. In 2016, just enough sixty-six-year-old patriots who were raised on a steady diet of freedom, faith, and free markets nudged the election in our favor. In 2020 and beyond, the twenty-six-year-olds are pulling us into Bernie-land. They have been indoctrinated, and we must save them—and their posterity.

THE *OTHER* PLEDGE OF ALLEGIANCE

Let's start with an example most of us can relate to—an honest question that we all need to answer. For those of us who attended college—or have kids in college—why is our allegiance to our alma mater so strong? I get it—we had good times on campus, we met lifelong friends we drank beer with, and we like cheering for our sports teams. And we want to support our kids or grandkids. But when was the last time you stepped back and looked at what that college or university actually stands for? Have you read the alumni newsletter? Attended events? Or looked at the classes the college offers? Unless you went, or sent your kids, to Liberty University, Hillsdale College, College of the Ozarks, West Point, or a handful of other schools, you will be mortified. If you still hold out hope that your school is the exception, take a few minutes and investigate. It's *your beloved school*, too! I promise you will question your allegiance.

Higher education is an insane asylum. You should know this already, but in case you have been blindly supporting your alma mater or the school of your offspring, you should know that the lunacy of sheer leftism is no longer confined to the Ivy League, UC-Berkeley, and University of Wisconsin–Madison. Every single school in between—large, small, public, private, Division I, II, or III, "religious" or secular, urban or rural—have become indoctrination camps. *All of them.* Your favorite school is not the exception to the rule. Your tuition dollars, your class dues, and the money you throw at the sports programs all go to further indoctrination.

Let me be very blunt: if you financially support your alma mater—or that of your kids—you are funding the enemy. *You* are funding the enemy. Why are you pumping dollars and support to a school that already has a massive endowment and then uses its influence to poison the next generation?

Stop! Stop now. Stop sending your money. And stop sending your kids.

This is a start, but crusading means taking the next step. Send your diplomas back. Mail them back—return to sender. *Thank you for the "education," but I can no longer support your leftist cause.* Then explain why. When the time is right—mark my words—Harvard

University will be getting the diploma it gave me back from me. Probably Princeton, too. When you send your diploma back, post it on Facebook and Instagram, tell everyone why, and ask, "Why don't you?"

If you just can't quit your alma mater, at least stop funding the school directly and start sending money to the groups on the campus that are fighting against the indoctrination. I guarantee you that they have a need for your money *way more* than the school does. Give to the conservative campus newspaper, the thriving Christian organization, the free-market business group, or the ROTC program on campus that could use a boost. Anything but the school; it's like giving straight to the Democrat Party—or actually the Socialist Party.

I never "pledged allegiance" to Princeton or Harvard. I went to both institutions before I truly understood the destructive nature of higher education, and frankly, I was still caught up in the "elite" rat-race narrative. I would never go again and will not encourage my kids to go. Yes, some students can be "salt and light" in these leftist bastions, and I support them. But most kids get gobbled up by the groupthink, because it's easier to compromise than to stick out like a conservative sore thumb.

Americanism is alive and well at some colleges and universities where the level of leftist infection is relatively contained. Seek them out. Support them. But otherwise, you need to know exactly what you are sending your kids and grandkids into. They are going into ideological war zones. If you don't teach them before they hit campus, you've already failed. If they're not ready, don't send them. I've met too many conservative parents who, predictably, bemoan children who left their households as patriotic conservatives and came back from college as America-hating socialists. I meet them at every event I do and every *FOX & Friends* diner I broadcast from. There are plenty of educational alternatives in today's information economy; a traditional college degree is not worth nearly what it was decades ago. Don't send your kids to a college and hope for the best; you might as well just register them as democratic socialists now. It would be faster and cheaper.

If your kids have already left college and are leaning toward leftism, you still have a chance. Yes, reality might mug them when they start paying taxes, but don't take the chance. Start by introducing them to Dennis Prager's PragerU videos on YouTube. Pick any topic they are misinformed on, and send them the corresponding five-minute video. Every subject is covered, and the research is bulletproof. You'll at least trigger a conversation; or, even better, I've met countless young adults who changed their worldview after watching the truth laid before them. A virtual degree from Prager University is worth exponentially more than most four-year degrees in America today.

COMMON SENSE VERSUS COMMON CORE

Let's continue down the delusion train. I hear this all the time: "I know there are lots of bad public schools in America, but my public school is excellent! I know the principal and some of the teachers and they're such good people. A few teachers are even secret conservatives." Question: Why do the conservatives think they have to hide? You know why. Because they are surrounded by Democrats and leftists who keep them in the closet. Just like the "I hate Congress, but I really like my congressman" that political pollsters often hear, parents fall into the same trap. "It's not *my* school." If you find yourself saying that, you, my friend, are lying to yourself. A lot of people assume that the bad schools are those "other" schools—inner-city schools, rural schools, underfunded schools. But the problem is *your* school. In fact, usually, it's the so-called elite public schools that are the *worst*—driven by leftist ideologues racing to create the most "woke" school district in the area.

I'll admit that in my blended family of seven kids, two of my kids currently attend public schools. I feel really guilty about it. We want to get them out as soon as possible, and we will, but at the beginning we were lying to ourselves, too. When they first enrolled in public school, we made the same excuses you do. "The school district is so great, it has such high test scores." Or "I pay all this money in property taxes, I should use the schools." Or "They just built a brand-new middle school. It's beautiful—even nicer than the local private school. And they give kids free iPads!" I'm here to tell you that *none of this matters.* Schoolwide test scores don't matter. Property taxes will be confiscated either way. New buildings don't teach your kids; teachers and curriculum do. And what is on those iPads? Not the Bible or an America-friendly version of American history; they're full of secularism and "racially appropriate" mathematics.

For those with kids in public schools who want to raise God-fearing citizens, sometimes you can't move your kids right away. I totally get that. You then have to work double overtime to overcome the poison pumped into their impressionable minds. The "isms" of previous chapters are the new lodestars of these schools. The "Tommy's Got Two Mommies" stories start in kindergarten. Grievance history starts in grade school. Overcoming the social indoctrination can be done, but it's incredibly counterproductive. You wake up, feed your kids, get them dressed, send them off to Democrat Camp, and then—pray. After school, they're tired, you're tired, they're busy, you're busy—and the cycle repeats itself. When do you deprogram them?

I'm not trying to make you feel guilty. I'm just as guilty! I forget to ask my kids what they studied at school that day or can't find the time to follow up with administrators when something looks amiss.

You can't wage cultural war on everyone all the time. I'm simply urging you to use common sense and consider the hard truths of today's public schools. Time is precious. What are your kids learning?

Remember, public schools are government schools. And just as Ronald Reagan warned, they have been taken over and weaponized. Common sense and local control, grounded in patriotism and excellence, have been replaced by Common Core standards and federal control, grounded in leftism. The leftists have been slowly taking over our schools and have used Obama's Common Core standards to accelerate their efforts, all in the name of equality. Today forty-one US states use Common Core, aided by federal dollars.

The Left purports to champion equality in education, but it's just a talking point—or a means to ram their leftist agenda down the throats of students. For this very reason, fighting for school choice is a no-brainer. It is the most transformational tactic toward equality. School choice leaves the decision of schooling to the family—parents and kids vote with their feet for the best possible school: public, charter, or private. Government education dollars—yes, vouchers!—follow the kids instead of going automatically to the local school. The best schools get bigger, and the worst schools go away—or have to improve in order to compete. This is the most straightforward way we could enable families in every financial situation to have a real choice.

That said, most of the "fancy" and "elite" *private* schools are just as "woke" as public schools. Private *does not equal better.* Finding an America-loving, history-teaching, excellence-demanding school is, first and foremost, the responsibility of parents. We are the gate-keepers. Consider how much time we spend picking vacation spots, dinner preferences, or our next big purchase. If we spent a fraction of that time, energy, and money examining the educational options of our kids, we'd find a better option than our local government school.

My wife and I just found an alternative for our two kids in public schools, and we will send them next year. We owe it to them.

But the quest is not easy. It's costly in terms of both time and money. It's unfair; you pay taxes! And it's really difficult. But it's common sense. The choice is, basically, between handing your kids over to leftist Democrats for twelve grades and taking back the power. There are exceptions, of course—especially in single-parent households and when both parents are employed—and there are many ways to make your public school better. But if you have the financial means or parenting space, the solution is pretty straightforward: homeschooling or sending your kids to a Christian or classical school that reinforces your values. Thankfully the stigma surrounding homeschooling has almost completely disappeared, and there are many resources that make it easier than ever. Academic cooperatives, internet learning, and shared athletic teams have grown and are widely available. Homeschooling is less difficult than you think—and I've never met a parent who regrets the investment.

If we choose to skip fighting in the realm of education, then we will always fight a retrograde action. Instead of holding ground and advancing Americanism, we'll be on the defense—and trying to deprogram kids who aren't taught the basic building blocks of logic and knowledge. I literally can't figure out how to do the Common Core math homework my third grader brings home from his government school. He's also not taught phonics but instead "experiential reading" and "personal exploration." Rather than learning how to form a sentence, he is encouraged to blather on the page about his emotions. Spelling, grammar, and critical thinking are all afterthoughts. Don't worry, "inclusive grading" is a new multiculturalist invention—so regardless of how poorly he does, he'll be okay. But he's white and "privileged," so maybe not.

Last year in Fairfax County, Virginia, the school district replaced its "chief academic officer" with a "chief equity officer." The same is happening across the country, as excellence is replaced by equity. True freedom says we can realize both excellence and equal opportunity, but that's probably too difficult for government schools to handle. "Gifted" and "talented" programs in government schools are being ended across the country because they're not sufficiently equitable—hat tip to New York City Mayor Bill de Blasio, who did just that. If some kids are allowed to excel, it widens the learning gap—so it's better to keep everyone down. The Seattle public schools just announced that traditional math is "racist," producing a report that included such profound questions as "Who gets to say if an answer is right?" and "How is math manipulated to allow inequality and oppression to persist?" Remember the line about the soft bigotry of low expectations? That is the essence of Common Core.

BULLYING BULLSHIT

In addition to the curriculum, "diversity" obsession, and never-ending climate change agenda, our schools are pushing a worldview that tells kids they are helpless victims to be shielded, coddled, and protected in every instance. The Left has seized onto a very powerful, anti-man tool: antibullying campaigns. When I was a boy, the term "bullying" was reserved for situations involving legitimate physical threats and actual violence. I was bullied, probably for good reason, actually, and I had to deal with it—learning from the fear, managing it, and overcoming it. My parents helped me deal with it, too. Today, schools encourage kids to see bullies behind every conflict. If a boy is too aggressive, he's bullying. If there's a disagreement, someone's the bully. And for every bully, there's a victim. My kids have come home from school saying they were bullied. I asked them what had happened and discovered it hadn't actually been bullying. I told them to shut up and deal with the issue.

I know that every generation says that kids these days are soft. But more than any previous American generation, kids today are actually conditioned to be helpless bed wetters. If kids do not develop some emotional resilience, they will be totally screwed when they go into the real world and have a tough boss or an unfair workplace. As a political tool, training kids to identify as victims sets up the pitch that "the government will take care of you." In case the true purpose of the antibullying efforts isn't clear, that's it.

The genderism lobby has long used "antibullying" as a cloak for its agenda, suggesting that anyone who doesn't sufficiently honor gay or transgender "pride" is threatening or bigoted. In their minds, real tolerance is not enough; unless you are celebrating, you are bullying. My current home state of New Jersey has taken this view to an entirely new level, launching a pilot program to try out a new LGBTQ curriculum for grammar, history, social studies, and—somehow—science and math classes. The curriculum will be *mandatory* by the 2020–21 school year, and parents will *not* be able to opt out. The indoctrination starts in fifth grade, but observers believe that it will soon start much earlier. If we kept some of our kids in government schools, they would soon be taught this. If they question it, *they* will be marked as bullies.

Overall, any form of conflict—including *perceived* conflict—sets off sirens today. And with boys, anything from name-calling to chivalry brings shrieks of "toxic masculinity." The tragedy is that we're not equipping kids to deal with the realities of life. The world is full of *real* bullies, not someone who made fun of your shirt but bullies with actual sticks, stones, guns, and bombs. We must equip boys and girls to confront those who seek to harm them. But that would require acknowledging that strength, including masculine strength, is inherently a good thing, a positive force in society. The best way to stop a bully is to be a strong male with a good heart or a courageous girl willing to stand up to the "mean girls." My kids will never be allowed to be bullies, and they'd better stand up to them—especially for kids who can't defend themselves. I'm not saying that bullying doesn't matter; I'm saying we're addressing it backward.

In my first book, IN THE ARENA, I wrote a great deal about raising kids with toughness, grittiness, courage, industriousness, and fortitude. In addition to civic-mindedness, free societies require men and women who live the martial values. And in the schools of yesteryear, it was okay to foster and encourage those values. No more. Walk your local public school hallways, and you'll see what schools really emphasize written all over the walls and halls: diversity, inclusivity, environmentalism, peace, self-esteem, and respect. Respect? That sounds great, and it is. My kids will be respectful of their teachers or pay the price. But that's not what is often reinforced. Instead, kids are taught to respect themselves, and the teachers bend to that will.

On the Left Coast, California passed a law in 2019 prohibiting schools to suspend students who are willfully disruptive and unruly. This is becoming the norm. In classrooms across the country— including my kids'—teachers are handcuffed and the kids run the show. Discipline is tepid because kids are coddled; they can't endure any bullying, unless they are the ones bullying the teacher.

Parents, please don't fall into the trap of "my kid is special" when it comes to respect for authority. If a teacher yells at your kid and gives him or her a punishment, reinforce the consequences of his or her actions—unless the punishment is a form of ideological indoctrination; that's an entirely different story. Kids are not wise human beings; they are minions who need to be forged. Government schoolteachers can't really do that anymore, so it's up to us, as it always has been.

CRUSADING FOR EDUCATION

I used to run an Iraq War veterans' organization called Vets for Freedom. In 2007, we brought a group of highly decorated war veterans to my former high school as part of a nationwide tour. We were invited by the principal to speak in front of the students—a few civics classes, not even the entire school. As we always did, we invited the local member of congress (in this case, Michele Bachmann) as well as local officials. The idea was to create an event where students could hear from veterans who had actually been in the war.

At other tour stops, we gave speeches aimed at building support for the war by talking about what was really happening on the ground. We would talk about the politics of war. But we made exceptions at school events; we would talk only about service and sacrifice and tell the stories of brave warriors. We understood the sensibilities of public schools, so we were very careful to reassure the principal that there would be no politics.

Just hours before the event was supposed to start, the principal, who was a friend of mine, called to tell me the event had been canceled. I was shocked. *Why in the world?* Well, it turned out that two or three parents—or maybe even *one* parent—from the school had called him to complain. I was told that one had threatened to stage a protest across the street from the school. A couple of parents had called to complain, and the principal had folded, canceling the event—a veterans' event in a patriotic town!

Here is the reason this matters so much. The principal was a friend and a good guy—from a conservative, pro-veteran school district. He was not and is not antiveteran or anti-American. In fact, he loves veterans and is a patriotic guy. But he canceled the event because government school administrators like him want one thing: to keep their jobs. They want no friction. They want no controversy. They want their job, and they want their pension. They never want to rock the boat. They fear nothing more than the "mob" showing up at their school. So when a few parents complained, he caved in, hoping it would all go away.

Instead, the opposite happened. We made sure that the local and national media knew about the story, and soon "Veterans blocked from high school" was splashed atop Drudge Report and across FOX News television screens. In the span of a few hours, the principal received thousands of angry phone calls—from both inside and outside the school district. It had not been my intention to berate him, but it was also a snub that could not be allowed to stand. We called out the cancellation for what it was—administrative cowardice resulting in blocking veterans from speaking at a public school in a patriotic community—and the principal was subjected to the very firestorm he had been hoping to avoid.

I remember driving out of Minnesota on our tour bus—televisions tuned to FOX News coverage of our snubbing—when my dear mother called me and said, "You have to make this stop, Pete! This is our community. We have to live here. You just drive in, light it on fire, and then leave!" The principal's voice mail box was full, and his phone was ringing off the hook. National media were running the story. He regretted his decision but couldn't undo it. I understand where my mom was coming from but disagreed with her very understandable sentiment. My agitation was new to her then; she's used to it now. Love you, Mom!

She spoke for a lot of people. Everyone, including myself, was made uncomfortable by the friction. Friends take sides. Jobs are threatened. Communities disagree. The lesson I learned from that was simple but extremely powerful. Agitation works! It's effective. A couple of personal phone calls were enough to change the mind of a school administrator. These are not courageous people—they have power in their fiefdoms, but they are not commanders in the 101st Airborne—they are *very* susceptible to both private pressure and public scrutiny.

The principal canceled the event, but our response had the larger consequence of making sure that the next time a veterans' group wants to hold an event at that high school, it's going to happen— even if someone complains. A few liberal complaints were effective, but in the long run, the collective pressure of thousands of patriots is even more effective. We have the numbers and the right stance; we simply need to stand up. Pressure works. Complaining works. Showing up works.

You need to be the one complaining. Leftists use this tactic extremely effectively; let's use the tactic right back at them. You need to be the one who calls the principal, who calls out the teacher, who shows up at the school board meeting. This isn't about making friends, this is about saving the country, dammit. We need to be the agitators—because the don't-rock-the-boat administrators are scared of agitation. If we complain and lose, we expose the insanity even more and we get others to complain—until the issue is too big to ignore.

That said, don't expect the same reaction that leftists get. When we conservatives complain, our grievances get second-class status. We are not in one of the leftists' self-proclaimed protected classes. As an example, I vigorously complained when the "holiday" program at one of my kids' schools made absolutely no reference to Christmas. I wasn't asking for a religious program, just a simple recognition of the reason for the season. The principal wrote me back, defending the school. He used all the familiar arguments. The program was already over; there wasn't much I could do. But this fall, I will be reaching out in advance to preemptively complain. We'll see what happens (if my kids are still in that school, after all).

The time is ripe. Our preschools, elementary schools, middle schools, high schools, and colleges are so infected with leftism that they've lost their common sense. So we have to fight back with commonsense Americanism. We are not debating the finer points of educational philosophy; we are fighting for the basics. Do your schools say the Pledge of Allegiance every day? If not, why the hell not? Start an effort to restore that—and dare your administrators to explain why they won't. If they refuse, they will look like the leftist loons they are. Then take it to the school board—and beyond.

To this point, stepping up should not be just reactionary. Don't look only for infuriating things that happen; be on the lookout for basics that are *not* happening. Do your schools teach capitalism? If not, why not? It's our economic system—why the hell would we not teach it? You know your school celebrates Earth Day and Gay Pride Day—but does it celebrate Patriot Day on September 11? Where is the Veterans Day event? How does the school leverage Constitution Day to highlight our founders? Ask questions. Demand straight answers. When the inevitable "holiday play" comes around, ask why Christmas is not included. *The school can't even mention Christmas?* Challenge the charade, and then see how many Christian parents join you. The number will be more than you imagine. Lots of people are thinking—and whispering—about these issues; they just need an agitator to make the first private, then public, comments.

Pick an issue, pick a day, stand on a hill, and dare the school to be against it. If the school still refuses to be transparent, call the local news station and newspaper. Raise hell on social media. Start a petition to call the principal. If nobody is listening, take it to your city council or state representative. Any action is better than sitting back and allowing the shallow currents of leftism to control the conversation. Remember, most administrators are cowards. They don't want any agitation, and they can't defend the indefensible.

Schools these days are run by the kids anyway; use that to your advantage. If you have a strong son, daughter, or grandchild who is patriotic and willing to take a stand, encourage him or her to do so. What better civics lesson could there be? They could rally students to wear patriotic T-shirts, or start a petition, asking their principals to celebrate our veterans on Veterans Day or pass out flags on Flag Day. Given a clear mission, kids are courageous—and effective. Look how climate change "walkouts" have amassed influence; use similar tactics to educate fellow students and expose the Left's agenda.

All we have to do is wake up to what is right in front of us, muster the courage to call it out, and stand firm in one immutable patriotic truth: that it's more important to do the right thing for your country than to be liked by parents who are blinded by the status quo. In the process of doing the right thing, you'll actually persuade many people who never thought to speak up.

I get it; taking such a stance can be really uncomfortable. But I've never, ever met a person who stood up and regretted it. Talk to patriots who have made a stand; they will say that it wasn't easy, and they did lose friends. But they never regret it, and they gain even more friends before all is said and done. And like anything else in life, standing up the first time is always the most difficult. It gets easier—and more effective—each time. You will learn what works and what doesn't. Your ranks will grow, and so will your influence. The school, the teachers, the principal will come to know your name—and they will think twice when they try their next leftist social experiment.

Activism on education is, I believe, the most useful form of active citizenship—taking local actions that have national consequences. By saving your kids' classroom, you are ultimately saving America—and the free world.

THE STATE OF ISRAEL

You might ask, What in the world does the State of Israel have to do with any of this? I live in the United States; why is Israel the "front line"?

Simply put: if you don't understand why Israel matters and why it is so central to the story of Western civilization—with America being its greatest manifestation—then you don't live in history. America's story is inextricably linked to Judeo-Christian history and the modern state of Israel. You can love America without loving Israel—but that tells me your knowledge of the Bible and Western civilization is woefully incomplete. If you're going to crusade, you need to know the totality of your mission.

This brief section is not intended to provide a full defense of Israel; but as an aspiring American Crusader, consider it homework. A great place to start, once again, is PragerU. Check out videos such as "Why Don't You Support Israel?," "Israel's Legal Founding," and "Why Does America Spend So Much on Israel?" After that, read *A Durable Peace: Israel and Its Place Among the Nations* by Benjamin Netanyahu. You'll quickly realize the depth of connection among education, Israel, and Americanism.

If you love America, you should love Israel. We share history, we share faith, and we share freedom. We love free people, free expression, and free markets. And whereas America is blessed with two big, beautiful oceans to protect it, Israel is surrounded on all sides by countries that either used to seek, or still seek, to wipe the nation off the map.

Israel is enemy number one for both Islamists and international leftists—which is reason alone to love it. The underlying reason for their hatred is anti-Semitism. Remember, fascism, Nazism, and socialism have never been "right-wing" ideologies; they are, and always have been, expressions of leftism. Hatred of Jews has a long history among leftists, and Islamists are sworn to subjugate and kill any Jew they can find. I learned that lesson firsthand in the wake of the Golden Mosque bombing in 2006 when I was serving in Iraq. On our first patrol into the city after the Al Qaeda attack, mosque loudspeakers were blasting one message: the mosque had been bombed by the Americans—and Jews. I remember thinking *There isn't a Jew within five hundred miles of Samarra—yet they get the blame?*

Welcome to the Middle East and college campuses. Today, as in Samarra, anti-Semitism is alive and well among our country's "elites" as they wage an unrelenting campaign to boycott, divest, and sanction (BDS) the state of Israel. The BDS movement, masked as a campaign for "human rights," was established by major Palestinian terrorist organizations in 2001 as a "nonmilitary" way to eradicate Israel. The goal is always the same: to eradicate the Jewish state. America's college campuses are full of groups pushing the BDS agenda.

The battle wages on Israeli soil as well. With each trip I take to Israel for *FOX Nation*, and on my personal time, I discover a new way in which Islamists and their leftist enablers seek to deny Jewish history and heritage. Today, Islamists in Jerusalem are attempting to claim that the Holy Temple built by King Solomon and rebuilt by Herod never existed. Apparently, they want us all to believe that Jews—from Abraham to Jesus—never sacrificed, built, or worshipped on that particular piece of real estate. "Temple denial" is yet another tool by which they seek to erase the Jews and the Jewish state. If that isn't delusional enough, on a recent trip to Bethlehem—

the birthplace of Jesus—I discovered that Palestinians now claim that Jesus was not in fact Jewish but instead a Palestinian. Try that one on for size—or watch my two *FOX Nation* documentaries on the subject: *Battle in the Holy City* and *Battle in Bethlehem*.

But if you don't know your Bible or your history, you might be seduced by these claims. As our founders understood, freedom without faith is untenable and unsustainable. The front lines of America are the front lines of our faith—which are Jerusalem and Israel.

I've been to Israel seven or eight times, and each time I am drawn deeper and deeper in my connection to both its biblical centrality and its modern relevancy. As a Baptist boy from the Midwest, I grew up with stories from the Bible but did not understand why they mattered so much to the larger world. Sorry, I was young and naive; Israel was a story, not geography. No more; now I understand. The story of Israel is a story of liberation and freedom, the same as America's.

With the right principles, freedom can thrive anywhere in the world. As we've seen, too many areas in the United States have rejected our founding principles. If we're going to survive, we're going to have to connect with freedom-loving people in other nations. We have domestic enemies, and we have international allies. It's time to reach out to people who value the same principles, relearn lessons from them, and form stronger bonds. Israel is the front line of this international bond. Thank God that President Trump and Israeli prime minister Netanyahu have made that bond stronger than ever.

After suffering the horrors of the European Holocaust—in which more than 6 million Jews were killed by the German socialists—the state of Israel was finally (re)established. Since that day, Israel has been attacked from all sides. If you read the Bible, you know that the Jewish people are far from perfect. God makes that abundantly clear. But God also stands with the people of Israel against their enemies and blesses those who bless Israel (Genesis 12:1–3). Israel continues to vanquish its Islamist foes—thanks to the big, beautiful wall and big, beautiful army it has built. Those fighting on the wrong side, the Islamists, are constantly getting their asses kicked—and they despise the Jewish people for defending themselves. America should stand with Israel because we honor God and love freedom.

Israel is an icon of freedom. But more than that, it is a living, breathing embodiment of freedom. Israel is the front line of Western civilization, a testimony to how life, liberty, and the pursuit of happiness can transform an embattled region and provide a standard of living unmatched elsewhere in the Middle East.

And that fact terrifies those on the left who hate America and Israel. That's why, in their minds, the nation must be condemned and destroyed. Because free people, guided by faith, are the exact opposite of what the Left wants. For us as American Crusaders, Israel embodies the soul of our American Crusade—the "why" to our "what." Faith, family, freedom, and free enterprise; if you love those, learn to love the state of Israel. And then find an arena in which to fight for her.

With the front lines identified, let's put a full-on American Crusade into action.

"You are about to embark upon the Great Crusade."

—General Dwight D. Eisenhower, D-Day Eve

FOURTEEN

MAKE THE CRUSADE GREAT AGAIN

Whether you like it or not, you are an "infidel"—an unbeliever—according to the false religion of leftism. You are marked for annihilation. Just like Islamism, you can submit now or later; or you can fight.

Enjoy Western civilization? Freedom? Equal justice under the law? *Thank a crusader.*

Let's make the crusade great again.

From the beginning, two thousand years ago, our Lord and savior Jesus Christ brought peace. His message was—and is—love. His statement in Matthew 10:34, "Do not suppose that I have come to bring peace to the earth. I did not come to bring peace, but a sword," was not a call to arms but a reference to the discord Christians face when they express their devotion. Christianity spread through divine revelation, reasoned persuasion, human mercy, and evangelical travel—followed by centuries of deadly persecution of believers.

It was not until the fourth century *after Christ* that the leader of the most powerful empire in the world converted to the faith and

Christianity picked up a sword. After the Roman emperor Constantine the Great converted to Christianity in the fourth century, that superpower effectively became the *Holy* Roman Empire. Christendom was officially born. The Romans had built military might to advance their power, and now Christians were safe behind the empire's shield. Christianity had a military—to *defend* itself.

Centuries later, the religion of Islam was born. Muhammad, its founder, was the polar opposite of Jesus. Muhammad was a warrior through and through. Islam did not bring peace but instead gained power through coercion and war. Muhammad built and led a vicious army and slaughtered his enemies, promising Paradise to his followers who died fighting for Islam. Islam never needed an army, because Islam *is* an army. Since its founding, with almost no interruption, jihad fed Islam's expansion. "Infidels" like you and me had three options when encountering Muslims: to convert to Islam, pay a submissive tax, or fight—to the death. (Leftism also offers these three options.) Since the seventh century—and up to today—Islam has been on offense.

By the eleventh century, Christianity in the Mediterranean region, including the holy sites in Jerusalem, was so besieged by Islam that Christians had a stark choice: to wage *defensive* war or continue to allow Islam's expansion and face existential war at home in Europe. The leftists of today would have argued for "diplomacy," sending Sir John Kerry to Jerusalem to broker peace by playing guitar with James Taylor. We know how that would have turned out. The pope, the Catholic Church, and European Christians chose to fight—and the crusades were born. Pope Urban II urged the faithful to fight the Muslims with his famous battle cry on their lips: "Deus vult!," or "God wills it!" The moment required followers of Christ to take up the sword in defense of their faith, their families, and their freedom. After centuries of fighting, the tide turned. Christianity in Europe was saved, Jerusalem was liberated, and Christians did not seek further war with Muslims.

During His time on Earth, Jesus was a spiritual warrior; but one thousand years after his crucifixion, his followers were forced to take up the sword to protect their families and in defense of their right to worship Him freely and peacefully. Contrary to what many leftist scholars and Democrats preach, Jesus never taught against self-defense. I'm not romanticizing the crusades; they were bloody and full of corruption, injustice, and unspeakable tragedy, especially against our Jewish friends. I've read the full histories of the crusades; they were complicated, flawed, and anything but clear cut. But the alternative—surrender—would have been horrific for billions of people around the globe.

Again, do you enjoy Western civilization? Freedom? Equal justice? *Thank a crusader.* If not for the crusades, there would have been no Protestant Reformation or Renaissance. There would be no Europe and no America.

But even after being halted by the crusades, Muslims never stopped fighting and expanding, both violently and nonviolently. Their jihad continued and expanded. Meanwhile, the European Church dropped its sword. As the continent became more secular, its resolve to defend itself also vanished. Today, the home of the crusades no longer has a vibrant Church or a fearsome army. Europe was twice bailed out by America in world wars, and the pope today leads interfaith services.

Thankfully, in the sixteenth and seventeenth centuries, another Christian army started sailing to a new continent to escape persecution from the now-corrupted church. Those Christians and freethinkers founded a new nation based on faith, freedom, and equal justice. From the beginning, this Christian nation had to fight for its right to exist, defeating the most powerful empire in the world since the Romans—the United Kingdom—first for independence, then again in the War of 1812.

Today, America has the only powerful, pro-freedom, pro-Christian, pro-Israel army in the world. The *only* one. As we proved in World War I, World War II, and since, we have no interest in taking other nations for our own. General Eisenhower called our effort to liberate Europe "the Great Crusade," correctly alluding to the fact that it was a war of defense and rescue. We in the United States do not try to forcibly convert our enemies; after soundly defeating them, we rebuild them. We don't fight because we hate our enemies and view them as less than human as Islamism does; we fight because we love our God-given freedoms.

Islamism attacked us on 9/11 and on countless other occasions, has infiltrated Europe, and is making inroads in America—thanks to leftists. Likewise, Christians around the globe are being attacked, killed, persecuted, and forced to flee—thanks to Islamists. And leftists couldn't give a damn; if anything, they think that Christians have it coming. Here we are again, just like the time after Muhammad, when peaceful Christians around the world are without an army.

We are surrounded, but we have a choice. One thousand years later, we don't *want* to fight, but we must. We need an American Crusade. Christians—alongside our Jewish friends and freedom-loving people everywhere—need to stand up for our faith, defend our freedom, and defeat leftism in all its forms, including Islamism. The 2020 election is the next battle we must win—but, like our enemies, we need to think bigger and longer term. Our cultural fight requires decisive action on all fronts: locally, nationally, and around the globe.

OUR BATTLE

It's one thing to see a news report of leftist cultural chaos and Islamist terror on the other side of the globe. But, as I've outlined, these threats are no longer outside our borders; they are now in our cities, our institutions, and our culture. Islam remade the Middle East, conquered northern Africa, and almost steamrolled through Europe. Thankfully, for the sake of human freedom everywhere, the crusades slowed its progress. Leftism today is trying to remake America. Will we mount our crusade? Islamists and leftists play the long game, and America is the next step in their geographical regression.

Biblical tenets of freedom, equal justice, and personal responsibility forged the American culture. Not so for leftists or Islamists, who share the goals of dependency, control, and submission. Islamism in Europe, aided by willfully blind leftists, is creating de facto "no-go zones" for infidels. Leftists say that this is a lie, but they are in denial of what is happening on their streets. They also won't look at the available counterevidence: *all modern Muslim countries are either formal or de facto no-go zones for practicing Christians and Jews.*

Leftists and Islamists have another thing in common: they strategize in terms of decades and centuries, not election cycles. As crusaders, to defeat them, we must do both.

I'm not asking you to paint your shield with a crimson cross, but I am asking you to paint your shield with the American flag, understanding fully what that flag stands for. Our American Crusade is not about literal swords, and our fight is not with guns. *Yet.* Until our crusader in chief, Donald Trump, showed up, our leaders were not seriously confronting the leftist invasion. Yes, voting is a weapon, but it's not enough. We cannot outsource or delegate our crusade. Arm yourself—metaphorically, intellectually, and physically. This is, by the way, why the Second Amendment exists. Let me repeat—slowly— for the benefit of leftist readers: I am not advocating any sort of violence in this book. The American Crusade is a war against destructive *ideas*. We are not calling for violence. I *am* saying that our founders would have compelled you to be prepared, because the clash is ongoing and only going to get nastier.

We didn't start this war. But we must win it.

THEY'RE AFTER *YOU*

On December 18, 2019—the day tongue-tied Speaker Nancy Pelosi and the Democrats in the House of Representatives voted to impeach him—President Trump tweeted the following crucial reminder: "In reality, they're not after me, they're after you. I'm just in the way." A few days earlier in a private lunch near the Oval Office, the president had said to my wife and me, "Well, I've been impeached! But you wouldn't know it here." Gesturing his hand around the room, he continued, "We will never stop fighting for the American people."

Truer words were never spoken. The clash of 2020 is going to focus on the reelection of Donald Trump; but the real clash—underneath it all—is for the soul of America. Yes, the leftist media and machine *hate* President Trump—but they hate *you* just as much, if not more. As patriots, we cannot let Trump continually be berated with impunity. Absorbing the daily barrage cannot be his responsibility alone.

It's easy to watch the political circus on television, even for me as a host of the highest-rated cable morning show in America, and think, "Trump's got it. He can defeat them single-handedly." But that's not true. Not even close! We are *all* in the arena now. The leftist talking heads, the shrieking marchers, the deep-state bureaucrats—they're not solely after Trump. They are after what he represents and who he represents. They're after me and you. They are after America.

Right now, President Trump is "in the way" of leftism—standing tall, wielding his Twitter sword. And although he has the most powerful platform in the world, he's still just one man. We need to reelect him in 2020, but imagine what we could accomplish if millions of American Crusaders followed his example in our own arenas. It's been done before.

OUR GATES OF VIENNA

The story of Polish crusaders throwing off the scourge of the USSR in the 1970s and 1980s is remarkable and instructive.

Poland has been a Catholic country for centuries and to this day guards its culture and sovereignty fiercely. However, as the citizens of a satellite nation of the Soviet Union after World War II, the Polish people suffered under decades of godless communist oppression under the guise of "equality." People of faith were persecuted, threatened, and even killed. But since nearly the entirety of the population of Poland identified as Christian, even the Soviet KGB could not extinguish the light of the Church.

At the same time, Polish communist leaders—puppets, traitors, and their enabling squishes—tried to form a "truce" with the Catholic Church on the condition that Christians would stay out of politics. The communists—the leftists—knew that if they could push the faithful outside the public square, they could freely advance their radical political agenda. God was the biggest impediment to complete government control, so God had to be eliminated. Sound familiar?

In a divine moment, Polish cardinal Karol Wojtyła became Pope John Paul II in 1978. The next year, the pope went on a weeklong pilgrimage to his homeland. The public gatherings drew almost one-third of the entire population of Poland; millions heeded his call. The Polish historian Adam Michnik, an atheist from a Jewish family, shared his impressions of that moment, writing, "In June, 1979,

I lived through one of those moments in my life that gave me a sense that I was alive for a reason. . . . I felt absolutely no sense of separation. Alongside me kneeled a Catholic priest, and no one on that square had any intention to divide people. It was natural that we were together." People of faith led the way, joining together with free people of all walks of life, to fight for their political freedom. Unlike in contemporary western Europe, Poles feel no need to separate their culture from Christianity—especially at the altar of "diversity."

About a year later, the Solidarity movement—a freedom-oriented political and social movement—began, led by an electrician and shipyard worker. Lech Wałęsa was not a member of the "elite," but he was a crusader who knew his people were being crushed under the weight of communism. His Solidarity movement was formally outlawed but nonetheless grew to over 10 million Polish citizens. The 1980s in Poland forged a unique alliance against socialism: church leaders, their members, and blue-collar workers. Sound familiar? Meetings in church basements across Poland addressed dreams of representative government and basic human freedoms. Church attendance grew as political engagement grew—and vice versa. Years later, after being surveilled, intimidated, and imprisoned, Wałęsa became the first democratically elected president of a free Poland.

In less than a decade, the power of faithful citizens' prayers and bold actions toppled the communist regime in Poland and ultimately began the domino effect of the collapse of the Soviet Union and its influence around the world. Thank God no one was whining about "separation of church and state" at that precarious moment. Tens of millions of people, in many countries, experienced personal freedom as a result of the church's engagement in their political system. Today Poland stands as a thriving, sovereign, and powerful example of what freedom-loving people can achieve—and maintain—if they respect their citizens enough to protect their borders, battle leftism, and fight for freedom.

Where did this strength of culture come from? Was that Christian strength born of the protest against the godless Soviet bear? Accentuated, yes. Born, no. Where did it come from? The legacy of the crusades. The Poles, part of the Slavic brotherhood of what we call eastern Europe, are no stranger to *slavery*, as all Slavs once were—hence the etymology. If we were to truly place the zenith of Christian strength in the Poles, that strength was born on September 11, 1683, at the gates of Vienna. (The Islamists and their long memory did not pick the date September 11, 2001, out of thin air.) On that day and the next, Poland's King John III Sobieski, the supreme commander of the Christian Coalition Army, and his knights defeated the Ottoman Empire's Islamic Army, ending the advance of Islam onto the continent of Europe. If Vienna had fallen, Muslims would have marched all the way to the Vatican and turned it into a mosque.

The Poles saved Western civilization and European Christendom. North African Christians, just like the Persians and half of India, fell to Islam—never to return. What the Poles recognize is that precious lives and treasure must sometimes be sacrificed to maintain culture, identity, faith, and freedom. Why most of western Europe wants to simply give theirs away for reasons of "guilt" is truly astonishing to most Polish citizens and leaders.

Right now, similar fights exist around our planet. Like the Poles, the freedom-loving citizens of Hong Kong are standing against the Chinese government—taking to the streets, waving the flag of the United States, and singing Christian hymns. Guided by faith, they do so at great personal risk to their lives and futures. If they lose, the communists will control their future.

You and I are not immune to history. Will we show the same courage in 2020 and beyond? What if we don't?

WHAT LOSING LOOKS LIKE

The prospect of losing the 2020 election—and its aftermath—makes me shudder. What if we do lose both? I'll keep this short, because it's too devastating to internalize. We've already seen glimpses of what losing this crusade will bring.

Globalism will erase our borders, sovereignty, and national identity.

Genderism will figuratively and literally turn our boys into girls and our girls into boys.

Socialism will suffocate our economy and bankrupt America—in one generation.

Secularism will bury God under the weight of government, sealing our cultural fate.

Environmentalism will close more of our factories and only make the planet worse.

Elitism will strangle us with political correctness until our thoughts are a crime.

Multiculturalism will magnify our differences, dividing and weakening us.

Islamism will grow and grow until it's powerful enough to grab everything.

Leftism will enslave us all with big government until it's enslaved by Islamism.

The First Amendment will apply only to politically correct leftist talking points, and the Second Amendment will be gone. Babies will be aborted in record numbers, and our schools will teach kids that all of this is a good, and necessary, thing.

America will decline and die. A national divorce will ensue. Outnumbered freedom lovers will fight back. The military and police, both bastions of freedom-loving patriots, will be forced to make a choice. It will not be good. Yes, there will be some form of civil war. It's a horrific scenario that nobody wants but would be difficult to avoid. If America is split, freedom will no longer have an army.

Communist China will rise—and rule the globe. Europe will formally surrender. Islamists will get nuclear weapons and seek to wipe America and Israel off the map. Freedom will fade, tyranny will rise.

This is not fiction, this is a preview. It's also not far-fetched. If our American Crusade does not succeed, not only will America be gone but human freedom will be finished. It won't happen overnight, but it will soon be irreversible. And there is nowhere else to sail to.

FOR GOD AND COUNTRY

Let's be clear about why we're in this fight. Yes, we fight for our God-given freedoms and for our families. But as in every crusade, this battle is for families and citizens we will never know. We fight so others can also be free.

I've had moments in my life when I've known the right thing to do and I was too selfish, too scared, or too naive to do it. I didn't act. I don't live life with regrets, but those moments shaped the decisions I make today. The experiences helped me create a "regret test" that I use for almost any crossroads in life. When facing a difficult choice, I try to step back from a situation, pull myself outside of the immediate blast radius of the decision, and ask: Which choice would I regret making the most? Not just tomorrow but in a year, ten years, or fifty years. The exercise is immediately clarifying. Making the right choice—the righteous choice—is always painful and difficult in the moment, but in the long term, deep down, you know you'll never regret it. You know creating short-term pleasure instead of long-term purpose is an empty proposition (hat tip to Hebrews 12:11). Sure, you'll lose things you enjoy, you'll miss people you love, and you'll endure the pain of change; but, considering what we face today, the last thing I want to be thinking on my deathbed is *What if . . . ?*

If you stand up to local government minions and present a patriotic argument, you might be ostracized. If you question political correctness at your job, you might miss a promotion. If you express your views on social media or organize a petition, one of your close friends—maybe even a family member—might call you a racist. Do you really care? Should you care? Of course not. Your eye is on a bigger prize. You're an American Crusader. It's time to dissolve the residual bonds of superficial relationships and realize that we are part of a larger story, a larger family.

In fact, we should expect this conflict. Earlier in this chapter, I quoted from one of my favorite verses, Matthew 10:34, where Jesus said, in part, "I did not come to bring peace, but a sword." The next verse, however, prepares us for what should come when we heed his message: "For I have come to turn 'a man against his father, a daughter against her mother; a daughter-in-law against her mother-in-law; a man's enemies will be the members of his own household.'" In quoting the Old Testament prophet Micah, Jesus is preparing his followers for what is to come. Jesus continues two verses later, "Whoever does not take up their cross and follow me is not worthy of me."

The same applies to our fight for freedom. Whoever is not willing to pick up the flag and fight for America is not living worthy of the gift our forefathers gave us.

In this cause, I've lost friends. Many. Some members of my extended family have no interest in speaking with me, and the feeling is mutual. People I used to admire send me nasty letters and emails telling me what a terrible person I am. Nonetheless, I've never felt more fulfilled in the fight for freedom, especially when I've applied the "regret test." You will never regret doing the right thing; instead, it's the most clarifying and liberating choice you can make.

When you choose to enter the freedom fight to save your country, your community, your school—on the front best suited to your skills and passion—something else amazing happens: You change. You become freer, bolder, and more clearheaded about what life is about.

When you fall in love with the gift America delivers—individual freedom to pursue our dreams—you want to share it with others who need it most. The American gospel! The pursuit of a cause and the relationships you form will take you to places of worldly fulfillment you would never have anticipated. You'll appreciate timeless, God-breathed truths that you never imagined. You will find reservoirs of energy you never knew you had, and you'll build relationships with wonderful people you never would have found—passionate patriots otherwise segregated from your consciousness.

There is a reason many soldiers who come back from combat become depressed. I did. I drank way too much and didn't want to leave the couch. It's often because when veterans come back to a modern society that's largely purposeless, they cannot find the sense of meaning and brotherhood that fulfilled and sustained them on the battlefield. It's understandable for all the reasons this book has outlined: our culture is becoming distracted, shallow, and trivial. However, when you get back to first principles, love the people around you, and love the pursuit of a cause that's bigger than you, it sets you back onto a "deployment" mind-set. You're back on the battlefield, here at home, with people you love and a clear sense of purpose.

I believed in the mission we had in Iraq and loved the daily grind. It was purposeful, focused, and fulfilling. Thankfully, I was able—eventually—to find similar arenas on this side of the pond. The American Crusade, with President Trump as our leader, is a pitch-perfect way to kindle or rekindle a mission greater than ourselves: the mission of America.

In the crusades of a thousand years ago, most of the fighters were common folks with no military experience at all. Sure, they were led by lords and knights, but the crusades could not have been waged or won without thousands of everyday Christians who relished having the chance to be a part of something much larger than themselves. The American Crusade is no different. This fight requires common sense, deeply held values, faith, and grittiness. We will have to do the heavy lifting. There is no certification or permission needed, no barrier to entry. What our fight requires is the same as what our founders wrote in the Declaration of Independence: to pledge our lives, our fortunes, and our sacred honor.

You don't have to be president or on television to fight and win. In fact, in the battle to recapture education, culture, and politics, you can do more than most. The first step is to stop being impressed by leftist-corrupted institutions. Free yourself from their brainwashing, and embrace freethinking. Have disdain for Ivy League snobbery. Despise the "elite" media and their self-righteousness. Detest feckless politicians—almost all of them. I used to look up to them almost as superheroes. Now I'm skeptical until proven wrong—because the majority of elected officials are weak, self-interested, and unworthy of trust.

Disdain, despise, detest, distrust—pick your d-words. But all of this must lead to action.

The leftist media want you to think that you and your like-minded friends are basically alone in what you believe. Polling is one way they try to sell this narrative. The truth is, you're part of a majority. Pick your title—moral majority, silent majority, or angry majority. They all apply. When you hear how impossible it is for Trump to win in 2020, remember 2016. "Trump will never be president," said Barack Obama,

Harry Reid, Bernie Sanders, Nancy Pelosi, Elizabeth Warren, Stephen Colbert, Rosie O'Donnell, George Clooney, Bill Maher, David Plouffe, and almost every "expert" in the left-wing legacy media.

When you decide to run for school board or city council—and work your ass off to win—remember 2016. Leftists want you to quit, because they are afraid that you won't fail.

Action inspires action. Courage multiplies courage. If we take action, we will turn the tide. When we stand up to the absolute idiocy of political correctness, others will see that the PC emperor has no clothes—and no argument. Others are inspired.

Either we win, or they win. And we can win—not "barely" but decisively—in the 2020 election and in our local communities in the years beyond. Here is what winning requires.

YOU

The American Crusade can be won, but not through "negotiation." Stale thinking and bipartisan "consensus" have betrayed us. This moment requires a total commitment to victory, which includes co-opting the successful tactics the Left has used for years. We must be smart, tough, proactive, and bold.

A great example is the work of Project Veritas and its undercover videos that expose the true motivation of leftists. It single-handedly shut down one of the most powerful and corrupt leftist organizations in America, the Association of Community Organizations for Reform Now, or ACORN, revealed the horrors of Planned Parenthood, exposed bias at CNN, and showed the world that organizers for Socialist Bernie Sanders secretly love gulags. They will do more. This is guerrilla warfare—real "journalism"—in the cause of Truth.

Another organization, TalNexus, is a liberty-oriented nonprofit in Hollywood that develops young conservative talent for careers in the entertainment industry. One of the projects it helped fund was a short film on Chairman Mao's horrific famine—and it was nominated for an Oscar! Imagine the horrors of communism on *Netflix*!

Yet another is Convention of States, a grassroots organization of patriots committed to triggering an "amending convention" to our Constitution by passing resolutions in the requisite number of state legislatures. The goal: to shrink the size and scope of the federal government, empower states' rights, and unleash individual liberty. Our founders gave us Article V of the Constitution for such a moment as this. There's no better organization for a crusader to join.

But as crusaders, we need to think about the areas in which we typically fall short, such as culture, media, and law. It is a fantastic thing that the Federalist Society aggressively populates our judiciary and law school faculties with originalist judges and professors. Instead of cutting a check to your alma mater, how about cutting one to Project Veritas, TalNexus, Convention of States, or the Federalist Society? Like them, we must expand the fight to all fronts of our culture.

Perhaps you know a right-leaning youngster with artistic talent or a bold camera wiz with a penchant for guerrilla journalism. Maybe you know a bold young patriotic entrepreneur. Their atypical pursuits need our financial encouragement. They need our moral support. Highly creative types have usually been swayed away from Americanism, so it is important that we champion these unique fighters.

Find these bold talents—maybe you are one of them?—and back them. We need to, as Project Veritas says, "Be brave. Do something." It will take squadrons of conservative storytellers, activists, and journalists willing to infiltrate existing left-wing institutions, subvert them, and eventually take them over—just as the Left has done since the 1960s.

Perhaps you don't have a creative bone in your body. Maybe you're not a millionaire able to fund conservative movies. My humble suggestion is to avoid engaging in a mere "war of ideas" with others online. Yes, our ideas work and leftist policies do not. But even if we win every social media debate, we lose ground everywhere else. That's because leftists don't really care about ideas; they care about power. That's why they ban us. So while we debate principles, they take over human resources departments, the faculty lounge, school boards, church boards, local committees, and town councils. We have the *principles*, but they have the *positions*. What President Trump is facing in the DC swamp (think Brett Kavanaugh) is similar to what we are facing locally. Fights over personnel and positions are crucial. Either you personally need to be the candidate for the board of regents, blue-ribbon commission, or school board, or you need to fight like hell to make sure those positions are denied to anti-American leftists.

If you are young (or not), get married and have children. Nothing more thoroughly develops empathy for future generations, and therefore the country, than making yourself directly responsible for your spouse and offspring. As previously stated, Europe suffers from plunging birth rates, which the globalists have used as a reason to import unskilled, noncontributing Islamist throngs from the Middle East. Even if you cannot run for office, aren't a millionaire, or have no creative talents, you *can* have a family of five or more. There is no higher responsibility.

If you are a male, your most important job is to be a good dad—no matter what your relationship status. Mothers, we know how important you are! Together, get those kids into Sunday School. Read books to them. Educate them about the miracle of America's founding. Protect them from evil—in all its forms. Childhood trauma and weak parents are a mental breeding ground for leftism. But if you love your spouse (and show it), care for your kids (and show it), you will strengthen the American fabric more than any politician or billionaire could dream of doing. You don't have to be perfect to do these things—Lord knows I'm aware of that—you just have to be intentional.

If you aren't old enough to lead a household, follow the lead of fourteen-year-old Charlie Hecht, who took home the "Unsung Hero Award" at the *FOX Nation* Patriot Awards I emceed in 2019. He noticed that his Virginia neighborhood was woefully lacking in American flags; so he started the "Patriotism Project" and partnered with Lowe's, which offered 20 percent off flags for anyone who would fly one at their house. He then went door-to-door with fliers explaining the deal. In short order, flags dotted the landscape of his town. He learned what we need to know: that average Americans love this country—we just need to wake them up!

His latest project: convincing local movie theaters to play the National Anthem before each film. I wouldn't bet against him.

President Trump has used his time in office to stock the federal judiciary with conservative justices; there will be more than two hundred by the time this book is printed. In a second term, he will only add more. Their judicial legacy will, in part, depend on the challenges you bring to the courts. Do you see a law, rule, or regulation that discriminates against freethinkers, people of faith, or gun owners? Challenge it. If the establishment won't change it, file a lawsuit. There are groups out there that will help you with the legal costs. If you lose, appeal—and alert the media.

Why can't we pray in school? Why can't we display the Ten Commandments? Where is "In God We Trust"—our nation's motto—in our school? Why can't my voucher apply to any private school? Why can't I carry my firearm? Why is abortion at any stage legal? Why was my Twitter account blocked? Why is there a boy in my daughter's bathroom? Why isn't English used exclusively here? Why do illegal immigrants get driver's licenses and free health care? You name it, you can challenge it.

Force the Left to defend its anti-American overreach. The courts—even the Supreme Court by the time President Trump leaves in 2024—will be with us, because the Constitution is with us.

Of course, you can run for office as well—and you should. But before you jump straight for the highest levels, don't forget local positions and offices. Remember, we need people, not just principles. Every school has a parents' group; put your name in to lead it. Many schools outsource the organization of school assemblies; take that job and bring in patriotic speakers. Run for school board member, city council member, mayor, or county commissioner. If your local school doesn't say the Pledge of Allegiance—why not? Make that single issue your platform, and watch your support swell. From issues of free speech to guns to refugee placement, the communities closest to us get a say.

Take a stand where you are. If your religious beliefs are sincerely held, don't bake a transgender wedding cake if you don't want to. I know the Left has given businesses that have done such things hell, but you have the Constitution—and the Trump judiciary—on your side. No patriotic parades in your town? Start one. Conservatives are sick and tired of other conservatives cowering like little chihuahuas at the first sign of leftist bellyaching. If you find yourself in the middle of a potential controversy, lawyer up and fight back. It worked for the Covington Catholic High School student Nick Sandmann, who was awarded a significant sum of money by fake-news CNN. You can win, though, only if you fight.

The next time conservative views are squelched in your local school, host a free-speech sit-in in your kids' school lobby and make your case. When local businesses declare "gun free zones," remember the Second Amendment, carry your legally owned firearm, and dare them to tell you it's not allowed. Find ways, large and small, to expose the cultural crosscurrents slanted against freedom-loving people.

You know what local politicians fear the most? A cell phone camera in their face when they are pulling a PC con job. Get their words on tape. Most politicians are cowards; when they hear from patriots, they back down. If they don't, they follow the establishment herd. Find, support, and defend politicians who fully embrace Americanism. They're out there. Even if you live in a blue community, sometimes all it takes is a couple of loud voices to stop initiatives such as "Tommy Has a Trans Mommy" being taught to five-year-olds.

All that said, we first and foremost need to win in 2020. But it's not enough to just vote. Volunteer to knock on doors. Make phone calls. Organize your neighbors. Meet with your pastor, and encourage your church to take a stand in the election—and beyond. Find influential people in your community, and convince them to put on their red hats—just like you. Winning in 2020 is a must, and the country needs you.

Then, with four more years of President Trump in the White House, get even more proactive. If you don't own a gun, buy one. Train to use it. And then buy more. If you're not in good physical condition, get off the couch and get into shape. Most of us will not save America from our keyboards; we're going to have to get out, pound the pavement, and outhustle the Left.

As you go along, be prepared to admit when you're wrong; after all, we're not the self-righteous Left. In my first book I argued for ending gerrymandering, which is a means of drawing the geographical boundaries of electoral districts to favor a certain party. I was wrong. Playing nice to placate the so-called middle has been a losing strategy for patriots for decades. Now I want to win, because the other side is stacked with enemies of freedom. Republican legislatures should draw congressional lines that advantage pro-freedom candidates—and screw Democrats. The alternative is happy-talk policy that elects more anti-American Democrats.

Speaking of my last book, the urgency of 2020 is even more fierce than when I wrote this In the Arena exhortation in 2016:

> If you're not going to enter the arena now, then when will you? If not in 2016—with America's cultural and civic decay in plain sight at home and American leadership falling apart across the world—then when? . . . There is a job you can do, a family you can lead, a cause you can champion, a group you can join, a team you can coach, a candidate you can support, a business you can start, a child you can raise, a tough assignment you can volunteer for. *Something!*

My point is, just get your ass out there. Whatever excuses you posit are pathetic or selfish, and you know it. You are invested enough to read this book; joining the American Crusade is an easy, and no-regrets, next step to take.

WHAT WINNING LOOKS LIKE

The road map is not entirely clear, but as history shows us, victory is possible. George Washington faced many dark days and hopeless nights while leading a ragtag army of regulars against the greatest army in the world. But it was faith, toughness, purposefulness, and perseverance that won the day. If we do that—if we truly crusade—here is a glimpse of what winning will look like:

> Our borders will be secured, our citizenship valued, and our flag respected. *Globalism, defeated.*
>
> Our boys will become strong, patriotic men, and our girls will become strong, patriotic women. Their differences will be elevated, not blurred. *Genderism, defeated.*
>
> Our free-market economy will flourish, while China will not

be able to cheat and compete—just like the Soviet Union. *Socialism, defeated.*

God will be revered and embraced, returning His blessing to America. *Secularism, defeated.*

Our birds will still chirp, rain will still fall, and crops will still flourish. And yes, the quality of our air and water will continue to improve because of American innovation. *Environmentalism, defeated.*

Our speech will be liberated and common sense restored. Elites will go back to just dressing better than the rest of us—or at least telling us they do. *Elitism, defeated.*

Martin Luther King, Jr.'s dream will be achieved: content of character before color of skin. Shared values, not diversity, will rule. *Multiculturalism and division, defeated.*

Overseas Islamism will be crushed (as ISIS was), and at home Islam will be forced to choose Americanism or go somewhere else. *Islamism, defeated.*

Power will be restored to We the People, empowering individuals over bureaucrats and states' rights over the federal government. *Leftism, defeated.*

The First Amendment will be broad and bold and the Second Amendment unfettered. Abortion will *finally* and forever be illegal and our government schools either abandoned or fully transformed. Prayer will be accepted in the public square. Education will be rigorous, not ideological. History and civics—not "social studies"—will spread the factually true story of American exceptionalism.

America will soar. Leftists will be relegated to the pedal-powered clown car, where they have been for most of American history. A more moderate, and pro-American, Democrat Party will emerge—restoring the balance that, prior to the twentieth century, was healthy for America. Rather than a messy national divorce, a new dawn will ensue for America. Communist China will fall—and lick its wounds for another two hundred years. Europe will still surrender, but pockets of freedom-loving resisters will remain. Islamists will never get a nuclear weapon but will be preemptively bombed back to the 700s when they try. Israel and America will form an even tighter bond, fighting the scourge of Islamism and international leftism that will never fully abate.

This is all possible. But only if we remember that history is not over. America is not inevitable, and if the twenty-first century is not an American-dominated century, it will not be a free century. American Crusaders like you will decide if we win.

SUPERHEROES LIKE US

It's Halloween night 2019. I am driving a gas-guzzling SUV full of seven little superheroes after a successful quest for candy calories. My wife, Jennifer—aka Captain Marvel—is our copilot. Suddenly my phone rings. The number is blocked, which can mean only one of two things: either FOX News or the White House. It's the worst possible timing. But I answer.

It's the president of the United States.

Shit! I have a car full of noisy, sugar-high kids, I'm in the middle of nowhere, and cell service is sketchy. So, while I still have reception, I pull onto a side road to park. My demanding hand motions and Jen's laser vision attempt to silence the mini-Avengers in the back seats. But they are all under the age of nine, and enforcement is futile.

So I step outside, hoping to maximize my phone signal and flee the giggling kids. *This is not a call I want to drop.* Oh, and by the way, I'm decked out in a head-to-toe Superman costume, my cape flapping furiously in the wind. My cape gets caught in the door, very unbecoming of Superman.

The familiar voice on the other end of the line informs me about three legal cases I've been championing for months—along with other allies—on behalf of brave warriors who were wrongly prosecuted for battlefield action. Barack Obama's rules of engagement threw those guys under the bus, and Donald Trump was considering presidential pardons for them.

The president wasted little time: "All the charges are being dropped, Pete."

My feelings of gratitude and relief were overwhelming. I could only imagine what the three heroes and their families were feeling. For a moment, I didn't even care that I was standing on the side of the road in red tights. It had been months—years—of fighting for their cases. But at that moment, as on every other day, the battle was beyond worth it.

Before hanging up the phone, the president said, in effect, "You never stopped fighting for these men. And the more I looked at their cases, I knew something had to be done. These are rough guys. But we sent them to do a job for our country, and we have to fight for our war fighters."

He ended with a compliment to me that I'll never forget and might put on my tombstone: "You're a fucking warrior, Pete. A fucking warrior." I thanked him for his courage, and he hung up. Soon thereafter, the world learned the news. I soon connected with all three families, who had already been notified of the president's decisions. It was a hallowed night.

Yes, this is a special case at some level. I happen to be a combat veteran who also happens to host a national television show. The president took note of those cases—through the efforts of several patriots—and the rest is history. But it would have been easy to sit back and do nothing. We heard "no" many times. We heard it was too complicated. The Pentagon bureaucracy tried to stifle us. The media said their cases were too toxic. Even well-meaning people told us to stop. Thank God we didn't.

I'm not Superman. Neither are you. But we are the next best thing—we are Americans. And if we make the choice to take the next step, to truly become American Crusaders, the future can—and will—be ours.

The call never comes at the right time. Life always gets into the way. Your cape will get caught in the door. The enemy is often more vicious than you thought. As we say in the army, "No plan survives first contact with the enemy." But if you persist, if you insist, and if you show courage, there is no force on Earth—especially the Left—that can hold you back.

See you on the battlefield. Together, with God's help, we will save America. Deus vult!

ACKNOWLEDGMENTS

Without my beautiful and brilliant wife, Jennifer, this book would not have been remotely possible. Thank you for your love, your support, and your incredibly insightful copyedits. This book is as much yours as mine.

Thank you to the Fox News Channel, and *Fox & Friends* specifically, for affording me the platform to share the views of this book every single day. What an honor. I am grateful for the opportunity to work with such talented professionals—and to travel the country meeting the patriots who make America great.

Thank you to my book agent, Tom Winters, as well as Mike Loomis, for their partnership on this project. A special shout-out to Stephen Limbaugh as well. And thank you to Kate Hartson and the entire team at Center Street and Hachette Book Group for investing in this book.

NOTES

CHAPTER 1: OUR AMERICAN CRUSADE

Page 4: Theodore Roosevelt, "Americanism," address to the Knights of Columbus, New York, October 12, 1915, http://www.theodore-roosevelt.com/images/research/txtspeeches/781.pdf.

4: Philip Davis, assisted by Bertha Schwartz, *Immigration and Americanization: Selected Readings* (New York: Ginn and Company, 1920), https://archive.org/details/immigrationameri00daviuoft/page/648/mode/2up/search/there+is+room+here, 648.

4: Cameron Cawthorne, "Omar Questions the Patriotism of American-Born Citizens," *Washington Free Beacon*, July 13, 2019, https://freebeacon.com/politics/omar-questions-the-patriotism-of-american-born-citizens/.

5: Greg Jaffe and Souad Mekhennet, "Ilhan Omar's American Story: It's Complicated," *Washington Post*, July 6, 2019, https://www.washingtonpost.com/politics/2019/07/06/ilhan-omar-is-unlike-anyone-who-has-served-congress-this-is-her-complicated-american-story/?arc404=true.

5: Mark Moore, "Ilhan Omar Suggests People Should Be 'More Fearful of White Men' than Jihadists in 2018 Interview," *New York Post*, July 25, 2019, https://nypost.com/2019/07/25/ilhan-omar-suggests-people-should-be-more-fearful-of-white-men-than-jihadists-in-2018-interview/.

6: Zachary Evans, "FBI Investigating Whether Ilhan Omar Married Her Brother," *National Review*, January 27, 2020, https://www.nationalreview.com/news/fbi-investigating-whether-ilhan-omar-married-her-brother/.

8: "The Red-Green Alliance and the Real Devil of Mogadishu," The Illustrated Primer, August 16, 2019, https://apelbaum.wordpress.com/2019/08/16/the-red-green-alliance-and-the-real-devil-of-mogadishu/.

CHAPTER 2: 2020: DEATH, DIVORCE, OR DAWN?

Page 26: Kevin Diaz, "Afghan Vet Pete Hegseth Will Run Against Amy Klobuchar," *StarTribune*, May 2, 2013, http://www.startribune.com/afghan-vet-pete-hegseth-will-run-against-amy-klobuchar/139873753/.

33: "Trump: 'I Was Elected to Represent the Citizens of Pittsburgh, Not Paris,'"
Washington Post, June 1, 2017, https://www.washingtonpost.com/video/
national/trump-i-was-elected-to-represent-the-citizens-of-pittsburgh-not-
paris/2017/06/01/11007d80-4707-11e7-8de1-cec59a9bf4b1_video.html.

34: Lydia Saad, "Socialism as Popular as Capitalism Among Young Adults
in U.S.," Gallup, November 25, 2019, https://news.gallup.com/poll/268766/
socialism-popular-capitalism-among-young-adults.aspx.

CHAPTER 3: AMERICANISM NOW, AMERICANISM FOREVER

Page 38: Avery Anapol, "Macron Calls Nationalism a 'Betrayal of Patriotism'
During Armistice Day Remarks," The Hill, November 11, 2018, https://thehill.
com/policy/international/416097-macron-during-armistice-day-remarks-
nationalism-is-a-betrayal-of.

40: Maegan Vazquez, "NY Gov. Andrew Cuomo Says America 'Was Never That
Great,'" CNN, August 16, 2018, https://edition.cnn.com/2018/08/15/politics/
andrew-cuomo-america-was-never-that-great/index.html.

47: Jenna Johnson, "Beto O'Rourke's Immigration Plan: No Wall, Few Specifics,"
Washington Post, January 15, 2019, https://www.washingtonpost.com/politics/
beto-orourkes-immigration-plan-no-wall-but-no-specifics/2019/01/15/f6e36fac-
15ea-11e9-90a8-136fa44b80ba_story.html.

50: "The Same Subject Continued: The Union as a Safeguard Against Domestic
Faction and Insurrection," *The Federalist Papers*, no. 10, November 23, 1787,
https://avalon.law.yale.edu/18th_century/fed10.asp.

54: Larry Kummer, "Choose: Open Borders or the Welfare State?," Fabius
Maximus Website, November 6, 2018, https://fabiusmaximus.com/2018/11/06/
predicting-results-of-immigration-in-sweden/.

CHAPTER 4: LEFTISM: HOW DEMOCRATS LEFT AMERICA

Page 64: Saul Alinsky, *Rules for Radicals: A Practical Primer for Realistic Radicals*
(New York: Vintage, 1989), https://chisineu.files.wordpress.com/2014/02/saul-
alinsky-rules-for-radicals-1989.pdf.

64: Julio Rosas, "'You Destroy Them': MSNBC Guest Offers Advice on Dealing
with White Trump Supporters," *Washington Examiner*, August 13, 2019, https://
www.washingtonexaminer.com/news/you-destroy-them-msnbc-guest-offers-
advice-on-dealing-with-white-trump-supporters.

81: Indicrat, "Reagan on Libertarians & Conservatives VS 'Liberal Fascists,'"
December 1975, YouTube, July 27, 2017, https://www.youtube.com/
watch?v=75Lc31h91BI&feature=emb_logo.

83: "Fascism," Merriam-Webster, https://www.merriam-webster.com/dictionary/fascism.

CHAPTER 5: GLOBALISTS: THE WORLD'S WORST CITIZENS

Page 88: Eugene Debs, September 1915, Eugene V. Debs Foundation, https://debsfoundation.org/.

88: Thomas D. Williams, "Pope Francis Proposes 'Europe First' Against Populist Nationalism," Breitbart, August 11, 2019, https://www.breitbart.com/europe/2019/08/11/pope-francis-proposes-europe-first-against-populist-nationalism/.

90: Associated Press, "Obama's 2005 Remarks Reflect Strong Stance on Controlling Immigration," November 2, 2018, https://apnews.com/afs:Content:2477111077.

94: Theodore Roosevelt, *History as Literature and Other Essays* (New York: Charles Scribner's Sons, 1913).

98: Douglas Murray, *The Strange Death of Europe: Immigration, Identity, Islam* (London: Bloomsbury Continuum, 2017).

100: Vicki Ikeogu, "Dayton Blunt in MN Forum: Anyone Who Can't Accept Immigrants 'Should Find Another State,'" *The Globe*, October 13, 2015, https://www.dglobe.com/news/3860425-dayton-blunt-mn-forum-anyone-who-cant-accept-immigrants-should-find-another-state.

103: Donald J. Trump, Twitter, June 8, 2018, https://twitter.com/realdonaldtrump/status/1005030839019802625?lang=en.

104: Daryl Morey, Twitter, October 6, 2019, https://twitter.com/dmorey/status/1181000808399114240?lang=en.

105: "Remarks by President Trump and Prime Minister Morrison of Australia Before Bilateral Meeting," September 20, 2019, White House, https://www.whitehouse.gov/briefings-statements/remarks-president-trump-prime-minister-morrison-australia-bilateral-meeting/.

106: Wu Yuehe, "United States, Don't Underestimate China's Ability to Strike Back," *People's Daily*, May 31, 2019, http://en.people.cn/n3/2019/0531/c202936-9583292.html.

109: Brendan Pringle, "Communist Propaganda Has Infiltrated More than 100 US Colleges, Posing as Chinese Language Institute," *Washington Examiner*, January 22, 2018, https://www.washingtonexaminer.com/communist-propaganda-has-infiltrated-more-than-100-us-colleges-posing-as-chinese-language-institute.

112: Michael R. Pompeo, "A Foreign Policy from the Founding," May 11, 2019, https://www.state.gov/remarks-at-the-claremont-institute-40th-anniversary-gala-a-foreign-policy-from-the-founding/.

113: Donald J. Trump, Twitter, July 14, 2019, https://twitter.com/
realDonaldTrump/status/1150381394234941448.

116: Domenico Agasso, Jr., "Pope Francis Warns Against Sovereignism: 'It Leads
to War,'" *La Stampa*, August 9, 2019, https://www.lastampa.it/vatican-insider/
en/2019/08/09/news/pope-francis-warns-against-sovereignism-it-leads-to-
war-1.37330049.

116: *Congressional Record*, vol. 57, pt. 5.

CHAPTER 6: GENDERISM: TOXIC FEMININITY AND BETA MALES

Page 118: ACLU, Twitter, November 19, 2019, https://twitter.com/aclu/status/11968
77415810813955?lang=en.

121: "Student Conservative Groups Decry Liberalism, Political Apathy on
Campus," *Daily Princetonian*, May, 2002, https://www.dailyprincetonian.com/
article/2002/05/student-conservative-groups-decry-liberalism-political-apathy-
on-campus.

126: LaVendrick Smith, "Dallas Child-Custody Battle Hinges on 7-Year-Old's
Gender Identity, Draws Attention of Abbott, Cruz," *Dallas News*, October
24, 2019, https://www.dallasnews.com/news/courts/2019/10/24/dallas-child-
custody-battle-hinges-on-7-year-olds-gender-identity-draws-attention-of-
abbott-cruz/.

134: "Martina Navratilova Apologizes for Transgender 'Cheating'
Comments," CNN, March 4, 2019, https://lite.cnn.com/en/article/
h_750d93039222ff808f3be16612cacf40.

136: "Portland Building Restrooms, 2/05/2019," The City of Portland, Oregon,
February 5, 2019, https://www.portlandoregon.gov/omf/article/713846.

CHAPTER 7: SOCIALISM: WILL IT WORK THIS TIME?

Page 143: Lawrence Reed, "Was Jesus a Socialist?," PragerU, July 6, 2019, https://
www.prageru.com/video/was-jesus-a-socialist/.

146: Walter E. Williams, *American Contempt for Liberty* (Stanford, CA: Hoover
Institution Press, 2015).

150: Adryan Corcione, "Who Is Karl Marx: Meet the Anti-Capitalist
Scholar," *Teen Vogue*, May 10, 2018, https://www.teenvogue.com/story/
who-is-karl-marx.

153: Franklin D. Roosevelt, "Letter on the Resolution of Federation of Federal
Employees Against Strikes in Federal Service," August 16, 1937, https://www.
presidency.ucsb.edu/documents/letter-the-resolution-federation-federal-
employees-against-strikes-federal-service.

158: Mona Charen, "Lovable Ol' Bernie?," RealClear Politics, December 24, 2019, https://www.realclearpolitics.com/articles/2019/12/24/lovable_ol_bernie_142022.html.

159: Matt Stevens, "Bill de Blasio on Income Inequality," *New York Times*, June 26, 2019, https://www.nytimes.com/2019/06/26/us/politics/bill-de-blasio-income-inequality.html.

CHAPTER 8: SECULARISM: DEPORTING GOD FROM AMERICA

Page 160: George Washington, "Thanksgiving Proclamation," October 3, 1789, Library of Congress, https://www.loc.gov/resource/mgw8a.124/?q=1789+Thanksgiving&sp=132&st=text.

169: Alexis de Tocqueville, *Democracy in America* (New York: Regnery Publishing, 2003).

171: Karin Dienst, "Princeton's Informal Motto Recast to Emphasize Service to Humanity," Princeton University, October 24, 2016, https://www.princeton.edu/news/2016/10/24/princetons-informal-motto-recast-emphasize-service-humanity.

172: "Shield and 'Veritas' History," Harvard GSAS Christian Community, http://www.hcs.harvard.edu/~gsascf/shield-and-veritas-history/.

175: Abraham Lincoln, "Second Inaugural Address," March 4, 1865, https://nationalcenter.org/LincolnSecondInaugural.html.

177: Democratic National Committee, "Resolution Regarding the Religiously Unaffiliated Demographic," August 2019, https://secular.org/wp-content/uploads/2019/08/DNC-Resolution-on-the-Nonreligious-Demographic.pdf.

178: Daniella Diaz, "Elizabeth Warren: 'My Faith Animates All That I Do,'" CNN, June 29, 2019, https://edition.cnn.com/2019/06/29/politics/elizabeth-warren-faith-life-decisions/index.html.

179: Daniel Burke, "How Pete Buttigieg Found God," CNN, August 17, 2019, https://edition.cnn.com/2019/08/16/politics/pete-buttigieg-religious-journey/index.html.

180: Caleb Parke, "Rabbi Wounded in Synagogue Shooting Urges Trump to Bring 'Moment of Silence' Back to Schools," Fox News, May 2, 2019, https://www.foxnews.com/politics/trump-rabbi-synagogue-moment-silence.

181: "Attorney General William P. Barr Delivers Remarks to the Law School and the de Nicola Center for Ethics and Culture at the University of Notre Dame," October 11, 2019, https://www.justice.gov/opa/speech/attorney-general-william-p-barr-delivers-remarks-law-school-and-de-nicola-center-ethics.

CHAPTER 9: ENVIRONMENTALISM: THE WAR ON WEATHER

Page 182: William Cummings, "'The World Is Going to End in 12 Years if We Don't Address Climate Change,' Ocasio-Cortez Says," *USA Today*, January 22, 2019, https://www.usatoday.com/story/news/politics/onpolitics/2019/01/22/ocasio-cortez-climate-change-alarm/2642481002/.

182: David Montgomery, "AOC's Chief of Change: Saikat Chakrabarti Isn't Just Running Her Office. He's Guiding a Movement," *The Washington Post Magazine*, July 10, 2019, https://www.washingtonpost.com/news/magazine/wp/2019/07/10/feature/how-saikat-chakrabarti-became-aocs-chief-of-change/.

184: "Transcript: Greta Thunberg's Speech at the U.N. Climate Action Summit," NPR, September 23, 2019, https://www.npr.org/2019/09/23/763452863/transcript-greta-thunbergs-speech-at-the-u-n-climate-action-summit?t=1582824447622.

185: Rob Verger, "Newsweek Rewind: Debunking Global Cooling," *Newsweek*, May 23, 2014, https://www.newsweek.com/newsweek-rewind-debunking-global-cooling-252326.

190: Youth Climate Strike, https://www.youthclimatestrikeus.org/platform?fbclid=IwAR1juKFlj-pdsGYFi5D-3vu_1wG7bik01VJDxAqdeeYJyb5pOGaRAM3rK8s.

190: "Youth Climate Demands," Rapid Shift, http://www.rapidshift.net/youth-climate-demands/.

196: "Cold Yet?," *Washington Times*, September 19, 2007, https://www.washingtontimes.com/news/2007/sep/19/inside-the-beltway-69748548/.

196: S. I. Rasool and S. H. Schneider, "Atmospheric Carbon Dioxide and Aerosols: Effects of Large Increases on Global Climate," *Science* 173 (1971): 138–41, https://pdfs.semanticscholar.org/4db2/1045b17ebcdd6a8c6adeb1f42eb5c2c39270.pdf?_ga=2.101301249.1213837356.1583856627-1227194247.1574373344.

197: Rob Bluey, "Q&A: The Politically Incorrect Book That Debunks Climate Change Myths," The Daily Signal, June 3, 2018, https://www.dailysignal.com/2018/06/03/qa-the-politically-incorrect-book-that-debunks-climate-change-myths/.

198: Henry Fountain, "Climate Change Is Accelerating, Bringing World 'Dangerously Close' to Irreversible Change," *New York Times*, December 4, 2019, https://www.nytimes.com/2019/12/04/climate/climate-change-acceleration.html.

200: Salvador Rizzo, "What's Actually in the 'Green New Deal' from Democrats?," *Washington Post*, February 11, 2019, https://www.washingtonpost.com/politics/2019/02/11/whats-actually-green-new-deal-democrats/.

201: J. V. Chamary, "The Science of 'Avengers: Endgame' Proves Thanos Did Nothing Wrong," *Forbes*, May 7, 2019, https://www.forbes.com/sites/jvchamary/2019/05/07/avengers-endgame-biodiversity/.

CHAPTER 10: ELITISM: THE POISON OF POLITICAL CORRECTNESS

Page 204: Tyler McCarthy, "Dave Chappelle Defends Freedom of Speech from 'Cancel Culture': 'First Amendment Is First for a Reason,'" Fox News, October 29, 2019, https://www.foxnews.com/entertainment/dave-chappelle-freedom-speech-cancel-culture-first-amendment-for-a-reason.

204: Alan M. Dershowitz, "The Dangerous Stalinism of the 'Woke' Hard-Left," Gatestone Institute, August 31, 2019, https://www.gatestoneinstitute.org/14794/the-dangerous-stalinism-of-the-woke-hard-left.

213: Janell Ross, "Obama Revives His 'Cling to Guns or Religion' Analysis—for Donald Trump Supporters," *Washington Post*, December 21, 2015, https://www.washingtonpost.com/news/the-fix/wp/2015/12/21/obama-dusts-off-his-cling-to-guns-or-religion-idea-for-donald-trump/.

222: Emily S. Rueb and Derrick Bryson Taylor, "Obama on Call-Out Culture: 'That's Not Activism,'" *New York Times*, October 31, 2019, https://www.nytimes.com/2019/10/31/us/politics/obama-woke-cancel-culture.html.

CHAPTER 11: MULTICULTURALISM: E PLURIBUS RACISM

Page 224: Colby Itkowitz, David Weigel, and Mike DeBonis, "House Democrats' Racially Charged Infighting Escalates," *Washington Post*, July 13, 2019, https://www.washingtonpost.com/politics/2019/07/13/house-democrats-racially-charged-infighting-escalates/.

224: Gen. Joseph Lengyel, Twitter, August 16, 2017, https://twitter.com/chiefngb/status/897842312704917505?lang=en.

225: "The 1619 Project," *The New York Times Magazine*, August 14, 2019, https://www.nytimes.com/interactive/2019/08/14/magazine/1619-america-slavery.html.

225: Katherine Kersten, "The New York Times '1619 Project' Revisited," Center of the American Experiment, December 9, 2019, https://www.americanexperiment.org/2019/12/the-new-york-times-1619-project-revisited/.

229: Karen Zeigler and Steven A. Camarota, "67.3 Million in the United States Spoke a Foreign Language at Home in 2018," Center for Immigration

Studies, October 29, 2019, https://cis.org/Report/673-Million-United-States-Spoke-Foreign-Language-Home-2018.

233: *Congressional Record*, vol. 57, pt. 5.

235: Ruben Navarrette, Jr., "Millions of Latinos Are Trump Supporters. Here's What They're Thinking," *USA Today*, November 26, 2019, https://eu.usatoday.com/story/opinion/2019/11/26/latinos-for-trump-supporters-hispanics-mexicans-attacks-immigrants-column/4224954002/.

237: Saritha Prabhu, "White Men Are Now the Democratic Party's Punching Bag. That's a Dangerous Bet to Make," *USA Today*, October 28, 2018, https://www.usatoday.com/story/opinion/nation-now/2018/10/28/white-male-bashing-trend-dangerous-saritha-prabhu-column/1778385002/.

238: Scott Martelle, "Opinion: No, President Trump, Washington's Slaves and Lee's Treason Are Not the Same Things," *Los Angeles Times*, August 16, 2017, https://www.latimes.com/opinion/opinion-la/la-ol-trump-statues-confederacy-20170816-story.html.

238: 'Fox & Friends Sunday Defends White Supremacist Charlottesville Protesters: 'There's a Reason Those People Were Out There,'" Media Matters, August 13, 2017, https://www.mediamatters.org/fox-friends/fox-friends-sunday-defends-white-supremacist-charlottesville-protesters-theres-reason.

Page 240: "Swain: If We Want to Come Together We Need to Move Away from Identity Politics and Multiculturalism," Grabien, August 14, 2017, https://grabien.com/story.php?id=122395.

CHAPTER 12: ISLAMISM: THE MOST DANGEROUS "ISM"

254: Steven A. Camarota, "The High Cost of Resettling Middle Eastern Refugees," Center for Immigration Studies, November 4, 2015, https://cis.org/Report/High-Cost-Resettling-Middle-Eastern-Refugees.

255: "Osama bin Laden Wanted Americans to Help Obama Save Humanity from Climate Change," Vice News and Reuters, March 2, 2016, https://www.vice.com/en_us/article/j59b3b/osama-bin-laden-wanted-americans-to-help-obama-save-humanity-from-climate-change.

258: "American Commissioners to John Jay," March 28, 1786, https://founders.archives.gov/documents/Jefferson/01-09-02-0315#TSJN-01-09-0315-fn-0001.

258: Brian Kilmeade and Don Yaeger, *Thomas Jefferson and the Tripoli Pirates: The Forgotten War That Changed American History* (New York: Sentinel, 2016).

259: "The Future of World Religions: Population Growth Projections, 2010–2050," Pew Research Center, April 2, 2015, https://www.pewforum.org/2015/04/02/religious-projections-2010-2050/.

CHAPTER 13: THE FRONT LINES: EDUCATION AND ISRAEL

Page 268: Zack Beauchamp, "The Ilhan Omar Anti-Semitism Controversy, Explained," Vox, March 6, 2019, https://www.vox.com/policy-and-politics/2019/3/6/18251639/ilhan-omar-israel-anti-semitism-jews.

CHAPTER 14: MAKE THE CRUSADE GREAT AGAIN

295: Brian Porter, "Catholic Church in Poland," George Mason University, http://chnm.gmu.edu/1989/exhibits/roman-catholic-church/introduction.

INDEX

leftist orientation of, 31–32, 70, 71–72
"mass reeducation" need and, 82
minimum wage, socialism and, 149, 150
praising bread lines, 159
Project Veritas exposing, 82, 303
shunning faith, supporting abortion,
178
veteran stance of Left and, 86
Sanders, Sarah Huckabee, 123
Saudi Arabia(ns), 210–211, 250–251
Second Amendment, 49–50, 56–57, 204,
294, 298, 307, 310
secularism, 161–181. *See also*
Christianity, Christ, and the Bible; God
and religion
abortion and, 66, 73–74, 123, 178–179,
202, 310
"Athens and Jerusalem" and, 173–174
authoritarian governments and, 174
the Bible as America's foundation
stone and, 174–177
Bible reading in schools and, 73
crusading against, 179–181
definition/meaning of, 165–167
Democrat party and, 177–179
"humanistic values" and, 178
Islamism and, 254
Marx, Marxism and, 172–173
prayer in public schools and, 73
replacing God with government, 71,
72–74
"separation of church and state" and,
165–167
tearing down connections to faith, 166
Ten Commandments in schools and,
73
Trump stemming tide of, 177
2020 election and, 298, 310
September 11 date significance, 297
Sharia law, 100, 250
"The 1619 Project" (*New York Times*),
225–226, 241
Sobieski, John III, King of Poland, 297
social justice, 70, 210, 211
social media. *See also* Twitter
social media, elitism and, 210–211

socialism, 139–159. *See also* Sanders,
Bernie
about: basics of economics, capitalism
and, 139–141, 146
definition and explanation of, 146–148
democratic, 146–147, 201
"economic justice/fairness" and,
147–148
"equality" and, 149–150
fantasies instead of facts, 159
frauds, formulas, fawning, and fear,
148–152
"free" stuff and, 148
government employees, unions and,
153–154
hiding behind capitalism success,
148–149
Islamism and, 254
Jesus Christ, faith/Christianity and,
141–146
Marx, Marxism and, 71–72, 74,
150–151, 159, 172–173
millennials and, 148
minimum wage and, 149, 150
Orwell on, 138
popularity, vs. capitalism, 34, 148
Scandinavian countries and, 147
secularism and, 177–179 (*See also*
secularism)
Thatcher on, 138
2020 election and, 298, 310
2020 Democrat candidates and, 31–32
unions, accountability and, 152–154
Solyndra debacle, 199–200
Somali Muslims in Minnesota, 99–102
Somali Omar. *See* Omar, Somali (Ilhan)
sports, genderism and, 132–134
squishes, 11–13, 14, 28
*The Strange Death of Europe:
Immigration, Identity, Islam* (Murray),
98
Swain, Carol, 240

T

TalNexus, 303–304
taxes, leftism/leftists and, 69, 71, 141, 159

Declaration of Independence and,
47–50
democracy and, 50–53
First Amendment, 56, 204, 223, 241,
298, 310
the Left, leftists and, 47, 48–49, 50,
56–57
Minneapolis teenager on Islamic
school and, 100
multiculturalism and, 228–229
Second Amendment, 49–50, 56–57,
204, 294, 298, 307, 310
"separation of church and state" and,
166–167
"separation of church and state"
myth, 166–167
as solution to America's problems,
41–42
supporting conservative positions, 307
US Senate, Pete's candidacy for, 25–28
USA Today, 235, 237

V

veterans, VA health care and, 84–87

W

Wałęsa, Lech, 296
Warren, Elizabeth, 31–32, 159, 170, 178,
207–208, 209, 236, 237, 303
Washington, George, 160, 167, 168–169,
238, 309
Washington Post, 47, 52–53, 196, 235
Waters, Maxine, 242
wealth tax, 71, 159
West, Kanye, 161–162
"white privilege," 125, 232–233, 236–241
Williams, Walter E., 146

Y

Yang, Andrew, 159

ABOUT THE AUTHOR

PETE HEGSETH is the co-host of *Fox & Friends Weekend*, America's #1-rated cable morning television show.

Pete is an army veteran of Afghanistan, Iraq, and Guantanamo Bay who holds two Bronze Stars and a Combat Infantryman's Badge for his time overseas. He still serves as an army major.

Pete is a graduate of Princeton University and Harvard University's John F. Kennedy School of Government. His first book, *In the Arena*, was published in 2016.

Pete and his wife, Jennifer, have seven kids, all future Crusaders.

PeteHegseth.com